D0439518

The Prince

by Niccolò Machiavelli

WITH RELATED DOCUMENTS

Translated, Edited, and with an Introduction by

William J. Connell

Seton Hall University

BEDFORD/ST. MARTIN'S   Boston ♦ New York

For Bedford/St. Martin's

Executive Editor for History: Mary V. Dougherty
Director of Development for History: Jane Knetzger
Senior Developmental Editor: Heidi L. Hood
Editorial Assistant: Carina Schoenberger
Senior Production Supervisor: Nancy Myers
Senior Marketing Manager: Jenna Bookin Barry
Project Management: Books By Design, Inc.
Text Design: Claire Seng-Niemoeller
Indexer: William J. Connell
Cover Design: Billy Boardman
Cover Art: Santi di Tito (1536–1603). *Portrait of Niccolò Machiavelli (1469–1527).*
© Scala/Art Resource, NY. Palazzo Vecchio, Florence, Italy.
Composition: Stratford Publishing Services
Printing and Binding: Haddon Craftsmen, an RR Donnelley & Sons Company

President: Joan E. Feinberg
Editorial Director: Denise B. Wydra
Director of Marketing: Karen Melton Soeltz
Director of Editing, Design, and Production: Marcia Cohen
Manager, Publishing Services: Emily Berleth

Manufactured in the United States of America.

0   9   8
j   i   h   g

For information, write: Bedford/St. Martin's, 75 Arlington Street, Boston, MA 02116
(617-399-4000)

ISBN-10: 0-312-14978-6
ISBN-13: 978-0-312-14978-9

Distributed outside North America by Palgrave Macmillan.

Acknowledgment

Translation of Niccolò Machiavelli, "The Thrushes," reprinted by permission of the copyright holder, Joseph Tusiani, Distinguished Professor, CUNY, Lehman College.

Foreword

The Bedford Series in History and Culture is designed so that readers can study the past as historians do.

The historian's first task is finding the evidence. Documents, letters, memoirs, interviews, pictures, movies, novels, or poems can provide facts and clues. Then the historian questions and compares the sources. There is more to do than in a courtroom, for hearsay evidence is welcome, and the historian is usually looking for answers beyond act and motive. Different views of an event may be as important as a single verdict. How a story is told may yield as much information as what it says.

Along the way the historian seeks help from other historians and perhaps from specialists in other disciplines. Finally, it is time to write, to decide on an interpretation and how to arrange the evidence for readers.

Each book in this series contains an important historical document or group of documents, each document a witness from the past and open to interpretation in different ways. The documents are combined with some element of historical narrative—an introduction or a biographical essay, for example—that provides students with an analysis of the primary source material and important background information about the world in which it was produced.

Each book in the series focuses on a specific topic within a specific historical period. Each provides a basis for lively thought and discussion about several aspects of the topic and the historian's role. Each is short enough (and inexpensive enough) to be a reasonable one-week assignment in a college course. Whether as classroom or personal reading, each book in the series provides firsthand experience of the challenge—and fun—of discovering, recreating, and interpreting the past.

Lynn Hunt
David W. Blight
Bonnie G. Smith
Natalie Zemon Davis
Ernest R. May

Preface

Why produce a new edition of Niccolò Machiavelli's *Prince*? Western society has arrived at a certain acceptance of and even level of comfort with the Florentine thinker. Nowadays we read *The Prince* knowing that it is a classic in the history of political thought. Unfortunately, considering this work as a classic softens our response even before we begin reading, making it difficult to identify with readers of the past and the effect *The Prince* may have had on them. One of the principal aims of this new English edition is to correct that problem by enabling first-time readers to understand how Machiavelli's *Prince* profoundly disturbed people in the past.

Furthermore, because Machiavelli's text has been interpreted in many different ways, it is important to offer readers a translation that is true to the sense of Machiavelli's original prose, yet also highly readable. Most English versions of *The Prince* have been translated by literary scholars or political theorists who have had little familiarity with the historical circumstances and the writing practices of the Florentine chancery where Machiavelli worked as secretary from 1498 to 1512 before writing *The Prince*. A better understanding of Machiavelli's idiomatic language has made it possible for this edition to give more accurate renderings of numerous passages.

Yet another reason for publishing a new edition is the opportunity to publish historical documents related to the writing, publication, and reception of *The Prince,* a number of which are translated here for the first time. These documents give students a fuller understanding of the context in which *The Prince* was composed, and help them grasp how people have found it to be at once compelling and repellent.

The introduction, "The Puzzle of *The Prince,*" provides background information on Machiavelli and his book to help readers begin to answer a number of important questions. If *The Prince* was so difficult for others to accept, why, then, did Machiavelli write it? Why did he refrain from publishing it during his lifetime? Can the book's shocking qualities be explained as a product of the times in which Machiavelli lived? Why do we say that modern political theory began with *The Prince,* and, if it did, what does that say about modern political theory? These are questions that students of Machiavelli have asked for many years, and in all likelihood they will continue to ask for many years to come. The introduction's thorough explanation of the history and context surrounding the composition and publication of *The Prince* provides the foundation students need to understand these issues. To give students a feeling for the geography of the places Machiavelli discusses, three maps at the end of the introduction include places named in *The Prince:* a map of Italy in Machiavelli's time, a map of Europe c. 1500, and a map of places in the ancient world.

The related documents that follow *The Prince* offer further keys to understanding Machiavelli's treatise and its historical reception and make useful starting points for class discussion. They include not only Machiavelli's famous letter to Francesco Vettori of December 10, 1513, in which he announces his writing of *The Prince* (Document 3), but also the first prefaces of *The Prince,* which before now have never been translated into English.

To further aid students, the appendix includes a chronology of Machiavelli's life and career, questions for consideration to prompt students to think critically about the explosive book they hold in their hands, and a selected bibliography to guide student research assignments.

ACKNOWLEDGMENTS

It is a pleasure to acknowledge the numerous friends and colleagues who, over a number of years, have encouraged and assisted this work. Cecil H. Clough, Julius Kirshner, John Najemy, John T. Scott, and Deanna Shemek read the translation in draft and made numerous helpful suggestions. Other scholars who have assisted the project in various ways include Sergio Bertelli, the late William Bouwsma, Julian Brooks, Alison Brown, Gene Brucker, Niccolò Capponi, the late Fredi Chiappelli, Samuel Cohn, Marcia Colish, Giles Constable, Felicia Else, Riccardo Fubini, Mark Iusim, Hugo Jaeckel, Jonathan Israel, Myra Jehlen, Donald Kelley, Dale Kent, Oleg Kudriavtsev, the late Paul O. Kristeller, Harvey Mansfield, Roger Masters, Thomas F. Mayer, Lloyd Moote, Athanasios Moulakis, Armando Petrucci, Franca Petrucci Nardelli, Nadia Selunskaia, Randolph Starn, the late Hugh Trevor-Roper, Marcello Simonetta, David Wootton, and Andrea Zorzi. At Seton Hall, my colleagues Peter Ahr, David Bénéteau, Eugene Cotter, Marta Deyrup, Nathaniel Knight, John Sweeney, and Gisela Webb were always ready to listen as I worked through particular points, and Jennifer Jamer assisted with the index. Stephanie Jed, John McLucas, and Paul Rahe introduced me to *The Prince* long ago when I was an undergraduate. The late Sebastian de Grazia offered much encouragement early on. For conversations that helped to keep the subject fresh over many years, I am indebted to Allen Allured, William Allured, the late Joseph Alsop, David Calleo, Joseph Ciccolini, Jean Cootes, the late Katherine Graham, the late Meg Greenfield, Robert Kagan, the late Lane Kirkland, Barbara Manley, Frank Manley, Nikos Pharasles, the late Harrison Salisbury, Salvatore Valente, and Lowell Weicker.

For external support in the form of valuable leaves from teaching, funding for research, and numerous occasions for discussion, I am grateful to the Institute for Advanced Study, the Columbian Foundation of New Jersey, Liberty Fund, UNICO National, and Villa I Tatti. Collaboration with the *Journal of the History of Ideas* and *Renaissance Quarterly* has helped to keep me sharp on Machiavelli scholarship. At Seton Hall I have received valuable institutional support from the Joseph M. and Geraldine C. La Motta Chair in Italian Studies, the Valente Italian Studies Library, and the Charles and Joan Alberto Italian Studies Institute. The personnel of the Biblioteca Malatestiana in Cesena and the Firestone Library of Princeton University responded to especially difficult queries. Mike Siegel of the Rutgers Cartography Lab drew the first versions of the three maps with his usual care. Photographs were supplied by Agnew's of London, the Morgan Library, and Young and Co. Brewery PLC.

The publisher, Bedford/St. Martin's, has done a splendid job of seeing the project through to completion. Natalie Zemon Davis, who commissioned this translation, and Lynn Hunt, who read the completed manuscript and with her usual good sense made many excellent suggestions, have been terrific as series editors. The readers for the press, to whom I am much indebted, were Christopher Celenza (Michigan State University), Charles Evans (Northern Virginia Community College), Paula Findlen (Stanford University), Kenneth Gouwens (University of Connecticut), William McCuaig, Stephen Miller (University of Maine), Deanna Shemek (University of California, Santa Cruz), and Michael Zuckert (University of Notre Dame). At Bedford/St. Martin's the project received steady support from Joan Feinberg, president; Denise Wydra, editorial director; Mary Dougherty, executive editor; Patricia Rossi, former publisher for history;

Katherine Kurzman, former acquisitions editor; Jane Knetzger, director of development of history; Heidi Hood, senior editor; Carina Schoenberger, editorial assistant; and Emily Berleth, manager of publishing services.

My wife, Nikki, has helped in more ways than can be imagined, and my young daughters, Zoë and Livia, have tolerated the project with patience and affection. My parents, William F. Connell and Marilyn Moore, have willingly and unwillingly listened to many discussions of Machiavelli. Above all, I am grateful to the many students who have joined me in reading *The Prince*.

William J. Connell

A Note about the Text and Translation

Machiavelli was a powerful and innovative writer of Italian prose, and this edition of *The Prince* attempts to restore the integrity of his prose in a new, more readable English translation. Not only was Machiavelli aware of the past meanings (in both Italian and Latin) of the important words he used—words such as "virtue," "liberty," "state," and "fortune"—he also imbued these words with new meanings that still reverberate in languages that are spoken throughout much of the world. The desire to determine in a precise way what Machiavelli meant when he used these and other key terms has resulted in a number of useful studies and glossaries.[1] And, reminiscent of the Renaissance controversy over translation *ad verbum* and *ad sensum,* the fascination with Machiavelli's vocabulary has encouraged many scholars to follow one of two divergent paths when translating *The Prince* into English. One popular approach tries to accommodate what the translator detects as Machiavelli's variable meaning by using a number of different English words to translate the same Italian word, depending on the immediate context. Thus the Italian word *virtù* will sometimes appear as its English cognate "virtue," but also as "craft,"

---

[1] Fredi Chiappelli, *Studi sul linguaggio del Machiavelli* (Florence: Le Monnier, 1952), and Chiappelli, *Nuovi studi sul linguaggio del Machiavelli* (Florence: Le Monnier, 1969), remain useful and perhaps underappreciated. For individual terms in Machiavelli's vocabulary, see J. H. Hexter, "*Il Principe* and *lo stato,*" in Hexter, *The Vision of Politics on the Eve of the Reformation* (New York: Basic, 1973), 150–78; J. H. Whitfield, "The Anatomy of Virtue," in Whitfield, *Machiavelli* (Oxford: Blackwell, 1947); Neal Wood, "Machiavelli's Concept of *virtù* Reconsidered," *Political Studies,* 15 (1967): 159–72; Russell Price, "The Senses of *virtù* in Machiavelli," *European Studies Review,* 3 (1973): 315–45; Price, "The Theme of *gloria* in Machiavelli," *Renaissance Quarterly,* 30 (1977): 588–631; Russell Price, "*Ambizione* in Machiavelli's Thought," *History of Political Thought,* 3 (1982): 382–445; Josef Macek, "La *fortuna* chez Machiavel," *Le Moyen Âge,* 77 (1971): 305–28; Marcia Colish, "The Idea of Liberty in Machiavelli," *Journal of the History of Ideas,* 32 (1971): 323–50; repr. in William J. Connell, ed., *Renaissance Essays II* (Rochester: University of Rochester Press, 1993), 180–207. Useful glossaries to Machiavelli's terminology appear as appendixes to Machiavelli, *The Prince,* ed. Quentin Skinner and Russell Price (Cambridge: Cambridge University Press, 1988); and Machiavelli, *The Prince,* trans. Harvey C. Mansfield, 2nd ed. (Chicago: University of Chicago Press, 1998).

"skill," "cleverness," "ability," "courage," and "power," depending on the passage in which it occurs. A problem with this approach is that the English reader loses contact with Machiavelli's careful manipulation of meaning-laden words in the original Italian.[2] A second popular approach to translating Machiavelli, usually followed here, is to attempt to consistently translate important recurring Italian terms with single English terms where sense allows.[3] Often this sort of translation goes by the name of "literal." Thus, in the present translation, *virtù* is translated as "virtue," and *stato* as "state," wherever they occur. To be sure, these words mean different things in Machiavelli's changing verbal contexts. Yet there is less agility demanded of the English reader in adjusting to Machiavelli's wording than some translators have supposed. The word "virtue," for instance, as it appears in this translation of *The Prince,* where it denotes Machiavelli's *virtù,* does not refer to a person's saintliness; yet its meaning is quite close to what we encounter when we speak in English of a drug's "virtues," or when we use the phrase "by virtue of," or call someone a "virtuoso." The advantage of the literal method is that the English reader gains closer access to Machiavelli's original, and he or she is less dependent on the translator's hidden choices.

Yet clearly there are instances when context and idiom interfere with a translator's desire to be consistent. To the scholar with some knowledge of the Italian language as it was written in the fifteenth and sixteenth centuries it often seems that Machiavelli's would-be literal translators are so devoted to his nouns that they have had little patience for such grammatical nuts and bolts as articles, pronouns, and participles. These elements frequently provide a meaningful context in which to situate the key words, and they are essential to understanding the historical idiom in which Machiavelli and his contemporaries wrote.[4] For example, one important point sometimes overlooked by English-language scholars is that Machiavelli's definite

---

[2] For this reason the Skinner and Price translation really requires its excellent "Notes on the Vocabulary of *The Prince.*" Wootton's translation, Machiavelli, *The Prince,* trans. David Wootton (Indianapolis: Hackett, 1995) compensates in the case of one important word by placing *virtù* in brackets after the various English renderings.

[3] This approach has been followed by Mansfield, de Alvarez, and Codevilla: Machiavelli, *The Prince,* trans. Mansfield; Machiavelli, *The Prince,* trans. Leo Paul S. de Alvarez (Irving, Tex: University of Dallas Press, 1980; repr. Prospect Heights, Ill.: Waveland Press, 1989); and Machiavelli, *The Prince,* trans. Angelo M. Codevilla (New Haven: Yale University Press, 1997).

[4] In this regard, the "literary" translators of Machiavelli have tended to do a better job than the "literal" ones. Perhaps the best is Machiavelli, *The Prince,* trans. James B. Atkinson (Indianapolis: Bobbs-Merrill, 1976).

articles (for example, *il, la, lo*) often have a possessive force dependent on a noun. Thus *lo stato* frequently needs to be translated as "his
(or "her," "their," etc.) state," rather than simply "the state."[5] Once this
possessive use of the definite article (still standard in modern Italian,
but not in French or English) is acknowledged in translation, one can
see that Machiavelli's language is more immediate and much less
abstract and "impersonal" than commonly believed. Machiavelli's frequent use of participles, reminiscent of what one finds in Greek, poses
an additional problem. Too many English translators have shied away
from Machiavelli's participles by translating them as participles in
English. Machiavelli's Italian generally requires that one give participles
more specific English meaning by translating them as verbs in dependent, or sometimes independent, clauses that are often conditional or
concessive.

The question of whom Machiavelli addresses in *The Prince,* long a
matter of debate, is complicated somewhat by the author's use of two
different forms of the second person pronoun, both of them translated
into English by "you." Machiavelli's most common form of "you" in *The
Prince* is *voi,* which was regularly used as a singular in Machiavelli's
time, although it also functioned as a plural, as in modern Italian. Some
scholars have preferred to read Machiavelli's *voi* as a plural, which
they think indicates that Machiavelli was thinking of a readership
beyond his single dedicatee, Lorenzo de' Medici the Younger.[6] A more
probable explanation, however, is that Machiavelli's *voi* is consistently
singular, and that it refers throughout only to Machiavelli's dedicatee.
Whenever Machiavelli introduces his second form of "you," the familiar *tu,* the "you" is someone in a hypothetical and often disadvanta-
geous situation. The *tu* of *The Prince* is thus not a familiar "you," but
rather an impersonal one that sets up imagined situations, which are
thus politely distanced from the dedicatee. By using both *voi* and *tu,*
Machiavelli distinguishes between a very real "you," the man to whom
he dedicates his book, and a nonspecific "you," introduced for the sake
of discussing the circumstances in which a prince may find himself.[7]

---

[5]Although Mansfield's translation misses the grammatical point, elsewhere he
grasps the conceptual one. See Harvey C. Mansfield, *Machiavelli's Virtue* (Chicago:
University of Chicago Press, 1996), 288: "When Machiavelli uses *lo stato* without a possessive pronoun . . . he seems always to imply one."

[6]Leo Strauss, *Thoughts on Machiavelli* (Glencoe, Ill.: Free Press, 1958; repr. Chicago:
University of Chicago Press, 1995), 77; Cecil Clough, *Machiavelli Researches* (Naples:
Istituto Universitario Orientale, 1967), 51–52.

[7]Machiavelli's use of *voi* and *tu* and their adjectival forms are recorded in the notes
of this translation.

One can understand what this translation attempts, and how it differs from a sample of other English translations, by comparing the renderings of one of Machiavelli's most famous sentences, which appears near the beginning of chapter 15 of *The Prince,* where he declares (in the present version): "But since my intent is to write a thing that is useful for whoever understands it, it seemed to me more appropriate to go after the effectual truth of the thing (*andare dreto alla verità effettuale della cosa*) than the imagination of it." Among the looser versions of the second part of this sentence are those of Bull ("to represent things as they are in a real truth"), Price ("to concentrate on what really happens"), and Sonnino ("to get to the bottom of things"). Atkinson, Mansfield, and Wootton mistranslate the word *dreto* as though it meant *diretto* or "direct," when in fact it is a shortened Tuscan form of the word *indietro,* or "behind." Theirs is thus a bold and confident Machiavelli, who aims, respectively "to go straight to the actual truth of matters," "to go directly to the effectual truth of the thing," and "to go straight to a discussion of how things are in real life." De Alvarez and Milner read Machiavelli's *dreto* properly as "behind" ("to go behind to the effectual truth of the thing," "to go behind to the effectual truth of the matter"), but they fail to notice the idiomatic connection between *dreto* and the verb *andare* ("to go"). Only Codevilla ("to go after the effective truth of the thing") and Adams ("to go after the real truth of the matter") seem to have noticed that the Italian idiom *andare dietro a,* as used in this passage, means "to follow" or "to pursue," without any guarantee that one will reach the goal.[8] Thus, properly considered, Machiavelli's phrase makes a claim that is rhetorically more modest than that he will represent the truth, go directly to it, or find it behind something that stands in his way. This sort of comparative exercise, in which one reviews the translations of a line next to the other—a practice somewhat akin to shooting fish in a barrel—has its drawbacks, of course. Chief among them is the fact that one's own translation will soon be swimming in the barrel with its fellows. All the same, the present translation aspires

---

[8]*The Prince,* trans. George Bull, intro. Anthony Grafton, new edition (London: Penguin, 1999), 49; *The Prince,* ed. Skinner and Price, 54; *The Prince,* trans. Paul Sonnino (Atlantic Highlands, N.J.: Humanities Press, 1996), 84; *The Prince,* trans. Atkinson, 255; *The Prince,* trans. Mansfield, 61; *The Prince,* trans. Wootton, 48; *The Prince,* trans. de Alvarez, 93; *The Prince and Other Political Writings,* trans. Stephen J. Milner (London: Everyman, 1995), 89; *The Prince,* trans. Codevilla, 57; *The Prince,* trans. Robert Adams, 2nd ed. (New York: Norton, 1992), 42. Codevilla is often quite good on diction, but he refuses to break up Machiavelli's long sentences and to distinguish the force of participles. For explanatory purposes Adams often adds words or phrases not present in Machiavelli's text.

to a more precise rendering of Machiavelli's idiomatic language than has been available hitherto.

THE ITALIAN TEXT

This is the first English translation of *The Prince* to benefit from Italian scholars' recent contributions to our knowledge of the original text. Especially valuable have been Giorgio Inglese's critical edition published by the Istituto Storico Italiano per il Medio Evo in 1994; the same scholar's annotated paperback edition, published by Einaudi in 1995; and an edition and commentary published by Rinaldo Rinaldi in 1999 in the UTET series of Machiavelli's *Opere*.[9] Inglese's critical edition makes available in careful transcriptions the early manuscript and printed variants of the text, and his Einaudi edition offers a detailed historical commentary that adds much of value to what was previously available. Rinaldi's edition follows the text established by Inglese with only a few exceptions, and his linguistic commentary is richer than any now available. Although all scholars acknowledge the utility of Inglese's labors, his text of *The Prince* has not won universal acceptance. In particular, Inglese's readings are sometimes determined by the assumption that the text of *The Prince* was complete in its present form in early 1514, even though there is evidence that Machiavelli continued to make small changes after that date. The present translation is therefore based on the text established by Mario Casella in 1929, which has long been the best available.[10] The differences between Inglese and Casella are of little consequence to the reader of an English translation. Although Casella's edition has served as the basis for the translation, in a few instances I have followed emendations proposed by Inglese or by his chief critic, Mario Martelli.[11] I have also frequently turned to the commentary of Jean-Louis Fournel

[9]Niccolò Machiavelli, *De principatibus,* ed. Giorgio Inglese (Rome: Istituto Storico Italiano per il Medio Evo, 1994); Machiavelli, *Il Principe,* ed. Giorgio Inglese (Turin: Einaudi, 1995); Machiavelli, *De principatibus,* ed. Rinaldo Rinaldi, in Machiavelli, *Opere,* 4 vols. in 5 (Turin: UTET, 1984–1999), 1:1, 103–409.

[10]Published in Machiavelli, *Tutte le opere storiche e letterarie,* ed. Guido Mazzoni and Mario Casella (Florence: Barbèra, 1929), 3–51.

[11]Martelli, "Sette proposte per il testo del Principe," *Interpres,* 16 (1997): 189–203; Martelli, *Saggio sul "Principe"* (Rome: Salerno, 1999). See also the small volume announcing the program for a new edition of Machiavelli's works: [Mario Martelli], *Edizione nazionale delle opere di Niccolò Machiavelli* (Rome: Salerno, 1997), 17–20. If Inglese appears extreme in claiming that Machiavelli completed *The Prince* entirely by early 1514, Martelli also appears extreme in claiming that significant revisions were made as late as 1518.

and Jean-Claude Zancarini in their recent French translation of *The Prince*.[12]

All of the additional translations that appear in this volume, including the related documents, are my own—with the exceptions of an excerpt of a quote from Reginald Pole in the introduction, which was translated by Nicholas Webb, and Document 4, a poem of Machiavelli's already elegantly translated by Joseph Tusiani, upon whose version I could not improve.

[12]Machiavelli, *Le Prince,* trans. Jean-Louis Fournel and Jean-Claude Zancarini (Paris: PUF, 2000).

Contents

Foreword   iii

Preface   v

A Note about the Text and Translation   ix

PART ONE
Introduction: The Puzzle of *The Prince*   **1**

An Extreme Book for Extreme Times   6
Humanists and Heretics   9
Machiavelli before *The Prince*   14
Writing *The Prince*   17
Living with *The Prince*   19
Rival Readings of Machiavelli in Early Modern Europe   22
The Prince and the Autonomy of Politics   26
MAPS   35

PART TWO
The Prince (On Principalities)   **39**

Dedicatory Letter to Lorenzo de' Medici the Younger   39
1/How many kinds of principalities there are,
and by what means they are acquired   41

2/On hereditary principalities — 41

3/On mixed principalities — 43

4/Why Darius' kingdom, which Alexander had occupied, did not rebel from Alexander's successors after his death — 51

5/By what means cities or principalities are to be administered that, before they were occupied, lived by their own laws — 53

6/On new principalities that are acquired by one's own arms and by virtue — 54

7/On new principalities that are acquired with the arms and fortune of others — 58

8/On those who achieved principalities through wicked deeds — 64

9/On the civil principality — 68

10/In what ways the strengths of all principalities should be measured — 71

11/On ecclesiastical principalities — 73

12/How many kinds of military there are, and concerning mercenary soldiers — 76

13/On auxiliary troops, mixed troops, and one's own — 81

14/What the prince should do concerning the military — 84

15/On those things for which men and especially princes are praised or criticized — 87

16/On liberality and parsimony — 88

17/On cruelty and compassion, and whether it is better to be loved than to be feared, or the contrary — 90

18/In what way faith should be kept by princes — 93

19/On avoiding contempt and hatred — 96

20/Whether fortresses and many other things made or done by princes every day are useful or useless — 104

21/What the prince should do to be thought outstanding — 108

22/On those whom princes have in their service for secret matters — 112

23/In what way flatterers are to be avoided — 113

24/Why the princes of Italy have lost their kingdom — 115

25/How much fortune is able to do in human things, and by
what means she may be opposed 116

26/An exhortation to seize Italy, and to set her free from the
barbarians 119

PART THREE

Related Documents 125

1. Niccolò Machiavelli, *Draft of a Letter to Giovan Battista
   Soderini,* September 13–27, 1506 125

2. Francesco Vettori, *Letter to Niccolò Machiavelli,*
   November 23, 1513 129

3. Niccolò Machiavelli, *Letter to Francesco Vettori,*
   December 10, 1513 134

4. Niccolò Machiavelli, *The Thrushes,* 1513 140

5. Riccardo Riccardi, *Machiavelli's Presentation
   of* The Prince *to Lorenzo de' Medici,* ca. 1515 142

6. Niccolò Guicciardini, FROM *A Letter to Luigi Guicciardini,*
   July 29, 1517 143

7. *Early Prefaces of* The Prince 145

   Biagio Buonaccorsi, *Prefatory Letter to Pandolfo Bellacci,*
   ca. 1516–1517 145

   Teofilo Mochi, *Preface to a Manuscript of* The Prince,
   ca. 1530 147

   Antonio Blado, *Dedicatory Letter to Filippo Strozzi,*
   January 4, 1532 147

   Bernardo Giunta, *Dedicatory Letter to Giovanni Gaddi,*
   May 8, 1532 150

8. Agostino Nifo, FROM *On Skill in Ruling,* 1523 153

9. Giovan Battista Busini, FROM *A Letter to Benedetto Varchi,*
   January 23, 1549 159

10. Benedetto Varchi, FROM *Florentine History,* 1565 161

11. Étienne Binet, FROM *On the Health of Origen,* 1629 163

12. Reginald Pole, FROM *Apology to Charles V,* 1539 164

13. Innocent Gentillet, FROM *Discourses against Machiavelli*, 1576 — 166

14. Christopher Marlowe, FROM *The Jew of Malta*, ca. 1590 — 170

15. Frederick the Great, FROM *The Refutation of Machiavelli's Prince*, 1740 — 171

16. Jean-Jacques Rousseau, FROM *On the Social Contract*, After 1762 — 177

17. Benito Mussolini, *A Prelude to Machiavelli*, 1924 — 179

18. Antonio Gramsci, FROM *Prison Notebooks*, 1932–1934 — 184

APPENDIXES

A Niccolò Machiavelli Chronology (1469–1527)   190

Questions for Consideration   193

Selected Bibliography   195

Index   199

PART ONE

Introduction:
The Puzzle
of *The Prince*

Niccolò Machiavelli, a writer from Renaissance Florence who lived from 1469 to 1527, is both emblematic of the time in which he lived and a harbinger of times to come. Machiavelli grew up amid the intellectual and cultural achievements of Florence at the time of Lorenzo de' Medici the Magnificent. As an adult, Machiavelli represented the Florentine Republic on diplomatic missions to Renaissance Europe's kings, emperors, and popes; he also collaborated on military projects with the great artists Leonardo da Vinci and Michelangelo. Throughout his life, Machiavelli was profoundly influenced by the Renaissance recovery and study of the civilization of the ancient Greeks and Romans. By studying Machiavelli we can learn much about the Renaissance.

But Machiavelli is also important because his writings, in particular *The Prince,* had an important impact on subsequent Western philosophy, science, and political theory. Machiavelli made a significant break with the idealism of earlier writers by offering a body of political theory that he said should be measured not by its adherence to abstract standards of truth and moral goodness, but by the beneficial material effects it would bring. In his emphasis on the real rather than the ideal, or "the effectual truth of the thing" (*The Prince,* chapter 15) rather than the moral truth, Machiavelli began what would become a

dominant trend in subsequent Western intellectual history. Many later philosophers and scientists openly acknowledged their debt to him.

Above all, Machiavelli remains famous today because of his ruthless advice to rulers in his best-known work, *The Prince*. Many guides to good government have been written, but Machiavelli's *Prince* is unique in the Western tradition because it was the first to argue explicitly that good government requires the skillful use of cruelty and deception to continually take what belongs to others.

For centuries Machiavelli's name was synonymous with evil. In part, this was due to Machiavelli's conscious abandonment of the moral principles central to Christianity and to most ancient philosophies. As a result, in 1559 the Catholic Church formally banned Machiavelli's writings. Protestants, too, denounced Machiavelli, whose ideas, they said, were responsible for the St. Bartholomew's Day Massacre of French Huguenots in 1572.[1] In early modern England, Machiavelli had such a reputation for wickedness that at least one writer thought the term "Old Nick," a name for the devil that is still used in Great Britain, referred originally to Machiavelli, because the Christian name Niccolò is an Italian form of Nicholas.[2] The taint associated with Machiavelli persisted for so long that in Russia, in 1936, during the first of Stalin's great purge trials, the prosecution considered it very damaging that one of the accused had written the preface for a Russian translation of *The Prince*.[3] More recently, the sinister interpretation of the Florentine writer led rap artist Tupac Shakur to rename himself "Makaveli: the Don Killuminati" shortly before his murder.

Machiavelli's reputation not only survives, but it has actually improved considerably. The Machiavelli to whom we allude today is kinder and gentler than the Machiavelli of centuries ago. No longer seen as evil through and through, people tend to invoke his name when someone tries to cleverly circumvent established procedures, or when they hope certain regrettable transgressions will result in benefits that outweigh any shortcomings. To be sure, there remains something unwholesome about Machiavelli's reputation, but many argue that he must have been misunderstood in the past, that he was merely a "realist" or a "results-oriented" thinker whose reputation suffered

---

Opposite: A sixteenth-century portrait of Niccolò Machiavelli, traditionally said to have been painted by Rosso Fiorentino, recently attributed to Andrea Boscoli. From a private collection.

Reproduced by permission of Agnew's of London.

Right: As this label from a twenty-first century beer bottle shows, Old Nick is still an English name for the devil. One theory is that the name originally referred to "Nick" Machiavelli.

Reproduced by permission of Young & Co.'s Brewery PLC.

undeservedly. As a result of the greater acceptance of his ideas, in recent decades Machiavelli has become especially famous in the world of business. Books with such titles as *The New Machiavelli: The Art of Politics in Business* have become standard fare for executives.[4]

Most of us still like to think of our leaders as trustworthy, compassionate, and generous. However, Machiavelli argues (especially in chapters 15–19 of *The Prince*) that the qualities of untrustworthiness, cruelty, and stinginess are useful to a ruler. And, when forced to act, the prince will be more successful if he exhibits these unattractive qualities rather than their opposites. Successful leaders, Machiavelli attempts to show, are really not very nice at all. Thus his harsh portrayal of sound leadership as necessarily ruthless and cold-hearted seems as hard to swallow today as it was when *The Prince* was first published.

As we read *The Prince,* it is hard to escape sharing some of the indignant emotions of earlier generations of readers. Today's reader, like earlier readers, reacts with horror at Machiavelli's description (in chapter 8) of how the young Liverotto of Fermo (Oliverotto Euffreducci) deceived and murdered his kindly uncle in order to seize the city of Fermo. Similarly, readers past and present have found it outrageous that Machiavelli congratulates Liverotto on how well he accomplished the overthrow of his uncle.

Another passage that still shocks readers is Machiavelli's account (in chapter 7) of the career of Cesare Borgia. Machiavelli holds up Borgia, the brutal and treacherous illegitimate son of Pope Alexander VI, as a model for the new prince. Especially memorable is Machiavelli's telling of the story of Remirro de Orco (Ramiro de Lorqua), a trusted follower of Borgia's, who was asked to bring order to an unruly area in central Italy known as the Romagna, a province that was being looted by local brigands. Remirro ended the violence by imposing harsh justice and executing many of the brigands, which made the people of the Romagna hate him. Once order was restored, and Borgia wished to gain the support of the people, he decided to arrest and execute his own lieutenant, Remirro. As Machiavelli describes it, when Remirro's body was put on display, the people of the Romagna were "at once stupefied and satisfied." Machiavelli praises the forceful logic of Borgia's approach to the problem of order in the Romagna. But Borgia's tactics are cruel; it is hard not to identify, at least in part, with the betrayed underling who was following his master's orders.

Thus we sometimes shudder as we read *The Prince*. These are not pleasant lessons. The fact that Machiavelli's advice runs counter to what we would like to hear about our leaders, and to what other writers have so often said leaders should do, once led a scholar to suggest that Machiavelli wrote *The Prince* as a satire of other political advice books.[5] The idea contains a kernel of truth, although it is hardly a full and satisfactory explanation. In Machiavelli's day there were a number of treatises, known as "mirrors of princes," which advised rulers to be just, merciful, and generous, and to use these qualities in winning the love and affection of their subjects. Clearly Machiavelli had these other treatises in mind when he wrote *The Prince,* as he borrowed many of his chapter titles from them.[6] And Machiavelli takes evident delight in coming to conclusions that are the opposite of those of the "mirrors of princes." Yet it is impossible to sustain the argument that he wrote *The Prince* purely as satire. Machiavelli's letters mention *The Prince* with only the highest seriousness. Certainly none of Machiavelli's contemporaries thought *The Prince* was a humorous work. In a lengthy book Machiavelli wrote on republics, the *Discourses on the First Ten Books of Titus Livy,* which has never been considered a satire, there are sober cross-references to *The Prince;* and *The Prince,* too, twice refers to the *Discourses* in a perfectly serious way. So it seems clear that Machiavelli intended these two books, *The Prince* on principalities, the *Discourses* on republics, to be complementary, and that people would read them with something approaching equal gravity.

This leaves us with the great puzzle concerning *The Prince*: to discover what Machiavelli intended to achieve by writing it. The question of Machiavelli's purpose has troubled readers of *The Prince* since it first began to circulate in manuscript in Florence, probably in 1516. In fact, Machiavelli's career and his other writings suggest that he did not really support rule by princes. Rather than a monarchical regime, Machiavelli seems genuinely to have preferred a republican form of government, in which sovereignty and authority reside in the citizens and their legitimate representatives, not in a single ruler. Machiavelli's *Discourses* show rather decisively that he preferred republics; even in *The Prince* Machiavelli praises republics for the passion they inspire in their citizens. (See especially chapter 5.) So why Machiavelli should have written a book that instructs men how to become princes, that teaches princes how to preserve their rule, and that promotes cruel and tyrannical techniques is even more puzzling.

AN EXTREME BOOK FOR EXTREME TIMES

To explain the troubling advice that Machiavelli delivers in *The Prince,* readers often suggest that the work reflects the difficult times in which the author lived. Extraordinary circumstances may have required the extraordinary measures Machiavelli recommends.

There is no question but that Machiavelli, who was born in 1469 and died in 1527, lived during a period in history that was both destabilizing and revolutionary. And he was well aware that great changes were taking place in European society during his lifetime. Still, it is worth noting that he did not always attribute to events the same importance that we would assign to them today. Thus in his writings Machiavelli never explicitly mentions the discovery of the Americas or the opening of a sea route around the African continent to India. In *The Prince,* when he lists the accomplishments of the Spanish king, Ferdinand the Catholic (see chapter 21), he does not mention the Spanish discoveries in the New World.[7] In the military, gunpowder weapons, especially siege cannons and the ancestors of rifles, known as arquebuses, were rapidly transforming how European wars were fought, but in *The Prince* Machiavelli emphasizes the tactics of foot soldiers armed with pikes and bucklers, the spears and shields of his day (see chapter 26).[8] In yet another area, the success of the printing press set off an information revolution that profoundly changed the worldview of sixteenth-century Europeans,[9] but Machiavelli, who did have some involvement with the printing industry, neglected to write about it, and his three greatest works—*The Prince,* the *Discourses,* and the *Florentine Histories*—

remained unpublished when he died. Clearly Machiavelli's perspective on his times was not the same as our own.

Machiavelli perceived other developments as more immediate and traumatic because they disrupted affairs in his native city, Florence, as well as his own life and career. Foremost among these was a series of foreign invasions of the Italian peninsula that began in 1494.

The Italy in which Machiavelli grew to adulthood still bore the scars of bitter political contests dating from the later Middle Ages. Struggles between the papacy and the Holy Roman Empire during the twelfth and thirteenth centuries resulted in divisions among and within the Italian cities, in which followers of the papacy were identified as "Guelfs" and rival followers of the Holy Roman Empire were called "Ghibellines." In the early fourteenth century, however, both the Empire and the papacy lost much of their influence over Italian affairs. Imperial power in Italy largely vanished after the abortive invasion of Emperor Henry VII of Luxemburg, who died in Genoa in 1314. Papal authority in Italy diminished during the Avignon papacy (1309–76) and the Great Schism (1378–1417). In addition to this power vacuum, the demographic collapse associated with the Black Death, which arrived in 1347–48, had the effect of disproportionately weakening Italy's midsize cities, paving the way for the largest Italian powers to assert themselves through a series of territorial acquisitions. Between 1350 and 1454 the duchy of Milan, the republics of Florence and Venice, the papacy (resurgent after the end of the schism in 1417), and the Kingdom of Naples expanded their dominions, annexing many of the peninsula's smaller states and feudal territories in order to create larger territorial states. Territorial expansion changed the nature of Italian politics and diplomacy, as the more distant and impersonal rule of a few controlling regimes replaced the face-to-face style of government of hundreds of formerly independent communes. The new territorial states established larger chanceries and more effective fiscal policies, and they secured broad statutory authority and more extensive policing powers.[10] They also discovered that they could no longer defend themselves adequately with their own citizen militias, so they hired troops of professional soldiers working under mercenary captains.[11]

To preserve their new states—both against the possibility that one Italian power might become dominant and against outside invaders— the major Italian powers agreed to the Peace of Lodi in 1454. The leading states agreed to settle their differences internally and to prevent meddling by foreign powers. One effect of the Peace of Lodi was what has sometimes been called the "birth of modern diplomacy"; the need to resolve problems quickly encouraged the Italian states to consult with one another frequently by means of ambassadors and other agents.[12] There were indeed wars in Italy between 1454 and the French invasion of 1494, some of them quite fierce, yet, all the same, an overall diplomatic balance was maintained, foreign armies were kept out, and the peninsula achieved a remarkable level of prosperity. In *The Prince,* Machiavelli remembers this period with nostalgia. (See chapter 11.)

Italian affairs changed dramatically in 1494, when King Charles VIII of France marched an army across the Alps into Italy to lay claim to the Kingdom of Naples. Although Charles was forced to retreat to France in 1495, his invasion irreparably upset the balance of power in Italy. Governments up and down the peninsula changed. Long-established ruling families were exiled or eliminated. City after city that had considered itself well defended found itself under attack by foreign troops, and all too often there were horrendous sackings involving thousands of innocent civilians. Well-disciplined foreign foot soldiers, especially from Switzerland and Germany, proved superior to Italian mercenary companies in battle after battle. Charles's invasion set a precedent for further invasions in coming years by other European rulers, including Emperor-elect Maximilian I, King Ferdinand the Catholic of Spain, Kings Louis XII and Francis I of France, and Emperor Charles V. In this atmosphere, under Popes Alexander VI and Julius II, the papacy became an aggressive territorial power. Papal imperialism was accompanied by startling abuses of the church's spiritual power, in order to raise money and forge alliances, and those abuses led, on the one hand, to outright religious skepticism, and, on the other, to increasingly urgent calls for church reform. For Italians who had prospered under the previous political order it seemed that a golden age had ended and that a new iron age had begun.

No doubt one can attribute much that seems harsh and unusual in *The Prince* to these difficult circumstances. Machiavelli claims to be a realist, someone who tries to explain "the effectual truth of the thing" (chapter 15), and it is important to understand that he was responding to an unusual historical situation when he wrote *The Prince.* The call for a new prince to lead Italy out of its troubles that appears in his final chapter (chapter 26) may appear idealistic, even messianic, today, but it was written in response to a deeply painful and very real historical situation that was affecting the Italian states. Machiavelli appears to be saying that simple political survival in such unpredictable and violent times requires an unusual adaptability and a willingness to break with traditional ways of doing things.

Yet, remarkably, Machiavelli's *Prince* does not claim to be a manual for extraordinary times. It does not come with a label that reads "Warning: Emergency Use Only." On the contrary, Machiavelli offers rules for navigating the seas of power politics that he claims were always valid and always will be. They are confirmed not only by his own experience and the experience of his contemporaries, but also by the experiences of the ancient statesmen and politicians whose history he studied, whom he mentions so frequently in his work, and whom he does not consider fundamentally different from the men of his own time. The dramatic historical events of the early sixteenth century may have prompted Machiavelli to write down his lessons for princes, but certainly many of his rules for taking and retaining political power have long-term value. Some remain effective in our own time, as Machiavelli's devotees in the business world attest. To understand why Machiavelli wrote *The Prince* we need to be attentive to the historical context and the circumstances under which he wrote, but if we are truly to grasp the challenge *The Prince* poses, we need to try to see it as more than a reflexive creation of its particular time, and to understand how Machiavelli believed he was writing for all time.

HUMANISTS AND HERETICS

Another approach to the puzzle of *The Prince* involves looking beyond the political circumstances described in the book to the intellectual context in which Machiavelli wrote. As most authors do when they write, Machiavelli was entering into a larger intellectual discussion when he composed *The Prince*. There were many other writers in Machiavelli's day who, like him, believed that they were communicating valuable truths to posterity.

One particularly important category of writer that influenced Machiavelli comprises the many authors of his and earlier generations who are known as humanists. First-time readers of *The Prince,* who are usually not familiar with the intellectual history of fifteenth- and sixteenth-century Italy, are invariably startled by Machiavelli's many examples from ancient Greek and Roman history. Although Machiavelli explains what is important in the examples he cites, and modern footnotes can usually supply whatever else is needed, the sheer abundance of these citations can be an obstacle to a full appreciation of *The Prince*. To better understand Machiavelli's purposes, it is necessary to consider his relationship to the intellectual movement known as Renaissance humanism.

Humanism had its beginnings in the early fourteenth century, when a number of poetically inclined literary hobbyists began to acquire a deep knowledge of classical antiquity, principally by studying the texts of ancient Roman and, later, Greek authors.[13] From the fourteenth through the sixteenth century, such humanists as Petrarch, Coluccio Salutati, Leonardo Bruni, Guarino Guarini, Lorenzo Valla, Poggio Bracciolini, Angelo Poliziano, Rudolph Agricola, and Desiderius Erasmus made the study of the literature of classical antiquity a basic part of the education of Europe's elites.[14]

Although he studied under humanist teachers as a young man in Florence, Machiavelli himself is usually not thought to have been a humanist; one of the hallmarks of a humanist was the ability to compose elegantly in Latin, and all of Machiavelli's major works were written in Italian. Machiavelli also frequently presents himself as a critic of the humanists. In the *Florentine Histories* he criticizes Bruni and Bracciolini for omitting domestic politics in their histories of Florence. In the *Discourses* he laments the fact that many people of his day imitate the forms of the civilization of classical antiquity but make no attempt to revive its substance.

Yet throughout his life Machiavelli read widely and deeply in the Latin classics. He was also attuned to a number of the intellectual controversies that resulted from the rediscovery of the writings and thought of classical antiquity. He was especially interested in ancient history, for instance, and in his critical approach to the writings of ancient historians he relied on the previous discoveries and methods of such humanists as Bruni, Valla, Bracciolini, Flavio Biondo, and Poliziano, who preferred to look for human rather than divine causes of historical events.

Also like many of these humanists, Machiavelli was interested in the ways offered by ancient philosophy for viewing the world from a perspective that differed from the Christian religion and theology of his day. Machiavelli appears to have been drawn especially to the ancient philosophy of Epicurus, which denied the existence of the human soul and an afterlife, held that the earth evolves without divine intervention, and based human morality on the pursuit of pleasure. In the later Middle Ages there was interest in Epicurus' beliefs in Florence, where several prominent Ghibellines were accused of Epicureanism, and some of these were condemned as heretics.[15] A subsequent revival of interest took place in the fifteenth century, with the discovery in 1417 by the Florentine humanist Poggio Bracciolini of a manuscript of a great philosophical poem by Lucretius, a follower of Epicurus: *On the Nature of Things,* written in the first century BCE. Lucretius' account of Epicureanism was far more elegant and systematic than anything that had previously been gleaned from other ancient texts. Fifteenth-century humanists had a number of reasons to be cautious in disseminating a work that was directly contrary to the scriptural and Aristotelian accounts of the universe, as well as to Christian morality. Nevertheless, *On the Nature of Things* was widely read, and one of the persons known to have copied the poem—because a manuscript in his hand survives in the Vatican library in Rome—was Machiavelli.[16]

In Machiavelli's own time, however, Renaissance humanism was increasingly following paths the former Florentine secretary cannot have been comfortable with. Down one road lay a new academicism; down the other a Christian Reformation. Machiavelli's *Prince* refused to follow either course.

With the acceptance of humanistic studies into the university curriculum, and with the success of the printing press, it became possible for larger numbers of Europe's humanists to have reasonable careers in which they could devote themselves to the study of antiquity for its own sake, without having to worry about the implications of their discoveries for contemporaries, or to find ways of making their research relevant. Humanist writers devoted increased attention to editions and commentaries of some of the more obscure classical texts, and to the compiling of such reference works as Polydore Vergil's *On the Discoverers of Things,* Erasmus' *Adages,* and Raffaello Maffei's *Urbane Commentaries.* One of the monuments of early-sixteenth-century scholarship was an extensive commentary on a Greek pharmacological text of the first century CE by Dioscorides Pedanius published by a chancery colleague of Machiavelli's, who also held a post in the Florentine university at Pisa.[17] The emphasis in this kind of work was on the sorting out of arcane details. It was far removed from what really interested Machiavelli, who, as he states numerous times, was hoping for a reform of politics, social organization, and military practice that would be guided, at least in part, by what could be learned from ancient history.

There were humanists in Machiavelli's day who sincerely sought thoroughgoing reform, but a reform of the church, which would have results quite different from the reforms Machiavelli was contemplating. Machiavelli wrote *The Prince* in 1513–14, several years before the Protestant Reformation began in 1517, when Martin Luther posted his Ninety-Five Theses in Wittenberg, but at a time when church reform was very much on the minds of writers and churchmen throughout Europe. Throughout the fifteenth century humanist intellectuals had been cautious about discussing church doctrine and practice. Many humanists followed ecclesiastical careers or found other employment in the church, and during the fifteenth century the church itself slowly became more vigorous in combating arguments it considered to be heterodox. The execution for heresy in 1417 of the Bohemian reformer Jan Hus and his follower Jerome of Prague seems to have had a deep impact on Italian humanists, judging from the large number of surviving manuscript copies of a letter of Bracciolini's describing Jerome's execution. Lorenzo Valla applied the critical methods of humanism to Christian texts and doctrine, challenging tradition on numerous points, with the result that in 1444 the Inquisition in Naples investigated him for possible heresy. An intellectual movement for church reform needed a broader consensus to survive, both within the church and among the laity, and by the end of the fifteenth century there were signs that such a consensus was materializing. Thus Girolamo Savonarola's preaching in Florence for a reform of the church won the adherence of most of the populace and also of humanist intellectuals like Marsilio Ficino and Giovanni Pico della Mirandola. Although Savonarola was executed on a trumped-up charge of heresy in 1498, his followers kept his ideas and his memory alive for decades thereafter.

It was the Dutch humanist Desiderius Erasmus who best typified the humanist movement for church reform at the time Machiavelli wrote *The Prince.* Erasmus was both a remarkable classical scholar and a devout Christian. He revered ancient philosophy in the Platonic and Ciceronian tradition for its emphasis on the personal dignity of the individual and the importance of education. The same principles, he believed, appeared in the New Testament, and so he argued that Christianity should return to the original "philosophy of Christ." Making skillful use of the printing press, Erasmus reached out to a large public, much of it of his own creation; through his popular educational dialogues, called the *Colloquies,* he trained many people to read his eloquent Latin. His most famous work, *The Praise of Folly,* written in 1510 and first published in 1511, attacked the corruption and venality of the church and it lambasted Pope Julius II. With the death of Julius II in 1513, and the election of the Medici pope Leo X, the Fifth Lateran Council, originally called by Julius II in 1512, made a serious effort to reform the church. But by the time the council closed in 1517, its attempt at reform would soon be engulfed in the storm that began with the Protestant Reformation.

Machiavelli seems to have had little regard for the contemporary movement for church reform: He seems to have thought that Christianity itself caused many of the problems in contemporary society. Like Erasmus, Machiavelli disliked Pope Julius II. In the *Discourses* Machiavelli even wrote that he had wished for Julius's assassination.[18] Yet Machiavelli's *Prince* reveals an undoubted admiration (especially in chapter 25) for the pope's abilities as a political and military leader. Machiavelli criticizes the one reformer he mentions by name, Girolamo Savonarola, both directly, as an "unarmed prophet" (in chapter 6), and indirectly, through praise of Alexander VI (in chapter 7), who had him put to death as a heretic. Although Machiavelli belonged to a religious confraternity like many of his fellow Florentines,[19] and although it is likely that he confessed to a priest on his deathbed,[20] a careful reading of his works reveals him as a man with little regard for Christianity, which he portrayed as a religion that mistakenly exalted weakness. As he later wrote in the *Discourses,*

> Our religion glorified humble and contemplative men more than active ones. Then it posited the highest good in humility, poverty, and in disdain for human things [. . .]. This way of life thus appears to have rendered the world weak, and given it in prey to wicked men, who are able to manipulate it safely, since mankind, in order to go to Heaven, thinks how to endure the beatings it receives, rather than how to avenge them.[21]

The Prince, too, is consistent with this disregard for the Christian religion. In chapter 19 Machiavelli likens the papacy to the Mameluke sultanate in Muslim Egypt. In chapter 6, in ironic remarks about Moses, he suggests that the author of the Pentateuch was not really God's agent, but rather a leader endowed with "virtue of spirit" just as the pagan princes Cyrus, Romulus, and Theseus (who, like Moses, were all born in questionable circumstances).

Although he appears not to have been a sincere Christian, Machiavelli recognizes that Christianity is the religion that holds sway in the Europe of his time, and that it is unlikely to disappear. Rather than follow the reformers, however, Machiavelli appears to be looking for ways to make Christianity better serve the ends of political regimes. The ruler Machiavelli praises most highly for his religious policy is Ferdinand the Catholic (in chapter 21), who did not reform the Spanish church, but manipulated it to increase his own power.

Thus, although Machiavelli's *Prince* addresses contemporary intellectual issues, such as the relationship of the present to classical antiquity and the proper role of the Church, the ideas Machiavelli put forth were far from typical. An understanding of Machiavelli's intellectual context helps to round out the picture, but it does not really solve the puzzle concerning the composition of *The Prince*. To better understand Machiavelli's reasons for writing *The Prince* we need to look more closely at Machiavelli himself.

MACHIAVELLI BEFORE *THE PRINCE*

Niccolò Machiavelli was born in Florence on May 3, 1469, the son of Bernardo Machiavelli, a notary, and his wife Bartolomea Nelli, a writer of religious poetry.[22] Niccolò was the third of four children, after two sisters, Primavera and Margherita; a brother, Totto, followed him. The Machiavelli family was one of the more distinguished of the city's patrician families. It traced its ancestry to minor nobility from the town of Montevarchi, in the Florentine *contado,* as the territory or "county" surrounding Florence was called. At home as a boy, Niccolò read Livy and Cicero as well as other Latin authors.[23] Bernardo provided his son with a fine humanist education, most appropriate for the career as a lawyer he probably hoped Niccolò would pursue.

Relatively little is known about Machiavelli's life prior to his election as second chancellor to the Florentine Signoria in 1498. For instance, we do not know why he failed to earn his law degree. There are some indications that the young Machiavelli may have been close to the Medici family before the family's exile in 1494, but the evidence is far from secure. On the other hand, the evidence is certain that Machiavelli belonged to a group in Florence that was strongly opposed to Girolamo Savonarola. The fiery Dominican preacher from Ferrara had come to political prominence after the exile of the Medici and the restoration of the Florentine republican constitution. Savonarola urged Florentines to purge themselves of their vices, by, among other things, constructing bonfires of vanities (paintings of pagan themes, luxurious dresses, licentious books, ladies' mirrors), and his message of religious renewal achieved considerable popular support. One of Machiavelli's earliest surviving letters describes a sermon of Savonarola's in disparaging terms.[24] In the immediate aftermath of Savonarola's execution in 1498, Machiavelli received his appointment as second chancellor after the office was vacated by a follower of Savonarola.[25] The second chancellor was the official in charge of the government's correspondence with territorial governors and local governments throughout the Florentine state in Tuscany. In addition,

Machiavelli was made secretary to the Ten of Liberty and Peace, a council in charge of military affairs. His career now determined, Machiavelli married Marietta Corsini, by whom he had five children.[26] Machiavelli also served as the republic's agent on a series of diplomatic missions to foreign rulers and governments. And, from 1507, Machiavelli served as chancellor to the Nine of the Militia—a position in which he organized and directed the affairs of a new military force consisting of inhabitants of Florence's subject territory in Tuscany. Machiavelli's work for the Florentine Republic in these posts continued until the return of the Medici family from exile in 1512. It provided the immediate experience in statecraft on which he drew when he began composing *The Prince* in 1513.[27]

The rich dispatches that survive from Machiavelli's diplomatic missions convey his first impressions of many of the persons described in *The Prince,* including Louis XII of France, the emperor-elect Maximilian, Pope Julius II, and Cesare Borgia. Perhaps the most interesting of these was from Machiavelli's embassy to Borgia in 1502 and 1503. Cesare was the bastard son of the Aragonese pope Alexander VI Borgia, who is notorious as one of the most corrupt and violent popes in history. Alexander had originally decided on an ecclesiastical career for Cesare and promoted him to the rank of cardinal, but when Cesare's older brother died and Alexander needed a marriageable son to advance his political ambitions, Cesare left the cloth at his father's behest. The pope then named his son captain general of the church and charged him with regaining papal authority over the province of the Romagna—a territory that had nominally belonged for centuries to the popes, but which over the years had been divided among numerous petty feudal lords, many of whom disputed papal jursidiction over their lands.

In a series of brilliant military campaigns, Borgia brought all of the Romagna under his sway and installed a new centralized regime there, while he and his father continued to plot extending their rule over other parts of the peninsula. Twice, in 1501 and 1502, Borgia nearly conquered Florence by force, and on both occasions only last-minute negotiations saved the city. Thus Borgia was no friend of the Florentines or of Machiavelli. Nonetheless, a certain admiration for this clever, ambitious, and ruthless opponent is evident in Machiavelli's official correspondence. In a dispatch of November 13, 1502, Machiavelli wrote to his Florentine superiors, "you have to understand that one is dealing here with a prince who governs by himself, and that whoever does not wish to write caprices and dreams has to check the facts, and that checking them takes time. . . ." A few weeks later he wrote of

Borgia, "one sees in him a luck unheard-of, a spirit and a hope that is superhuman in being able to achieve its every wish."[28] Machiavelli remarked on Borgia's decisiveness, his secrecy, and his boldness, and similar admiring phrases recur in Machiavelli's famous description of Borgia in chapter 7 of *The Prince,* where he vigorously describes Borgia as the model of how a prince ought to conduct himself.

Another important aspect of Machiavelli's experience in government was his attempt to establish a Florentine militia. Contrary to what Machiavelli argues in chapter 12 of *The Prince,* citizen militias had not gone out of use in fifteenth-century Italy because of laziness and corruption in the governments of the Italian states. Instead, the militia decayed as an institution because hired mercenary troops were more effective. New technology, including artillery and firearms, demanded professional expertise. Moreover, the steadily growing economies of the major urban centers of the peninsula during the Renaissance made hired military assistance more affordable, because governments could recruit soldiers from outside areas, especially from the poorer agricultural and pastoral areas of Italy. Regardless of their expertise and availability, Machiavelli emphasized the unreliability of mercenary forces, because these soldiers had little reason to risk their lives in battles when their own homes and lands were not at stake. Even when mercenary troops were victorious, Machiavelli argued, their captains would be tempted to seize power from their employers. It was Machiavelli's idea to establish a central Florentine agency, the Nine of the Militia, which would arm and train Tuscan peasants in the techniques of modern infantry warfare.

To Machiavelli's enduring dismay, this Florentine militia was never adequately tested. Its one significant achievement occurred at the end of a long war with Pisa, when Machiavelli and his troops of peasants maintained a blockade that forced the city to surrender to Florence on terms in 1509. In 1512, when an imperial army marched through Tuscany in an attempt to restore the exiled Medici family to Florence, Florentine leaders sent Machiavelli's militia out in the wrong direction, with the result that the enemy marched unhindered to the large subject town of Prato, just twelve kilometers from Florence. Probably it made no difference, but mercenary forces, rather than Machiavelli's militia, defended Prato, and the enemy captured and mercilessly sacked the town. News of the calamity in nearby Prato inspired terror in Florence, causing the collapse of the republican regime that employed Machiavelli. The Medici family was restored to Florence and quickly reestablished its control over the city. Although Machiavelli attempted to stay on in his post, on November 10, 1512, he was removed from office and required to remain in Florentine territory for a period of one year.

Misfortune followed misfortune. In February 1513 Machiavelli's name was found on a list dropped accidentally from the pocket of a man arrested for plotting to overthrow the Medici family and restore the republic. Machiavelli was arrested as a possible participant. He claimed that the arrested conspirator had never contacted him, and suggested that the list consisted of those the conspirator planned to approach for a possible plot, rather than of those who had already agreed to it. Even under torture he refused to confess, and he was sentenced to life in prison. However, when Cardinal Giovanni de' Medici of Florence was elected Pope Leo X on March 11, 1513, the government declared a general pardon as part of the festivities, and Machiavelli was released from prison. Machiavelli went out to his family farm at Sant'Andrea in Percussina, where the occasional literary pursuits he had engaged in during his career in government now became his major occupation.

WRITING *THE PRINCE*

Machiavelli was not happy in retirement. It remained his avowed aim to serve again in government. Such service probably would have been in the government of a prince, notwithstanding Machiavelli's public experience with and private preference for a republican system of government. This goal seems the most likely explanation for the subject of Machiavelli's most famous work, which he now began to write. Such an explanation finds confirmation in the famous letter that Machiavelli wrote to his friend Francesco Vettori on December 10, 1513 (Document 3), in which he expressed his intention to dedicate *The Prince* to Giuliano de' Medici, the brother of the new pope, Leo X, in the hope that Giuliano would find a way of employing him. This is also the message of Machiavelli's eventual dedicatory letter, addressed instead to Giuliano's nephew, Lorenzo de' Medici the Younger. In order to achieve his goal of employment, Machiavelli set to work using the tools of his former trade as secretary: pen and ink.

Giuliano de' Medici had probably been an acquaintance of Machiavelli's when he was a young man, before the exile of the Medici in 1494. Thus Machiavelli sent Giuliano two sonnets from prison, in February or March 1513, requesting Giuliano's intervention on his behalf, and he wrote a third sonnet, "The Thrushes" (Document 4), to Giuliano several months after his release. The poems indicate a certain familiarity, and one scholar has argued recently that Machiavelli wrote

"The Thrushes" as a dedicatory sonnet, later discarded, for *The Prince.*[29] At the time of Machiavelli's writing of *The Prince,* from summer 1513 to early 1514, it was well known that Pope Leo was considering either creating a new principality for Giuliano in north-central Italy, probably in the Modenese territory previously controlled by the dukes of Ferrara, or bestowing on him the papal fief of the Kingdom of Naples. In fact, in May 1513 Pope Leo called his brother Giuliano to Rome and removed him from authority in Florentine affairs. From a practical point of view, then, while he was writing *The Prince,* Machiavelli probably hoped to be working not in Florence, but in Modena, in a territory as famous for its feuds and its brigands as was Cesare Borgia's Romagna, or perhaps in Naples, where there was the likelihood of a significant military campaign to dislodge the Spanish. Reading *The Prince* in light of these considerations, it becomes easier to see why Machiavelli emphasizes Cesare Borgia's experience in the Romagna in chapter 7, why Machiavelli devotes so much attention to military affairs, and why he is so careful in describing Ferdinand the Catholic, the conqueror of Naples, to the point of deliberately not naming him in chapter 18.[30]

Giuliano, however, increasingly lost favor with the pope. In Rome he became famous for a dissipated lifestyle and for consorting with artists, poets, and astrologers while neglecting papal and family business. In early 1515, moreover, the papal court learned that Machiavelli was hoping to be hired by Giuliano. On February 14, 1515, Giuliano received a letter from Pietro Ardinghelli, a papal secretary in Rome, in which Ardinghelli described a conversation with Cardinal Giulio de' Medici:

Cardinal de' Medici asked me yesterday, in very strict confidence, if I knew whether Your Excellency had taken Niccolò Machiavelli into your service, and when I replied to him that I had no news of it, nor did I believe it, his most reverend lordship spoke to me the following formal words: "I don't believe it either; however, because there is news of this from Florence, I remind him that this suits neither him nor us. . . . Write to him on my behalf that I advise him to have nothing to do with Niccolò; and I say this not so as to teach him what he needs to do, but moved by love, etc."[31]

The prohibition on Machiavelli's service with Giuliano was quite clear. How this was communicated to Machiavelli is not known, but he must have found out about it, since in 1515 he stopped pursuing a job with Giuliano, and instead he turned his attention to Giuliano's nephew,

Lorenzo de' Medici the Younger, who at that time was the de facto ruler of Florence.

Although *The Prince* was written for Giuliano, it was dedicated to Lorenzo. Consequently there has been much discussion of the extent to which Machiavelli may have revised *The Prince* before presenting it to Lorenzo. There is such a concentration of thought and continuity of style in *The Prince* that some scholars believe that Machiavelli composed the entire text as we now have it, including the dedicatory letter, in the period 1513–14. The only modification many of these scholars will admit is the substitution of Lorenzo's name for Giuliano's in the dedicatory letter, although some accept that Machiavelli may have inserted a reference to the *Discourses* at the beginning of chapter 2. Debate continues on these questions, but a majority of scholars now accepts that Machiavelli probably wrote chapters 1–25 with Giuliano in mind in 1513–14, but added the dedicatory letter and chapter 26 (the "Exhortation") at the time of the work's presentation to Lorenzo. Insertions in the existing text that Machiavelli may have made in 1515 include the reference in chapter 2 to the *Discourses,* which he had begun to write by 1515, and part of chapter 3, since there is a probable reference (hitherto unnoticed) to the death of the French king Louis XII, which took place during the night of December 31, 1514–January 1, 1515.[32]

The Prince as we now have it is essentially the text that Machiavelli presented to Lorenzo de' Medici the Younger in 1515 in the hope of securing employment. Although the copy Machiavelli gave Lorenzo appears not to have survived, the earliest manuscript copies that exist were written shortly afterward, in 1516 or 1517.

There is no indication that Lorenzo ever read Machiavelli's treatise. Machiavelli's dedication and presentation of the work seem to have been an utter failure. According to an account that purports to give Machiavelli's own version of the affair, and which is consistent with all that is known of the young Lorenzo's character (Document 5), when Machiavelli went in person to present his manuscript of *The Prince* to Lorenzo, there was another man who came to offer the young Medici lord a brace of hunting dogs. Attracted by the dogs, Lorenzo ignored Machiavelli entirely.

LIVING WITH *THE PRINCE*

The failure to win a job must have been devastating for Machiavelli. By 1515 Machiavelli was already immersed in writing his next book, the *Discourses on Livy,* which was about republican rather than princely governments. Notwithstanding the difference in subject matter, there is an underlying consistency between the two books. Both offer hard-edged, often shocking, recommendations for the holders of power; both are dismissive of political idealism as well as Christianity; both claim to present new rules based on the study of things as they have actually happened, rather than how they ought to happen. Certainly Machiavelli kept *The Prince* near his desk as he was writing the *Discourses,* because he cites it at several points. Possibly he thought of publishing the two books together, or of revising *The Prince* so that together with the *Discourses* he could provide a unified treatment of politics in both principalities and republics, because the *Discourses* remained unpublished and in certain respects unfinished when Machiavelli died.[33]

Yet even while Machiavelli was immersing himself in the history of the Roman Republic, *The Prince*—his unpublished job application—began to take on a life independent of its author. Although the book remained unpublished, manuscript copies began to circulate in Florence in 1516–17. Machiavelli himself probably shared the book with friends in the Guicciardini family; Niccolò Guicciardini referred to *The Prince* in a letter to his father written in 1517 (Document 6). Biagio Buonaccorsi, a former colleague of Machiavelli's in the Florentine chancery, must also have received a copy, because he copied the earliest surviving manuscripts. But hostile criticisms of the book were appearing at the same time; Biagio Buonaccorsi prefaced one of these early manuscript copies with a letter urging that the work be defended against "those who, out of malignity or envy, might wish, according to the practice of these times, to bite and to lacerate [*The Prince*]" (Document 7). Machiavelli's *Prince* was already winning notoriety for itself and for its author.

It must have been difficult to be the author of an infamous book that was not formally published and was circulating only in manuscript. Certainly in his later years Machiavelli changed his feelings about *The Prince.* The pride so evident in the letter of 1513 to Vettori (Document 2), announcing the writing of *The Prince,* all but vanished. According to friends who knew him toward the end of his life, Machiavelli explained that he had written the book as a trap for the Medici rulers of Florence. By encouraging the Medici to be tyrannical, he hoped to encourage conspiracies that would result in their downfall. (See Documents 5 and 12.) It seems reasonable to discard this explanation in the light of what we now know concerning the intended dedication to Giuliano and Machiavelli's desperate search for an appointment in 1513. It is nonetheless interesting to note that the older

Machiavelli was embarrassed by the overt message of *The Prince* and felt the need to invent a covert one. Indeed, according to one of Machiavelli's younger friends, Benedetto Varchi, Machiavelli so regretted having written *The Prince* that before he died in 1527 he attempted to "eliminate" the work (see Document 10), a possible reference to the destruction of manuscript copies.

One further episode may possibly reveal Machiavelli's changing response to his treatise. In 1520 *The Prince* did not yet have a reputation strong enough to prevent Machiavelli's winning a job. In that year, the year following the death of Lorenzo the Younger, he finally gained his long-sought entry to Medici circles. Some friends in Florence introduced Machiavelli to Cardinal Giulio de' Medici (later Pope Clement VII), who in 1515 had vetoed his being hired by Giuliano. Cardinal Giulio first sent him on a minor diplomatic mission to Lucca, and then arranged a commission with a salary from the Florentine university in Pisa for Machiavelli to write his *Florentine Histories*. One of the most curious episodes in the history of *The Prince* dates from this period; in 1523 a rewritten, Latin version of *The Prince* was published in Naples in an edition that gave as its author the eminent philosopher Agostino Nifo. Nifo's book bore the title *On Skill in Ruling* (Document 8). Nifo preserved most of Machiavelli's arguments and examples, although he rearranged them and added many examples of his own. He also "sanitized" the book by suppressing passages (such as Machiavelli's praise of Cesare Borgia) that might be considered risky or irreligious. Machiavelli was a jealous protector of his intellectual property, so it is remarkable that no mention of Nifo's work survives in his ample correspondence. It seems probable that Nifo acted with Machiavelli's knowledge. Nifo was, like Machiavelli, both a client of the Medici and a colleague in the university at Pisa. Machiavelli may have thought that by having his work cleaned up, rewritten in Latin, and formally published under someone else's name, he would be able to deny that *The Prince* was the explosive work his contemporaries were already thinking it was. Machiavelli's contemporaries were certainly aware of the similarities of the two works. In 1532, in the preface to the Florentine edition of *The Prince* (Document 7), the printer Bernardo Giunta states that he is simply publishing in the original a work previously published in Latin under someone else's name—possibly as a way of defending himself against the charge of disseminating a morally dangerous work.

Machiavelli was old and weak when, in 1527, the Medici family was exiled from Florence again and the Florentine Republic was restored.

He seems to have hoped to be called into service to create a new militia, but to his tremendous disappointment, the new republic ignored him—both because there were rivals for the available posts, and also because he had tried so hard in the previous fifteen years to find favor with the Medici. Machiavelli died on June 21, 1527. *The Prince* was still unpublished.

RIVAL READINGS OF MACHIAVELLI IN EARLY MODERN EUROPE

How *The Prince* came to be published in Rome in 1532, as part of a project to publish Machiavelli's works five years after his death, is still something of a mystery. Certainly a number of Machiavelli's friends were behind the enterprise. These friends helped find the printer and secured the proper permissions. The book was printed with a privilege granted by Pope Clement VII, a fact that now seems ironic given that only a few decades later the church placed *The Prince,* along with all of Machiavelli's works, on the papacy's *Index of Forbidden Books.* Although Machiavelli already appears to have had a reputation for being "Machiavellian" in Florence before his death, the reputation seems not to have spread to Rome by 1532.

One of the most cogent explanations for the posthumous publication of Machiavelli's works makes the project appear almost accidental when set against the storms that would rage about Machiavelli in later years.[34] In the 1530s one of the greatest quarrels among Italian writers concerned the proper dialect to use for literary works in the Italian language, the *volgare.* It seems likely that the initial project of publishing Machiavelli's writings was undertaken in order to present Machiavelli to the public as an exemplary writer of prose in the Florentine dialect. Thus, the Roman printer of the first edition of *The Prince* had no idea of the potentially dangerous ideas contained in the work he was publishing, to judge from the preface he wrote for it (Document 7). The Florentine printer of a rival second edition, which appeared five months later, was necessarily more cautious and defensive (Document 7), as Machiavelli's notoriety was well-established in his native city.

Machiavelli's writings sold well. Venice, the printing capital of Europe, discovered the profitability of Machiavelli's works; most of the numerous editions of Machiavelli's writings published before 1550 appeared in Venice. Also by 1550, European interpretations of Machiavelli had firmly coalesced around two rival readings of his works,

IL PRINCIPE DI NICCHOLO MACHIA
VELLO AL MAGNIFICO LOREN·
ZO DI PIERO DE MEDICI·

LA VITA DI CASTRVCCIO CASTRA·
CANI DA LVCCA A ZANOBI BVON
DELMONTI ET A LVIGI ALEMAN·
NI DESCRITTA PER IL
MEDESIMO.

IL MODO CHE TENNE IL DVCA VA·
LENTINO PER AMMAZAR VITEL
LOZO, OLIVEROTTO DA FER·
MO IL·S·PAOLO ET IL DV
CA DI GRAVINA ORSI
NI IN SENIGAGLIA,
DESCRITTA PER
IL MEDESIMO·

Con Gratie, & Priuilegi di, N.S. Clemente
VII, & altri Prinċpi, che intra il termino di. X.
Anni non ſi ſtampino, ne ſtampi ſi uendino:
ſotto le pene, che in eſsi ſi contengono.
M. D. XXXII.

Title page of the first edition of Niccolò Machiavelli, *Il Principe,* published in Rome, January 3, 1532, under a privilege granted by Pope Clement VII.

23

readings that cannot help but appear extreme in the light of modern scholarship, but which continue to affect the way we approach Machiavelli's writings. For one important group of readers, Machiavelli was nothing short of an agent of the Devil. Other early modern readers preferred to read him as the apostle of secular republicanism. The diabolical Machiavelli appears in full bloom for the first time in the *Apology to Charles V*, a work written by an English cardinal, Reginald Pole, in 1539 (Document 12). According to Pole,

Machiavelli [was] a certain Florentine, entirely unworthy to have been born in that noble city. But just as Satan's progeny are everywhere, intermingling with the sons of God, . . . so this son of Satan, trained in all forms of wickedness in the midst of the many sons of God, was born in that noble city and has written things which stink of Satan's every wickedness. Among other works, he composed *The Prince* (for this is the title he has given to one of his books), in which he portrays for us such a prince that, if Satan were to reign in the flesh and were to have a son, to whom he were to bequeath sovereignty after his death, he would give him no other instructions than those found in this book.[35]

Although this work of Pole's remained in manuscript and was not published until the 1700s, Pole was an influential cleric who in the conclave of 1549–50 was nearly elected pope. In the late 1540s and early 1550s Machiavelli's writings came to the attention of the Roman Inquisition, and in 1557 they were among the condemned works placed on the *Index*.[36]

Machiavelli thus became a principal target of Counter-Reformation writers, but in the sixteenth century Protestants also perceived him as an enemy, especially French Calvinists. One can trace a considerable amount of the antipathy toward Machiavelli expressed by the Huguenots to anti-Italian sentiments that flourished in France during the sixteenth century.[37] It did not help Machiavelli's standing among the Huguenots that the persecution of French reformers was supported and sometimes instigated by the queen regent, Catherine de' Medici, who was none other than the daughter of Lorenzo the Younger, the dedicatee of *The Prince*. In particular, the Huguenots blamed the queen for the Saint Bartholomew's Day massacre of August 24, 1572, in which nearly seventy thousand people died. Indeed, Catherine had set events in motion by ordering the assassination of the Huguenot leader Admiral Coligny.

Protestant denunciations of Machiavelli spread to England with out-rage over the Saint Bartholomew's Day massacre, as Christopher Marlowe acknowledged in his play *The Jew of Malta,* in a speech by a character called "Machiavel" (Document 14). In England the demonization of Machiavelli continued apace, sometimes with brilliant results. Thus it is hard not to see the influence of the diabolical Machiavelli in the character Iago of *Othello,* and Shakespeare's *Macbeth* reads like an attempt to refute the message of chapter 8 of *The Prince* concerning Liverotto of Fermo's seizure of power. For the ambitious person who murders a legitimate prince there are terrible consequences, Shakespeare says.

Innocent Gentillet's *Discourses against Machiavelli* of 1576 (Document 13) was perhaps the most famous work to passionately denounce the Machiavellian cynicism the Protestants imagined at work behind the throne of France's Catholic rulers. The *Discourses against Machiavelli* were influential not only in England, where they were published in translation, but also, surprisingly, in Catholic Europe; a leading Jesuit polemicist, Antonio Possevino, wrote a major attack on Machiavelli that was based entirely on the book by the Calvinist Gentillet (who was unacknowledged), without any direct reading of Machiavelli.

But even in Calvinist Geneva there were people who were ready to defend Machiavelli. On two occasions Gentillet came to blows with refugees from Italy who considered his *Discourses* slanderous toward their nation. In fact, in Italy, a number of persons associated with the reform movement in the sixteenth century were readers of Machiavelli or had even known him personally, for instance, the Florentine Pietro Carnesecchi, who was burned as a heretic in 1567.[38] And it was probably in Italy that what became the dominant "republican" interpretation of *The Prince* in early modern Europe developed in the later sixteenth century. The Florentine historian and scholar Bernardo Segni cited Machiavelli's *Prince* as an authority in the notes of his Italian translation of Aristotle's *Politics,* published in 1551.[39] The aging Machiavelli had told his friends that *The Prince* was secretly a work aimed at bringing down tyrants, and in the second half of the sixteenth century the idea that *The Prince* contained a secret republican doctrine became more common. The Italian jurist Alberico Gentili, who became a law professor at Oxford, wrote that Machiavelli really intended *The Prince* as a book against princes.[40] There is a copy of the first edition of *The Prince* bound together with the *Discourses on Livy,* now owned by the Princeton University library, said to have belonged to Queen Elizabeth I of England, with a note on the title page that reads (in Latin): "This author was an enemy of tyrants."[41] Benedict de Spinoza, Pierre Bayle, and Denis Didérot later seconded the view that *The Prince* was really written against tyrants. This view culminated in a note in the second edition of Jean-Jacques Rousseau's *On the Social Contract,* which called *The Prince* "the book of republicans," because it taught the people why they should resist their princes (Document 16).

THE PRINCE AND THE AUTONOMY OF POLITICS

During the upheavals of the French Revolution and the Napoleonic Wars Machiavelli's writings remained of great interest throughout Europe. Although Machiavelli continued to have defenders who viewed him as a secret democratic hero, the prevailing view still held that Machiavelli had been a counselor to tyrants. After the defeat of Napoleon Bonaparte at the battle of Waterloo in 1815, English propagandists claimed that there had been a copy of *The Prince* in the emperor's personal baggage. All the same, informed interpretations of Machiavelli were about to undergo a dramatic change as the result of a discovery first published in those years.

As noted, throughout the early modern period, at the heart of the Machiavelli puzzle lay the question of his intention in writing *The Prince.* Surprisingly, the most important piece of documentary evidence concerning Machiavelli's actual intent, the letter he wrote to Francesco Vettori on December 10, 1513, in which he mentioned his hope for employment with the Medici (Document 3), remained unknown, although several people probably read it in the later 1700s, if not earlier. When a professor at the University of Bologna, Angelo Ridolfi, first published this letter in the appendix to a small volume on Machiavelli's aims,[42] it marked the beginning of a great shift in thinking about Machiavelli and *The Prince.*

After the publication of the Vettori letter, which gradually became known through its inclusion in subsequent editions of Machiavelli's collected works and correspondence, the rival interpretations of the early modern period underwent some modification. Although Machiavelli's detractors might still condemn *The Prince* as immoral and anti-Christian, the discovery of Machiavelli's personal hardships and his desire for employment made it harder to demonize him. Even more pronounced was the impact of the letter's publication on the arguments of Machiavelli's defenders.

It no longer seemed reasonable to believe that Machiavelli had written *The Prince* as a veiled attack on tyrants. Later in life Machiavelli may have tried, among friends and in his own defense, to argue that *The Prince* was secretly a work against princes. But the letter of 1513 proved beyond a reasonable doubt, at least at the time it was written, that *The Prince* was intended as a book of advice that was sincere, even if sometimes hard to swallow.

The realization that Machiavelli was serious about both the counsel for monarchs contained in *The Prince* and the counsel for republics contained in the *Discourses* gave rise, in the nineteenth and early twentieth centuries, to a new interpretation that attempted to transcend the scholarly quarrel over Machiavelli's republicanism by portraying him as a supreme political technician. Attributing to Machiavelli a perspective on politics much broader than that of a dogmatic republican, Machiavelli's defenders found it possible to interpret *The Prince* and the *Discourses,* which previous generations read as contradictory, as complementary parts of a coherent political vision. Notwithstanding Machiavelli's preference for republics, critics argued that he offered good practical advice for princes, too. And they showed how Machiavelli's teaching in the *Discourses,* which suggests that republics need prince-like figures when they are being founded or reformed, was not necessarily inconsistent with what he had argued in *The Prince.*

The rise of nationalism also encouraged people to abandon the old interpretations of Machiavelli as friend either of tyrants or republics. Especially in Machiavelli's own Italy, readers saw the call for a national leader that appears in chapter 26 of *The Prince* as prophetic of the unification of Italy first achieved in 1860. The fact that the new Italian government was neither an absolute monarchy nor a democratic republic, but rather a constitutional monarchy with an elected parliament, made Machiavelli's radical distinction between principalities and republics (in chapter 2 of *The Prince*) and the differences between *The Prince* and the *Discourses* appear less important to Italian readers.

Equally important in encouraging new ways of looking at Machiavelli and *The Prince,* not just in Italy but throughout the Western world, was the growing influence of scientific ways of thinking, especially in the field of political economy, which were encouraged by the industrial revolution. An emphasis on solving real problems, rather than on the construction of ideal goals for society, led readers to admire Machiavelli's empiricism and his study of the "effectual truth" (chapter 15), and to treat him not as either a committed republican or a follower of princes, but as someone who was interested in studying political power for whatever form it existed.

The idea that Machiavelli was first and foremost a student of the techniques of power, rather than a conspiratorial republican or an advocate of monarchy, found its most eloquent and influential expression in the writings of an Italian philosopher from Naples, Benedetto Croce (1866–1952). According to Croce, it was Machiavelli's great discovery that politics has rules that are distinct from the rules that govern other sorts of human behavior. Throughout Western history, in the centuries before Machiavelli, Croce argued, religion and common understandings of morality conditioned political behavior. Religion and accepted morality had established the policies that leaders were supposed to follow and the goals toward which they were supposed to strive, no matter how frequently they may have departed from them in actual practice. In Croce's interpretation, Machiavelli instead postulated that the real goal of politics is the state's simple survival. One could derive the rules of politics from this need to survive, and could therefore determine them without making any reference to religious and moral considerations. According to Croce, what Machiavelli discovered was "the autonomy of politics."[43] Machiavelli's politics offered a set of tools to anyone who cared to learn to use them, whether a prince or his people, whether for good or for evil.

Machiavelli allocated politics and ethics, which ever since the ancient Greeks had been considered closely joined in the Western intellectual tradition, to separate realms of human activity. Although Croce acknowledged that this could lead to abuses, he treated the autonomy of politics as an established fact—a discovery as revolutionary and as solid as the European discovery of the New World. In his writings, Croce showed how European intellectuals actually tried various stratagems to bring politics and ethics back together again, but met with little success, so powerful was Machiavelli's insight.[44] To use Machiavelli's political science in the service of a good state, Croce thought, would be a correct starting point for reconciling politics and ethics.[45] But the question of what constituted a good state would have to be decided within the realm of ethics, which had its own separate rules. And with politics operating according to its own rules, people might take wrong actions, even commit great crimes, for reasons that were purely political, without reference to the just, the good, or the moral.

Croce was pessimistic about the consequences of Machiavelli's discovery of the autonomy of politics, but he treated it as a fact from which there was no turning back. Other writers, contemporaries of Croce's, embraced this conclusion, but without Croce's reluctance. Croce's influence is easy to see in two famous interpretations of Machiavelli developed in the 1920s and 1930s by two very different men: Benito Mussolini, the leader of Fascist Italy from 1922 until 1944 (see Document 17); and Antonio Gramsci, one of the leaders of the Italian Communist Party, who suffered an excruciating imprisonment because of his opposition to Mussolini's regime, and who died shortly after his release in 1937 (see Document 18). For Mussolini, a former Socialist journalist, who read a great deal and was a prolific writer, Machiavelli offered a practical guide to the exercise of political power stripped of the false liberal democratic pieties that Mussolini thought were the enemy of true national greatness. Mussolini thought Machiavelli made it possible to rule more effectively because he revealed the brutal truths about political power. Among many other laudatory things, Mussolini wrote that Machiavelli had taught him that "when men no longer believe something, they can be made to believe it by force."[46] Like Mussolini, Antonio Gramsci thought that Machiavelli had effectively revealed the true nature of political power. According to Gramsci, Machiavelli stripped political power of the false ideological and ethical apparatus with which those who wielded power had defended themselves. Political power was up for grabs. The contest for power was now open to all comers, and it would be the working class, with the Communist party acting as a "modern prince," that would follow Machiavelli's precepts by seizing political control, without regard for tradition, morality, or ethics.

There is a curse of sorts implicit in the idea that politics operates entirely by its own rules. Although it may appear to be liberating if political actors are freed from the restraining forces of tradition and morality, political power that one acquires as Liverotto of Fermo acquired it, and exercises as Cesare Borgia exercised it—methods that Machiavelli, and later Mussolini and Gramsci, explicitly or implicitly endorsed—is a power that rests on naked fear. When one pursues politics as though it really were autonomous, the atmosphere in which it operates tends to become one of cruelty and fear. There is much to be said for the argument that the autonomy of politics is an idea fundamental to modern totalitarianism.

Did Machiavelli himself believe in the autonomy of politics? At times it appears that he did. Again and again he reduces the political life to a simple question of survival. Even in the Roman republic, as Machiavelli describes it in the *Discourses,* the Roman patricians regularly and successfully employed violence and deceit in order to maintain control of the plebs. The rules for the behavior of princes laid down by Machiavelli in chapters 15–20 of *The Prince* evidently hold for politicians in republics, too. In the end there is a paranoid quality to the politics *The Prince* describes, whether in principalities or republics.

To better understand what is missing from Machiavelli's understanding of politics, it helps to consider a passage of *The Prince* that is uncharacteristic of Machiavelli's political writing: one of the few passages that treats not warfare and survival, but the peaceful management of a city. At the end of chapter 21, "What the Prince Should Do to Be Thought Outstanding," Machiavelli writes:

> A prince must also show himself to be a lover of the virtues by giving hospitality to virtuous men, and he must honor those who are excellent in an art. Next, he must encourage his citizens to be able quietly to practice their trades, in commerce, in agriculture and in every other human occupation, so that one man is not afraid to improve his properties for fear they will be taken from him, and another is not afraid to open a business for fear of taxes. But he must prepare rewards for whoever wants to do these things, and for whoever thinks to increase his city or his state in whatever way. Beyond this, at the appropriate times of the year he should keep his people occupied with feast-days and spectacles. And because every city is divided into guilds or wards, he should take account of those collectivities, meet with them sometimes, and offer himself as an example of humanity and munificence, while nonetheless always keeping firm his dignity's majesty, for he does not want this ever to be lacking in anything.

The passage is in part nostalgic. Machiavelli has in mind the Florence of his youth, in which Lorenzo the Magnificent the Elder, the grandfather of the dedicatee of *The Prince,* was famous for comporting himself in this way in his dealings with the citizens of Florence. Most important, though, the passage appears as an afterthought to the discussions of the prince's behavior in chapters 15–20. The implication is that only after a prince has mastered the harsh lessons of the earlier chapters may he take the time to tend to these domestic affairs, which Machiavelli presents as rather simple concerns.

In the late twentieth century (especially during and after the 1980s), as the regimes of communist eastern Europe entered a period of final crisis, one of the themes that emerged was the diminished role under communism of what political theorists call "civil society." Civil society comprises the intermediate groups and organizations, businesses, unions, religious associations, and civic groups that in most Western democracies serve as buffers between the citizen and the state. The health of civil society continues to be of great interest to many scholars, especially political scientists—who tend to discuss politics in ways quite different from Machiavelli's. Although Machiavelli consistently praises what he calls the *vivere politico* or the *vivere civile* in all of his works, he pays almost no attention to its practical workings.[47] Amid the invasions, siege preparations, coups d'état, and breaches of faith that figure so prominently in *The Prince*, only one brief paragraph depicts ordinary life as desirable.

NOTES

[1] See Document 14.

[2] For instance, Samuel Butler (1612–1680) wrote in his *Hudibras,* "Nick Machiavel . . . gave his name to our old Nick." Ernst Leisi, "On the Trail of Old Nick," in Andreas Fischer, ed., *The History and the Dialects of English: Festschrift for Eduard Kolb* (Heidelberg: Carl Winter, 1989), 53–57, has suggested a morality play character called "Old Iniquity" as the real source, but the evidence is slender and the Machiavellian derivation remains possible.

[3] The trial record is published in People's Commissariat of Justice of the USSR, Report of Court Proceedings, *The Case of the Trotskyite-Zinovievite Terrorist Centre,* August 19–24, 1936 (Moscow, 1936), 138–39. The case against Lev Kamenev, who wrote the preface, is described in Chimen Abransky, "Kamenev's Last Essay," *New Left Review,* 15 (May–June 1962): 34–42. See also Mark A. Iusim, *Makiavelli v Rossii: Moral' i politika na protiazhenii piati stoletii* (Moscow: Institut Vseobschei Istorii RAN, 1998), 196–208. Interestingly, Nikolai Ryzhkov, *Perestroika: Istoriia predatel'stv* (Moscow: Novosti, 1992), 354–56, claims to have seen Stalin's marked-up personal copy of Machiavelli.

[4] Alistair McAlpine, *The New Machiavelli: The Art of Politics in Business* (New York: Wiley, 1998).

[5] Garrett Mattingly, "Machiavelli's *Prince*: Political Science or Political Satire?" *The American Scholar,* 27 (1958): 482–91.

[6] Allan H. Gilbert, *Machiavelli's Prince and Its Forerunners: The Prince as a Typical Book "de Regimine Principum"* (Durham, N.C.: Duke University Press, 1938). See also Felix Gilbert, "The Humanist Concept of the Prince and *The Prince* of Machiavelli" (1939), reprinted in Gilbert, *History: Choice and Commitment* (Cambridge, Mass.: Harvard University Press, 1979), 91–114.

[7] Machiavelli was certainly informed about these voyages, as he worked closely in the Florentine chancery with a cousin of Amerigo Vespucci. There is a general allusion to the voyages of discovery in the preface to book 1 of the *Discourses*.

[8] In his later works, the *Discourses* and the *Art of War,* Machiavelli instead gives firearms a more positive role in combat. See Allan H. Gilbert, "Machiavelli on Fire Weapons," *Italica,* 23 (1946): 275–86.

[9] See Elizabeth Eisenstein, *The Printing Press as an Agent of Change: Communications and Cultural Transformation in Early Modern Europe,* 2 vols. (Cambridge: Cambridge University Press, 1979), and on the consequent "Early Modern Information Overload," see *Journal of the History of Ideas,* 64 (2003): 1–72.

[10]On the territorial states, see Julius Kirshner, ed., *The Origins of the State in Italy, 1300–1600* (Chicago: University of Chicago Press, 1995); James S. Grubb, *Firstborn of Venice: Vicenza in the Early Renaissance State* (Baltimore: Johns Hopkins University Press, 1988); and William J. Connell and Andrea Zorzi, eds., *Florentine Tuscany: Structures and Practices of Power* (Cambridge: Cambridge University Press, 2000).

[11]William Caferro, *Mercenary Companies and the Decline of Siena* (Baltimore: Johns Hopkins University Press, 1998).

[12]See Riccardo Fubini, "Diplomacy and Government in the Italian City-States of the Fifteenth Century," in Daniela Frigo, ed., *Politics and Diplomacy in Early Modern Italy: The Structure of Diplomatic Practice* (Cambridge: Cambridge University Press, 2000), 25–48, and Garrett Mattingly, *Renaissance Diplomacy* (London: Cape, 1955).

[13]Ronald G. Witt, *"In the Footsteps of the Ancients": The Origins of Humanism from Lovato to Bruni* (Leiden: Brill, 2000). See also Paul O. Kristeller, "Humanism and Scholasticism in the Italian Renaissance," in Kristeller, *Studies in Renaissance Thought and Letters,* 4 vols. (Rome: Edizioni di Storia e Letteratura, 1956–1996), 1: 553–83.

[14]Anthony Grafton and Lisa Jardine, *From Humanism to the Humanities* (Cambridge, Mass.: Harvard University Press, 1986); Paul F. Grendler, *The Universities of the Italian Renaissance* (Baltimore:"Johns Hopkins University Press, 2002), 199–248.

[15]Joseph A. Mazzeo,"Dante and Epicurus," *Comparative Literature,* 10 (1958): 106–20.

[16]Sergio Bertelli and Franco Gaeta, "Noterelle machiavelliane. Un codice di Lucrezio e di Terenzio," *Rivista storica italiana,* 73 (1961): 544–57. The manuscript offers little indication of how Machiavelli read the work, but compare the very interesting marginal notes of another early modern reader of Lucretius in M. A. Screech, *Montaigne's Annotated Copy of Lucretius: A Transcription and Study of the Manuscript, Notes and Pen-marks* (Geneva: Droz, 1998). In general, see Alison Brown, "Lucretius and the Epicureans in the Social and Political Context of Renaissance Florence," *I Tatti Studies,* 9 (2001): 11–62.

[17]Discussed in Peter Godman, *From Poliziano to Machiavelli: Florentine Humanism in the High Renaissance* (Princeton: Princeton University Press, 1998). The hypothesis (237) that this chancery colleague, Marcello Virgilio Adriani, prevented the publication of *The Prince* is simply a guess, but the rivalry with Machiavelli was real.

[18]*Discourses,* 1.27.

[19]He enrolled in the Company of Piety in 1495. See Oreste Tommasini, *La vita e gli scritti di Niccolò Machiavelli nella loro relazione col machiavellismo,* 2 vols. in 3 (1883–1911, repr. Bologna: Mulino, 1994–2003), 2:1, 386 n. 1.

[20]Giuliano Procacci, *Machiavelli nella cultura europea dell'età moderna* (Bari: Laterza, 1995), 423–31, corrects a number of misunderstandings, confirms a well-known letter as a forgery, and gives the name of the likely confessor.

[21]*Discourses,* 2.2.

[22]The classic biography remains Roberto Ridolfi, *The Life of Niccolò Machiavelli,* trans. Cecil Grayson (London: Routledge and Kegan Paul, 1963). See also Pasquale Villari, *The Life and Times of Niccolò Machiavelli,* trans. Linda Villari, 2 vols., new ed. (1892; repr., New York: Greenwood Press, 1968). Three good brief treatments are: J. R. Hale, *Machiavelli and Renaissance Italy* (New York: Macmillan, 1960); Quentin Skinner, *Machiavelli: A Very Short Introduction* (1981; repr., Oxford: Oxford University Press, 2000); and Maurizio Viroli, *Niccolò's Smile: A Biography of Machiavelli,* trans. Anthony Shugaar (New York: Farrar, Straus and Giroux, 2000).

[23]One can obtain an idea of his early reading from the record book kept by his father: Bernardo Machiavelli, *Libro di ricordi,* ed. Cesare Olschki (Florence: Le Monnier, 1954).

[24]The letter is published in *Machiavelli and His Friends: Their Personal Correspondence,* trans. and ed. James B. Atkinson and David Sices (DeKalb, Ill.: Northern Illinois University Press, 1996), 8–10.

[25]The details of the election are presented in Nicolai Rubinstein, "The Beginnings of Niccolò Machiavelli's Career in the Florentine Chancery," *Italian Studies,* 11 (1956): 72–91, and further discussed in Clough, *Machiavelli Researches,* 13–24.

[26]He was not faithful to Marietta. Machiavelli had several mistresses, and his correspondence indicates sexual relations with men, too. One contemporary called him a "rascal" (*ribaldo*).

[27]On Machiavelli's career in the chancery, see the essays of Robert Black, "Machiavelli, Servant of the Florentine Republic," and John M. Najemy, "The Controversy Surrounding Machiavelli's Service to the Republic," both in *Machiavelli and Republicanism*, ed. Gisela Bock, Quentin Skinner, and Maurizio Viroli (Cambridge: Cambridge University Press, 1990), 71–117; and Godman, *From Poliziano to Machiavelli*. Working conditions are described in Fredi Chiappelli, "Machiavelli as Secretary," *Italian Quarterly*, 14 (1971): 27–44.

[28]Second legation to Cesare Borgia, dispatches of November 13, 1502, and January 8, 1503, here translated from Machiavelli, *Opere*, ed. Corrado Vivanti, vol. 2 (Turin: Einaudi, 1999), 705–6, 790–91. On the importance of this legation for Machiavelli's later theoretical writings, see Gennaro Sasso, *Machiavelli e Cesare Borgia: storia di un giudizio* (Rome: Edizioni dell' Ateneo, 1966).

[29]Hugo Jaeckel, "I 'tordi' e il 'principe nuovo.' Note sulle dediche del 'Principe' di Machiavelli a Giuliano e a Lorenzo de' Medici," *Archivio storico italiano*, 156 (1998): 73–92.

[30]See the important work of Clough, *Machiavelli Researches*, 40–67.

[31]Oreste Tommasini, *Vita e scritti*, 2:2, 1064–65. Carlo Dionisotti's clever suggestion, in his *Machiavellerie: Storia e fortuna di Machiavelli* (Turin: Einaudi, 1980), 36 n. 8, that this veto indicates *The Prince* was already in circulation is not supported by the manuscript tradition, and there were already sufficient reasons for Cardinal Giulio to issue such an order.

[32]The phrase "so long as he was alive (*vivendo lui*)" (p. 49 below) and the harsh criticism directed at Louis XII are possible indicators that Louis XII was dead at the time of composition. For other reasons Mario Martelli, in "La struttura deformata: sulla diacronia del cap. III del *Principe*," *Studi di filologia italiana*, 39 (1981): 77–120, has already suggested that part of chapter 3 was written at a stage subsequent to 1513–14.

[33]Cecil H. Clough, "Niccolò Machiavelli's Political Assumptions and Objectives," *Bulletin of the John Rylands Library*, 53 (1970): 30–74. For suggestions concerning the state of Machiavelli's manuscript of the *Discourses* prior to its posthumous publication, see Clough, *Machiavelli Researches*, 90–105.

[34]Procacci, *Machiavelli nella cultura europea*, 5–41.

[35]Here translated by Nicholas Webb in *Cambridge Translations of Renaissance Philosophical Texts*, vol. 2: *Political Philosophy*, ed. Jill Kraye (Cambridge: Cambridge University Press, 1997), 275.

[36]Procacci, *Machiavelli nella cultura europea*, 99.

[37]See Henry Heller, *Anti-Italianism in Sixteenth-Century France* (Toronto: University of Toronto Press, 2003).

[38]Carnesecchi is mentioned in Document 9.

[39]*Trattato dei governi di Aristotile*, trans. Bernardo Segni (Venice: Bartolomeo detto l'Imperador, 1551).

[40]Alberico Gentili, *De legationibus libri tres*, trans. Gordon J. Laing, 2 vols. (New York: Oxford University Press, 1924), 2: 156: "It was not his purpose to instruct the tyrant, but by revealing his secret counsels to strip him bare, and expose to him the suffering nations. . . . The purpose of this shrewdest of men was to instruct the nations under the pretext of instructing the prince. . . ."

[41]The 1532 editions of these two works by the printer Antonio Blado of Rome are bound in a single volume: Princeton University, Firestone Library, Rare Books, 7510.606.1532.

[42]In an appendix to Angelo Ridolfi, *Pensieri intorno allo scopo di Nicolò* [sic] *Machiavelli nel libro "Il Principe"* (Milan: Destefanis, 1810).

[43]Benedetto Croce, *Elementi di politica* (Bari: Laterza, 1925), 60; Croce, *Indagini su Hegel e schiarimenti filosofici*, 2d ed. (Bari: Laterza, 1967), 174–86. See also Isaiah Berlin,

"The Originality of Machiavelli" in Berlin, *Against the Current: Essays in the History of Ideas*, ed. Henry Hardy (New York: Viking, 1980), 25–79.

[44]Benedetto Croce, *Storia della età barocca in Italia: pensiero, poesia e letteratura, vita morale* (Bari: Laterza, 1929), 77–98.

[45]A. Robert Caponigri, *History and Liberty: The Historical Writings of Benedetto Croce* (London: Routledge and Kegan Paul, 1955), 147–48.

[46]See Benito Mussolini, "Preludio al 'Machiavelli'," *Gerarchia*, 3, no. 4 (April 1924): 205–9; reprinted in Mussolini, *Opera omnia*, 44 vols., ed. Edoardo and Duilio Susmel (Florence, 1956–80), 20: 251–54; and the discussion in Renzo De Felice, *Mussolini il fascista* (Turin, 1966), 1: 465–66. See also Paolo Paolini, "Mussolini e Machiavelli," *Otto/Novecento*, 19:1 (1995), 195–203, who argues that Mussolini's reading of *The Prince* may have inspired him to order the assassination of Giacomo Matteotti several months later. According to De Felice, just prior to studying *The Prince*, Mussolini was reading Plato's *Republic*.

[47]See Maurizio Viroli, *From Politics to Reason of State: The Acquisition and Transformation of the Language of Politics, 1250–1650* (Cambridge: Cambridge University Press, 1992), 126–77.

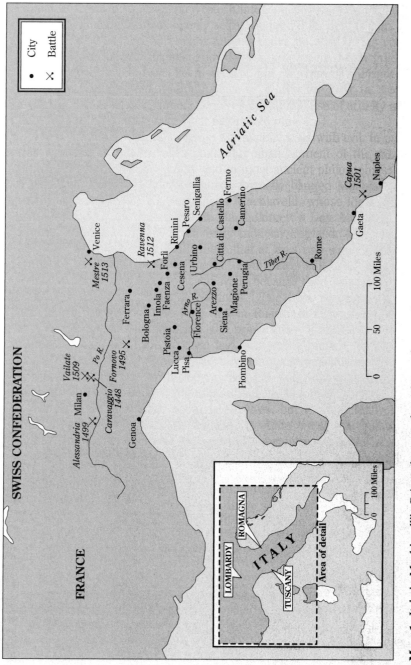

Map 1. Italy in Machiavelli's *Prince*, fourteenth to sixteenth centuries.

35

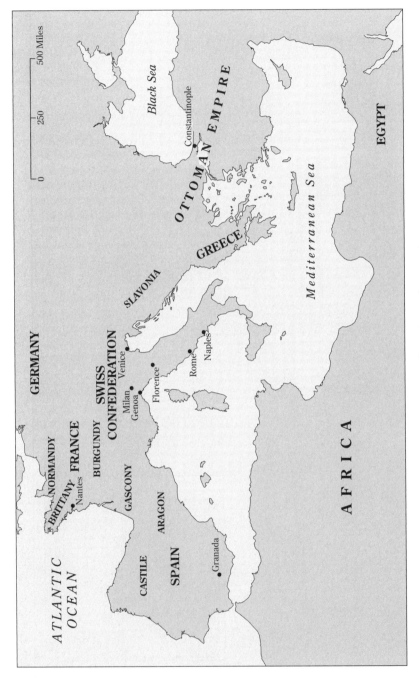

Map 2. The larger world of Machiavelli's *Prince*, fourteenth to sixteenth centuries.

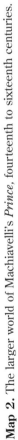

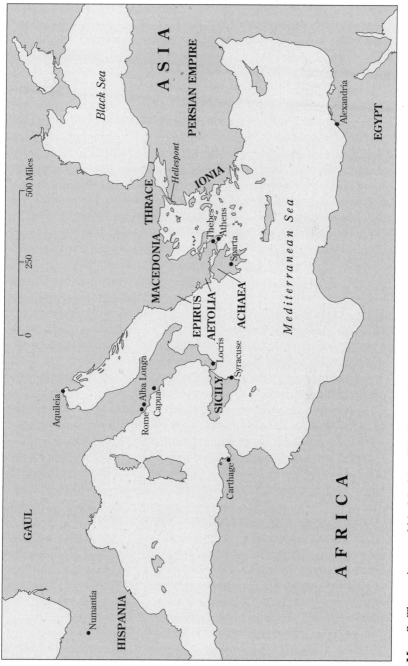

Map 3. The ancient world in Machiavelli's *Prince*, eleventh century BCE to fifth century CE.

PART TWO

The Prince

(On Principalities)[1]

DEDICATORY LETTER

Niccolò Machiavelli to the Magnificent Lorenzo de' Medici the Younger:[2] greetings.[3]

It is customary most of the time for those who desire to acquire grace with a prince to come before him with those things among their own that they hold most dear, or in which they see him delight the most. Hence one sees many times that princes are presented with horses, arms, cloth of gold, precious stones and similar adornments worthy of their greatness.[4] Therefore, since I desire to offer myself to Your[5] Magnificence[6] with some evidence of my devotion to you, and

---

[1] *The Prince* is a title that dates from the first printed edition of 1532. Prior to the death of Machiavelli (hereafter abbreviated as "M") in 1527, he and others referred to this work as *On Principalities.*

[2] Lorenzo di Piero de' Medici the Younger (1492–1519) was the grandson of Lorenzo de' Medici the Magnificent (1449–1492). Beginning in the spring of 1513 the younger Lorenzo administered the affairs of the Medici family in Florence. In October 1516 he became duke of Urbino.

[3] The salutation is in Latin.

[4] The initial part of the dedication appears to be modeled on the opening of a speech by Isocrates, *To Nicocles,* 1–2.

[5] "Your" (*vostra*). It was common in the early sixteenth century to use the second person plural, *voi,* and its related forms, when addressing a single person as "you," although it was also used as a plural. Since M additionally uses the second person singular, *tu,* and its forms, especially as an impersonal pronoun in hypothetical situations, these variations are indicated in the notes.

[6] In the fifteenth and sixteenth centuries the principal males of the Medici family (as well as those of several other patrician lineages in Italy) were customarily addressed with the unofficial honorific of "magnificent" (*magnifico*).

since I have not found among my valuables anything that I hold more dear or estimate so highly as the understanding of the deeds of great men, which I have learned through long experience of modern things and constant reading about ancient things, these I have with great diligence over a long time thought out and examined, and now, reduced into a small volume, I send them to Your Magnificence.

And, although I judge this work unworthy of your presence, nonetheless I very much trust that on account of your humanity it may be accepted, considering how no greater gift could be given by me to you than to give you the ability in a very short time to understand all that I, in so many years and through so many hardships and perils to myself, have known and understood. I have not embellished this work, nor stuffed it with fulsome clauses or with pompous and magnificent words or with any of the other pandering or outward adornment with which many are accustomed to describe and embellish their material. For I wanted either that it be honored on no account whatsoever, or that only the variety of the material and the weightiness of the subject should make it welcome. Nor do I want it to be imputed presumption if a man of low and basest state[7] should dare to discourse on and give rules for the conduct of princes. For just as those who sketch landscapes place themselves low in the plain to consider the nature of mountains and of high places, and to consider the nature of low places they place themselves high atop the mountains, similarly, to understand well the nature of peoples it is necessary to be a prince, and to understand well the nature of princes it is necessary to be of the people.

May Your Magnificence therefore take up this small gift in the spirit with which I send it. And if it is diligently studied and read by you, you will understand in it an extreme desire of mine that you should arrive at that greatness that fortune and your other qualities promise you. And if Your Magnificence, from the peak of Your Magnificence's height, sometimes will cast your eyes on these low places, you will understand how undeservedly I endure a great and continuous malignity of fortune.

[7]In this translation *stato* is given as "state," unless otherwise indicated, so the reader may better gauge M's use of this important term. Sometimes, as here, the meaning is often close to "status" or "estate."

CHAPTER 1

How many kinds of principalities there are, and by what means they are acquired[1]

All states, all dominions that have had and do have command[2] over men, have been and are either republics or principalities. Principalities are either hereditary, in which the lineage of their lord has been prince for a long time, or they are new. The new ones are either completely new, as was Milan for Francesco Sforza,[3] or they are like limbs added to the hereditary state of the prince who acquires them, as is the Kingdom of Naples for the king of Spain.[4] Dominions that are thus acquired are either accustomed to living under a prince or used to being free, and they are acquired either with the arms of others or with one's own, either by fortune or by virtue.[5]

[1]In the earliest manuscripts the chapters are not numbered. The chapter titles have been translated from Latin, although some early manuscripts give the titles in Italian.

[2]*Imperio* ("command," "rule," or "empire") usually retains some of the force of the Latin root, *imperium,* which was the power of command given to generals in ancient Rome. Sometimes the word refers to the Roman Empire or the Holy Roman Empire.

[3]Francesco Sforza (1401–1466) was a mercenary captain who became duke of Milan in 1450. He is mentioned in chapters 7, 12, and 14.

[4]Ferdinand II, king of Aragon, also known as Ferdinand the Catholic (r. 1479–1516), first partitioned the Kingdom of Naples with Louis XII, king of France (r. 1498–1515), according to terms agreed upon in the treaty of Granada in 1500. Then Ferdinand took the rest of the kingdom from Louis in 1502–4. On Ferdinand, see also chapters 3 and 21.

[5]In this translation *virtù* is given consistently as "virtue." As M uses it, "virtue" has no specific moral or Christian meaning. Instead the word refers to a person's or a thing's intrinsic and essential strength, regardless of whether this is morally good or bad. In English we use the word in a similar way when we speak of the "virtue" of a medicine, when we use the phrase "by virtue of," or, when, in perceiving the essence of something, we say we perceive its "virtual reality."

CHAPTER 2

On hereditary principalities

I shall leave out reasoning on republics because on another occasion I have discussed them at length.[1] I shall apply myself only to the

[1]This refers to M's *Discourses on the First Decade of Titus Livy,* a lengthy work of political theory written in the form of a commentary on Titus Livy's early history of Rome. A slight chronological difficulty is evidenced by the fact that *The Prince* seems to have been largely written in 1513–14, whereas the *Discourses* appear to have been written later, mostly in 1515–17. This sentence, and another reference to the *Discourses* (in chapter 8),

principality; I shall weave full cloth around the guiding threads stated above; and I shall debate how these principalities may be governed and maintained.

I say therefore that in states that are hereditary and accustomed to the lineage of their prince there are many fewer difficulties in maintaining them than in new ones, for it suffices only not to break with the orders of one's ancestors and then to govern according to circumstances. So that if such a prince is of ordinary industry he will always maintain himself in his state, unless an extraordinary and excessive force deprives him of it. And even should he be so deprived, whenever the occupier experiences some mishap he reacquires it.

We have in Italy, among our examples, the duke of Ferrara, who survived the attacks of the Venetians in 1484 and those of Pope Julius in 1510 for no other reason than that he had grown old in that dominion.[2] For the prince by birth has fewer reasons and less need to offend, from which it proceeds that he is more loved; and, if extraordinary vices do not make him hated, it is reasonable that his own subjects naturally should wish him well. And in the antiquity and continuity of his dominion the memories of revolutions and the reasons for them are extinguished, because each succession always leaves the indentations for the construction of the one that follows.[3]

---

appear in the early surviving manuscripts of *The Prince*. Because these date at the earliest from 1515, however, M probably inserted the phrase in the draft copy of his unpublished *Prince* after he started the *Discourses*. Three references to *The Prince* that appear in the *Discourses* (2.1, 3.19, 3.42) confirm that at some stage of composition M saw the two works as complementary. Some scholars have argued that this sentence must refer to an early section of the *Discourses* possibly written prior to *The Prince*, or to a previous and now lost work "on republics" that eventually became part of the *Discourses*, but no other evidence that would confirm this has survived.

[2]"Duke" here refers to the Este rulers of Ferrara, who held titles as papal dukes of Ferrara and imperial dukes of Modena and Reggio. Ercole I d'Este (r. 1471–1505) was at first defeated by the Venetians in 1482, but he was subsequently defended by a coalition of Italian states, with peace being made in 1484. Alfonso I (r. 1505–1534) was attacked by Pope Julius II (r. 1503–1513) in 1510, but the following year he regained the territory he had lost. Papal claims to the Este lands remained an ongoing problem for Pope Leo X at the time of M's writing.

[3]M distinguishes between *innovazioni* (innovations, revolutions) and the hereditary principality's orderly *mutazioni* (changes of government, successions). The hereditary principality is constructed progressively, like a row of buildings, with indentations at the end, so that each future building locks into an existing one.

CHAPTER 3

On mixed principalities

But the difficulties are in the new principality. And first, if it is not wholly new, but like a limb (so that all together it may be called almost "mixed"), its troubles arise in the first place from a natural difficulty that exists in all new principalities, which is that men willingly change their lord if they believe they will be better off, and this belief makes them take up arms against him. In this, however, they deceive themselves, because they then see by experience that they have become worse off. This follows from another natural and ordinary necessity that stipulates that one always has to offend those of whom one becomes a new prince, both with men-at-arms and with the infinite other injuries that a new acquisition brings with it. The result is that you[1] have as enemies all those you have offended in occupying that principality, and you cannot maintain as friends those who have put you there, because you cannot satisfy them in that way that they had earlier supposed and because you cannot use strong medicines against them, since you are obligated to them. For always, even though a prince is very strong when it comes to armies, he needs the favor of the provincials to enter into a province. For these reasons Louis XII, king of France, quickly occupied Milan and quickly lost it. And to take it from Louis the first time all that was needed were Ludovico's own forces,[2] because those people who had opened the gates to the king, when they found themselves deceived in their opinion and in the future good they had presupposed, could no longer endure the annoyances of the new prince.

It is indeed true that when lands that have rebelled once are regained for a second time they are lost with greater difficulty, for their lord, having taken the occasion from their rebellion, is less hesitant to secure himself by punishing the criminals, clearing up his suspicions, and providing for his weakest points. Thus if the first time all that was needed to make France[3] lose Milan was for a Duke Ludovico to make noise at her borders, to make him lose it the second time he had to have all the world against him, and his armies either had to have been

---

[1]An impersonal use of *tu*.

[2]Louis XII (r. 1498–1515) captured Milan in September 1499 from Duke Ludovico Maria Sforza, also known as Ludovico il Moro (1452–1508). Louis lost control briefly in February 1500, when Ludovico reentered the city, but in April 1500 the French recaptured Milan and Ludovico was taken prisoner to France, where he died in 1508.

[3]"France" stands for "the king of France."

eliminated or to have fled Italy,[4] and this proceeds from the causes stated above. Nonetheless both the first and the second time it was taken from him. The universal reasons of the first loss have been gone over. It remains now to tell of the causes of the second loss, and to see what remedies he had there, and which ones may be available to whoever is in his circumstances so that he may be able to maintain himself better in his acquisition than did France.

I say, therefore, regarding these states that are added to the old state of the acquiring prince, that when they are acquired they are either of the same province and the same language, or not. When they are, it is very easy to keep them, especially when they are not used to living in freedom, and to possess them securely it is enough to have eliminated the line of the prince who was ruling them. For as for other matters, if their former conditions are maintained for them and there is no disparity of customs, men live quietly, as it has been seen that Burgundy, Brittany, Gascony and Normandy have done, which have been with France for so much time,[5] and although there is some disparity of language, nonetheless their customs are similar and they are easily compatible with one another. Whoever acquires such provinces, if he wants to keep them, must have two concerns: one is that the bloodline of their former prince be eliminated; the other is to alter neither their laws nor their taxes, so that in a very brief time the acquired state becomes, together with the old principality, a single body.

But when one acquires states in a province that is foreign in its language, customs and orders, here the difficulties are; and here one needs great fortune and great industry to hold them. And one of the best and quickest remedies would be that whoever acquires the state should go there in person to live. This would make the possession more secure and lasting, as the Turk has done in Greece: despite all of the other orders observed by the Turk to hold that state, if he had not gone there to live,[6] it would not be possible for him to keep it. For when you[7] stay there, disorders are seen as they arise and you may quickly remedy them. When you are not there, they become known when they are great

---

[4]Louis XII lost Milan for the second time after the battle of Ravenna (April 11, 1512), in which he was opposed by the Holy League. Although the French won the battle, the death of their general, Gaston de Foix, forced them to retreat from Italy. On the battle, see also chapters 13 and 26.

[5]Normandy was joined to the French Crown in 1204, Gascony in 1453, Burgundy in 1477, and Brittany in 1491.

[6]Sultan Mehmet II, known as Mehmet the Conqueror" (1432–1481), took Constantinople in 1453; in 1465 he made it the capital of the Ottoman Empire.

[7]An impersonal use of *tu,* here, and in the following two sentences.

and when there is no longer remedy. Beyond this, the province is not despoiled by your officers: the subjects are satisfied by their close recourse to the prince, for which they have more reason to love him if they wish to be good, and if they wish to be otherwise they have more reason to fear him. If any outsider should wish to attack that state, he is more cautious about it. So that if the lord lives there he can lose it only with very great difficulty.

The other best remedy is to send colonies to one or two places, that they may be like shackles[8] for that state. For it is necessary either to do this or to keep many men at arms and footsoldiers there. Not much is spent on colonies; and at no expense to the lord, or at little, he sends and keeps them there, and he only offends the persons from whom he takes their fields and their houses to give them to the new inhabitants, and they are only a very small part of that state. And the persons he offends, since they remain dispersed and poor, are never able to harm him. And all the others remain, on the one hand, unharmed, and for this they should not complain, and, on the other hand, fearful of making a mistake, lest what happened to those who were despoiled of their property should happen to them. I conclude that these colonies do not cost much, are more faithful, and offend less; and the offended are not able to do harm, being poor and dispersed, as is said. In this regard one should note that men ought either to be coddled or eliminated.[9] For they avenge light offenses, but they are unable to avenge grave ones, so the offense that is given a man should be such that one does not fear his revenge.

But if instead of colonies he keeps men at arms there, he spends a great deal more, since he has to consume all of the revenues of that state in guarding it, so that the acquisition becomes a loss for him. And he is much more offensive, because he harms that whole state by moving his army and its lodgings about, at which everyone feels unease, so that each person becomes his enemy. And these are enemies who are able to do him harm, since, although defeated, they remain in their own homeland. From every perspective, therefore, this defense is as useless as the defense with colonies is useful.

Whoever is in a foreign province should also, as is said, make himself the leader and defender of its less powerful neighbors, and contrive to weaken the powers in the province, and be on guard lest through

---

[8]M uses the Latin word *compedes.* According to Livy, 32.37.4, Philip V, king of Macedon (238–179 BCE) referred to three cities in which he kept garrisons—Demetrias, Chalcis, and Corinth—as "the shackles (*compedes*) of Greece."

[9]See also *Discourses,* 2.23.

some accident an outsider as powerful as himself should enter the province. And it will always be the case that an outsider will be brought there by those in the province who are discontented, whether from excessive ambition or from fear, as was once seen when the Aetolians[10] brought the Romans into Greece, and in every other province that the Romans entered they were brought in by the provincials. And the order of things is that immediately after a powerful outsider enters a province, all the inhabitants who are less powerful ally themselves with him, since they are moved by an envy they have against whoever has been powerful over them. So that with respect to these who are less powerful he suffers no trouble whatsoever in winning them over to himself, because immediately all of them together make a compact with the state he has acquired in that province. The outsider has only to see to it that they not gain too many forces and too much authority, and with his own forces and with their favor he can easily cut down those who are powerful, so that he remains in everything the arbiter of that province. And whoever does not manage this point well will quickly lose whatever he acquired, and for as long as he keeps it he will have infinite difficulties and annoyances in it.

The Romans observed these points well in the provinces they seized. They sent colonies, they dealt with the less powerful without increasing their power, they reduced the powerful, and they did not permit powerful outsiders to gain reputation there. And I want the province of Greece to suffice as my single example. The Romans were brought in by the Achaeans and the Aetolians[11] of their own accord; the kingdom of the Macedonians was reduced;[12] Antiochus was chased out.[13] Nor did the merits of the Achaeans and the Aetolians ever cause the Romans to allow them to increase their state in any way. Nor did the persuasions of Philip ever induce them to be his friends without reducing him. Nor was the power of Antiochus able to make them consent to his keeping any state in that province. For the

[10]The Aetolian League was a confederacy of city-states in central Greece. In 212 BCE it entered into an alliance with Rome against Philip V of Macedon, who was supporting Carthage against Rome in the Second Punic War.

[11]The Achaean League was a confederacy of Greek city-states in the Peloponnesus. At first it provided somewhat reluctant support to the Romans against Philip V, but in 198 BCE, encouraged by the Roman general Titus Quinctius Flamininus, the league entered into an alliance with Rome.

[12]Philip V was defeated at the battle of Cynoscephalae in 197 BCE.

[13]Antiochus III, known as "Antiochus the Great" (ca. 242–187 BCE), king of Asia Minor and Syria, invaded Greece and was decisively defeated by the Romans, who forced him to terms in 188 BCE.

Romans did in these circumstances what all wise princes should do. Such princes have not only to beware of present disorders, but also of future ones, and to make every effort to obviate these, for if one sees them earlier from a distance, one can easily remedy them, but if you wait for them to come near to you, the medicine will not be in time, because the sickness has become incurable. And from this it comes about that, as the doctors to a consumptive say, during the beginning of his illness it is easy to cure and difficult to recognize, but, with the passage of time, if no one recognizes or medicates it at the beginning, it becomes easy to recognize and difficult to cure. So it happens in matters of state: for if a prince recognizes them at a distance, which is something given only to a prudent man, the evils that are born in a state are quickly cured; but when, because he did not recognize them, they are allowed to grow such that everyone recognizes them, there is no longer a remedy.

For this reason the Romans, who saw problems at a distance, always remedied them. And they never allowed them to continue in order to avoid a war, because they knew that war is not averted, but it is postponed to the advantage of others. For this reason they wanted to make war against Philip and Antiochus in Greece in order not to have to make it against them in Italy. And they were able for the time being to avoid both the one and the other war, but they did not want that. Nor did they ever like, what today is in the mouths of the wise men of our times, "to enjoy the benefit of time";[14] but instead they liked very much to enjoy the benefit of their own virtue and prudence. For time pushes everything forward, and it can bring with it good as well as evil, and evil as well as good.

But let us return to France[15] and examine whether, of the things that have been said, he has done any of them. And I shall speak of Louis,[16] and not of Charles,[17] since on account of his having held territory in Italy longer he is the one whose steps have been better seen. And you[18] will see how he has done the contrary of those things that should be done to hold a state in a foreign province. King Louis was brought into Italy by the ambition of the Venetians, who wanted to

[14]Faced with uncertainty, most Florentine writers and statesmen advocated a policy of temporizing. Compare Francesco Guicciardini, *Ricordi*, B.79.

[15]The king of France.

[16]Louis XII.

[17]King Charles VIII of France (r. 1483–1498) invaded Italy in September 1494 and withdrew in October 1495.

[18]*voi*: addressing the dedicatee.

gain half of the state of Lombardy through his coming. I do not want to blame this decision taken by the king, for, when he wanted to get a foothold in Italy, because he had no friends in this province, and on the contrary, all of its gates were locked against him on account of the behavior of King Charles, he was forced to accept whatever friendships he could have. And it would have resulted in a decision well taken for him if in his other actions he had not made any errors. Thus when the King had acquired Lombardy he immediately regained the reputation of which Charles had deprived him. Genoa surrendered; the Florentines became his friends; the marchese of Mantua, the duke of Ferrara, the Bentivoglio, my lady of Forlì, the lords of Faenza, of Rimini, of Pesaro, of Camerino, of Piombino, the Lucchese, the Pisans, and the Sienese[19]—all presented themselves before him in order to be his friend. And the Venetians were then able to consider the shamelessness of the decision they had made, since to acquire a couple of towns in Lombardy they had made the king lord of two-thirds[20] of Italy.

Let anyone now consider with how little difficulty the king would have been able to maintain his reputation in Italy if he had observed the rules set out above, and kept safe and defended all of those friends of his, who, because they were a great number and weak and fearful (some fearful of the church and some of the Venetians), would always have needed to stay with him, and by their means he easily could have assured himself of whoever remained great there. But no sooner was he in Milan than he did the contrary when he gave aid to Pope Alexander[21] to occupy the Romagna. Nor did he realize that with this decision he was making himself weak, by shedding his friends and those who had thrown themselves in his lap, and making the church strong, by adding to its spiritual power (which gives it so much authority) so much temporal power. And having made a first mistake, he was constrained to follow through until, in order to place a limit on

---

[19]In 1499, when Louis XII invaded Italy, Genoa belonged to the duchy of Milan; Florence was an independent republic; Mantua was ruled by Marchese Francesco Gonzaga; Ferrara was ruled by Duke Ercole I d'Este; the Bentivoglio family were lords of Bologna; Countess Caterina Sforza Riario ruled Imola and Forlì; Astorre Manfredi was lord of Faenza; Pandolfo Malatesta was lord of Rimini; Giovanni Sforza was lord of Pesaro; Giulio Cesare Varano was lord of Camerino; Jacopo IV Appiano was lord of Piombino; and Lucca, Pisa, and Siena were independent republics.

[20]Most manuscripts read "two-thirds," although Casella followed a manuscript that gives "one-third." Probably M included the French claim to the Kingdom of Naples (roughly one-third of Italy) in arriving at this figure.

[21]Pope Alexander VI (r. 1492–1503), formerly Cardinal Rodrigo Borgia.

the ambition of Alexander and so that he could not become lord of Tuscany, the king was constrained to come into Italy.

It was not enough for him to have made the Church great and to have shed his friends, for out of his desire for the Kingdom of Naples he partitioned it with the king of Spain. And where he was once the supreme arbiter of Italy, he brought in a partner, with the result that the ambitious men of that province[22] and those who were discontent with him had someone else to turn to. And where he could have left a king who would have paid him tribute in that kingdom,[23] he removed him in order to install one who was capable of expelling himself. It is a thing truly very natural and ordinary to desire to acquire. When men do it who are capable, they always will be praised or not criticized. But when they are not capable and want to do it anyway, here is the error and the blame. Thus if France had been able with his own forces to attack Naples, he should have done it; if he could not do it, he should not have partitioned it. And if the partition that he made of Lombardy with the Venetians merited excuse, since with that he got his foothold in Italy, this partition merits blame because it was not excused by that necessity.

Thus Louis made these five errors: he eliminated the lesser powers; he enhanced the power of someone[24] who was powerful in Italy; he brought into Italy an outsider who was very powerful;[25] he did not come to live there; he did not put colonies there. These errors, so long as he was alive,[26] could not have harmed him still, if he had not committed the sixth, which was to take their state away from the Venetians.[27] For if he had not made the Church great nor brought Spain into Italy, it would have been very reasonable and necessary to cut down the Venetians; but after he made those first two decisions he should never have consented to their ruin, for, since they were powerful, they would always have warded the others off from their invasion

---

[22]Italy.

[23]Frederick I of Aragon, who became king of Naples in 1496. He was betrayed by his cousin, Ferdinand the Catholic, in the secret treaty of Granada (1500), by which France and Spain agreed to partition the kingdom of Naples. In 1501 Frederick was forced from the throne.

[24]Pope Alexander VI.

[25]Ferdinand the Catholic.

[26]A possible indication that Louis, who died the night of December 31, 1514–January 1, 1515, was dead when this passage was written.

[27]Louis XII led the League of Cambrai when it defeated Venice at the battle of Vailate (the name of a nearby village) on May 14, 1509. The battle is also known as Agnadello (another nearby village) or Geradadda (after the general area along the Adda river). After the battle, most of Venice's territories on the Italian mainland rebelled.

of Lombardy. For, on the one hand, the Venetians would not have consented to such an invasion unless they themselves were to become the lords of Lombardy; and, on the other hand, the other powers would not have wanted to take Lombardy away from France to give it to the Venetians, and they would not have had the courage to go and cast out both of them.

And if anyone should say King Louis surrendered the Romagna to Alexander and the Kingdom of Naples to Spain in order to avoid a war, I reply with the reasons stated above, that one should never allow a disorder to happen in order to avoid a war, because it is not avoided but it is deferred to your disadvantage. And if anyone else should invoke the promise that the king had given to the pope, to make that invasion for him in exchange for the annulment of his marriage[28] and the cardinal's hat for Rouen,[29] I reply with what will be said by me below concerning the promises of princes and how they ought to be observed.[30]

Thus King Louis lost Lombardy because he did not observe any of those rules that have been observed by others who have taken provinces and have wanted to keep them. Nor is any of this a miracle, rather it is very ordinary and rational. And on this subject I spoke with Rouen at Nantes,[31] when Valentino (since this was how Cesare Borgia, the son of Pope Alexander, was commonly called[32]) occupied the Romagna. For when the Cardinal of Rouen told me that the Italians did not understand war, I replied to him that the French did not understand states, since, if they understood them, they would not allow the Church to come into such greatness. And by experience it is seen that the greatness of the Church and of Spain in Italy was caused by France, and her own ruin was caused by them. From this one extracts a general rule that never or rarely fails, that whoever causes someone else to become powerful is ruined, for he causes that power either with craft or with force, and both of these qualities are suspect to whoever has become powerful.

---

[28]Louis divorced his wife, Jeanne, the sister of his predecessor, Charles VIII, in order to marry Charles's widow, Anne of Brittany, in October 1498. The bull of annulment was granted by Pope Alexander VI and personally delivered to France by the pope's illegitimate son, Cesare Borgia.

[29]Georges d'Amboise (1460–1510), archbishop of Rouen and principal adviser of Louis XII, was named cardinal by Alexander VI on September 17, 1498.

[30]In chapter 18.

[31]During M's first legation to France. He was at Nantes at the end of October and beginning of November 1500.

[32]In 1498 Louis XII gave Cesare Borgia title to the French duchy of Valentinois, with territory in the vicinity of Valence. Hence the name Valentino.

CHAPTER 4

Why Darius' kingdom, which Alexander had occupied, did not rebel from Alexander's successors after his death[1]

When the difficulties that exist in holding a newly acquired state are considered, anyone might marvel at how it happened that, when Alexander the Great became lord of Asia in a few years, and died when he had barely occupied it, so that it seemed reasonable that all of that state should have rebelled, nonetheless, the successors of Alexander maintained it, and in keeping it they had no difficulty other than what arose among themselves because of their own ambition. I reply that the principalities of which there is memory are found to be governed in two different ways: either by a prince, with everyone else as his servants, who, as ministers, by his grace and leave, assist in governing that kingdom; or by a prince and by barons, who hold that rank not by the grace of their lord but by the antiquity of their blood-lines. Barons such as these have states and subjects of their own, who recognize them as lords, and have a natural affection toward them. Those states that are governed by a prince and by servants hold their prince in more authority, because, in all his province, there is no one who recognizes anyone but the prince as his superior, and, if they obey anyone else, they obey him as a minister and officer, and toward the prince alone do they bear particular love.

In our times the examples of these two different kinds of government are the Turk and the king of France. The whole monarchy of the Turk is governed by one lord: the others are his servants. And since his kingdom is divided into sanjaks,[2] he sends different administrators to them, and he substitutes and transfers them as he pleases. But the king of France is placed in the middle of an ancient multitude of lords in that state who are recognized by their subjects and loved by them. They have their own hereditary privileges: the king cannot take these away from them without danger to himself. Thus whoever considers the one and the other of these states will find difficulty in acquiring the state of the Turk, but great ease in keeping it once he is defeated. Conversely, he will find more ease in some respects in occupying the Kingdom of France, but great difficulty in holding it.

---

[1]Alexander III of Macedon, known as "Alexander the Great" (356–323 BCE), conquered the Persian Empire of King Darius III (ca. 380–330 BCE).

[2]*sanjaks:* a name given to administrative districts in the Ottoman Empire.

The causes of the difficulty in being able to occupy the kingdom of the Turk are in not being able to be called in by the princes of that kingdom, nor to hope to be able to facilitate your[3] invasion by the rebellion of those the Turk has around him. This arises from the reasons stated above, for since they are all slaves and obligated to him, it is more difficult to corrupt them, and even if they should be corrupted, one may hope for little that is useful from it, since they cannot bring their people along with them for the reasons noted. Hence it is necessary for whoever attacks the Turk to think that he will find him wholly united, and he must hope for more from his own forces than from the disorders of others. But if the Turk were defeated and routed in open battle, in such a way that he could not raise armies again, he need not worry about anything save the bloodline of the prince, since when this is eliminated there remains no one he need fear, since the others do not have credit with their people, and just as the victor could place no hope in them before his victory, so he should not fear them after it.

The contrary happens in kingdoms governed like that of France, because with ease you[4] can enter there by winning to yourself some baron of the kingdom, for always one finds some malcontents and some who want to revolt. Those people, for the reasons stated, are able to open the way for you to that state and to ease your victory. But then this, if you want to hold your own, brings with it infinite difficulties, both with those who helped you and with those whom you defeated. Nor is it sufficient for you to eliminate the bloodline of the prince, because there remain those lords, who make themselves the leaders in new troubles, and since you can neither content them nor eliminate them, you lose that state whenever the opportunity comes.

Now if you[5] will consider what the nature of Darius' government was, you will find it similar to the kingdom of the Turk. And for this reason it was necessary for Alexander first to cast him down completely and take the field from him. After this victory, once Darius was killed, that state remained secure for Alexander for the reasons set forth above. And his successors, if they had been united, could have enjoyed it for themselves at their leisure. Nor did tumults arise in that kingdom other than those that they themselves incited. But as for states ordered like that of France, it is impossible to possess them in

---

[3] An impersonal use of *tu.*
[4] *tu:* used impersonally throughout this paragraph.
[5] *voi.*

such tranquility. From this fact arose the frequent rebellions against the Romans by Spain, by France,[6] and by Greece. On account of the many principalities that existed in those states the Romans were always uncertain of their possession so long as the memory of these endured. But when the memory of those principalities was eliminated through the power and duration of their empire, the Romans became their secure possessors. And later, when the Romans were fighting among themselves, each was able to bring along part of those provinces according to the authority he had assumed in them. And since the bloodlines of their former lords were eliminated, the provinces recognized only the Romans. Thus, when all of these things are considered, no one will marvel at Alexander's ease in keeping his state in Asia, and at the difficulties that others, such as Pyrrhus[7] and many others, have had in keeping what they acquired. This is a thing that arises not from the great or small virtue of the victor, but from the difference in their situations.

[6]The Roman province of Gaul is here called "France."
[7]Pyrrhus, king of Epirus (319–272 BCE), was a brilliant general who won victories against the Macedonians, the Romans, and the Carthaginians but failed to subjugate their lands.

CHAPTER 5

By what means cities or principalities are to be administered that, before they were occupied, lived by their own laws

As has been said, when those states that are acquired are accustomed to live with their own laws and in liberty, there are three ways of trying to hold them. The first is to destroy them. The second is to go there in person to live. The third is to allow them to live with their own laws, while extracting tribute from them and creating inside a state of the few,[1] who will keep it friendly to you,[2] for, since this state is created by that prince, it knows that it cannot exist without his friendship and power, and it has to do everything to support him, and it is easier to hold a city used to living in freedom by means of its own citizens than in any other way if one wants to preserve it.[3]

[1]An oligarchy.
[2]An impersonal use of *tu.*
[3]That is, not destroy it.

As examples there are the Spartans and the Romans. The Spartans held Athens and Thebes by creating states of the few, although they lost them again.[4] The Romans, in order to hold Capua, Carthage and Numantia, destroyed them,[5] and they did not lose them. They wanted to hold Greece almost as the Spartans did, by making it free and leaving it to its own laws, and this did not succeed for them, so that they were forced to destroy many cities of that province in order to hold it. For in truth there is no secure way to possess them other than their destruction. And whoever becomes master of a city accustomed to living in freedom and does not destroy it may expect to be destroyed by it, because in rebellion it always takes refuge in the name of liberty and its ancient constitution,[6] which neither through the passage of time nor through benefits are ever forgotten. And whatever is done or provided, if the inhabitants are not divided or scattered, they do not forget its name or their constitution, and immediately in every accident they run back to them, as Pisa did one hundred years after it had been placed in servitude by the Florentines.[7]

But when the cities or the provinces are used to living under a prince, and his bloodline is extinguished, they do not know how to live in freedom, because on the one hand they are used to obeying, and on the other hand, not having the old prince, they are not able to agree to make one of their own a new prince. The result is that they are slower to take up arms, and a prince may with more facility win them over and rely on them. But in republics there is greater life, greater hatred, more desire for revenge. Nor does the memory of their ancient liberty ever allow them to rest, nor can it, so that the most secure way is to eliminate them or live there.

CHAPTER 6

On new principalities that are acquired by one's own arms and by virtue

Let no one wonder whether I shall introduce the greatest examples in the speech I shall make concerning principalities that are wholly new,

---

[4]In 404 BCE, after winning the Peloponnesian War, Sparta created in Athens a regime of Thirty Tyrants that was overthrown in 403 BCE. In 382 BCE, Sparta created an oligarchy in Thebes that was overturned in 378 BCE.

[5]Capua was destroyed in 211 BCE, Carthage in 146 BCE, and Numantia in 133 BCE.

[6]*constitution:* the Italian is *ordini,* usually translated as "orders."

[7]Pisa was taken by Florence in 1406; it rebelled in 1494 when Charles VIII invaded Italy; it was retaken by Florence in 1509.

both in their prince and in their state. For, since men always walk in paths beaten by others, and they proceed by means of imitation in their actions, and since one cannot completely hold to the paths of others, nor arrive at the virtue of those whom you[1] imitate, a prudent man should always enter by paths beaten by great men and imitate those who have been the most excellent, so that if his virtue does not arrive there, at least it gives off some scent of it. And he should do as the prudent archers do when the place they wish to strike appears to them too far off. Since the archers know just how far the virtue of their bow reaches, they place their aim much higher than the intended place, not in order to reach a place so high with their arrow, but to be able, with the help of so high an aim, to achieve their goal.

Thus I say that in wholly new principalities, in which there is a new prince, one finds greater or lesser difficulty in maintaining them depending on whether he who acquires them is more or less virtuous. And because this event—becoming a prince from being a private man—presupposes either virtue or fortune, it appears that the one or the other of these two things in part mitigates many difficulties; nonetheless, he who has relied less on fortune has kept more of what he has acquired. It becomes even easier if, because he does not have other states, the prince is constrained to come live there in person.

But to come to those who by their own virtue and not by fortune became princes, I say that the most excellent are Moses, Cyrus, Romulus, Theseus and similar persons. Although one ought not to reason about Moses, since he was a mere executor of the things that were ordered of him by God, yet he should be admired, if only for that grace that made him worthy of speaking with God. But let us consider Cyrus, and the others who have acquired and founded kingdoms. You[2] will find them all admirable, and if their particular actions and orders are considered they will appear no different from those of Moses, who had so great a teacher.[3] And if their actions and life are examined, it is not seen that they got anything from fortune other than opportunity, which gave them the material so as to be able to introduce into it whatever form they chose.[4] And without that opportunity, the virtue of their spirit would have been wasted; and without that virtue, the opportunity would have come in vain.

---

[1]An impersonal use of *tu*.

[2]*voi*.

[3]M suggests, without positively saying so, that Moses may have done all that he did by himself.

[4]The passage looks ahead to chapter 26.

It was therefore necessary for Moses to find the people of Israel in Egypt, enslaved and oppressed by the Egyptians, so that in order to escape servitude they were disposed to follow him. It was suitable that Romulus not settle in Alba Longa, and that he should have been exposed at his birth,[5] if he was to become the king of Rome and the founder of that fatherland. It was necessary that Cyrus find the Persians discontented under the empire of the Medes, and the Medes soft and effeminate because of their long peace. Theseus would not have been able to demonstrate his virtue if he had not found the Athenians dispersed. Thus these opportunities made these men happy, and their own excellent virtue caused the opportunities to be revealed whence their fatherlands were ennobled and became very happy. Those who, like these men, become princes in virtuous ways, acquire their principalities with difficulty, but hold them with ease. And the difficulties they have in acquiring the principality arise in part from the new orders and methods they are forced to introduce in order to establish their state and their security. One should consider how there is nothing more difficult to treat, nor more doubtful to succeed in, nor more dangerous to manage than to make oneself a leader who introduces new orders. For the introducer has as enemies all those who are doing well under the old orders, and, as his defenders, all those who would do well under the new orders are lukewarm. This lukewarmness arises in part out of fear of their adversaries, who have the laws on their side, and in part from the incredulity of men, who do not truly believe in new things unless they see that they arise from solid experience. Whence it arises that whenever those who are hostile have the opportunity to attack, they do it in a partisan way; and those others defend the new orders lukewarmly, so that, together with the orders, the one who introduces them is imperiled.

It is necessary, therefore, if one wants to discuss this part well, to examine whether these innovators stand by themselves, or if they depend on others. That is, whether to carry out their work they need to beg,[6] or whether instead they can use force. In the first case they always come to ill and do not accomplish anything. But when they rely on themselves, and they are able to use force, then rarely is it that they are imperiled. From this it arose that all the armed prophets were victorious

---

[5]Moses (according to Exodus 2:3–10) and Cyrus (according to Herodotus, 1.108–114) were also exposed at birth.
   [6]Or "to pray" (*pregare*).

and the unarmed ones were ruined. For beyond the things already said, the nature of peoples is changeable, and it is easy to persuade them of one thing, but it is difficult to keep them in that persuasion. For this reason it is suitable for them to be ordered in such a way that when they no longer believe, one can make them believe by force. Moses, Cyrus, Theseus and Romulus would not have been able to make their peoples observe their constitutions for long if they had been unarmed, as in our times happened to Brother Girolamo Savonarola.[7] He was ruined in his new orders when the multitude began not to believe him and he had no way to hold firm those who had believed, nor to make the unbelieving believe. For this reason such men as these have great difficulty in their journey, and all of their dangers are along the way, and it is best that they overcome them with virtue. But when they have overcome them, and when they begin to be held in veneration since they have eliminated those who used to envy them their quality, they remain powerful, secure, honored and happy.

To such lofty examples I want to add an example that is lesser, but that still has some similarity with those, and I want it to suffice for all the other similar examples, and this is Hiero the Syracusan.[8] That man, from being a private citizen, became the prince of Syracuse, nor did he get anything from fortune other than the opportunity. For when the Syracusans were oppressed they elected him as their captain, hence he was worthy of being made their prince. And he was of such great virtue, even in his fortune as a private man, that he who writes about him says "that he lacked nothing appropriate to kingship save a kingdom."[9] Hiero eliminated the former military and established a new one; he abandoned former alliances and took up new ones;[10] and since he had alliances and soldiers that were his own, he was able on such a foundation to build any building whatsoever, so that he endured much labor in acquiring and little in maintaining.

---

[7]Girolamo Savonarola (1452–1498) of Ferrara was a Dominican friar who became famous as a preacher in Florence. He exercised a strong influence over the city's republican government after the exile of the Medici family in 1494, introducing major changes in the constitution. He came into conflict with Pope Alexander VI, with the result that he was burned as a heretic, but Savonarola's numerous followers remained politically active in Florence for decades after his death.

[8]Hiero II (ca. 306–215 BCE) was a general, tyrant, and later king of Syracuse.

[9]Here M quotes Justin, 23.4. Other phrases in the paragraph echo Polybius, 7.8. See also the dedicatory letter of the *Discourses*.

[10]Hiero was first an ally of Carthage; however, in 263 BCE he changed sides and became an ally of Rome.

CHAPTER 7

**On new principalities that are acquired with the arms
and fortune of others**

Those who, through fortune alone, pass from being private persons to
being princes do so with little labor, but they maintain themselves with
a great deal of labor. And they have no difficulty on the way, because
they fly into place, but all of the difficulties arise once they are in
place. Cases such as these are when a state is granted to someone for
money, or by the grace of whoever concedes it, as happened to many
persons in Greece, in the cities of Ionia and the Hellespont, where
they were made princes by Darius[1] so that they would hold their cities
for his security and glory, and as was also done to those emperors
who, from being private persons, attained the empire by corrupting
the soldiers. These persons rely simply on the will and fortune of whoever has granted it to them, and those are two things that are very
volatile and unstable, and they neither know how nor are able to maintain that rank. They do not know how, because, if he is not a man of
great genius and virtue, it is not reasonable that after always having
lived in private fortune a man should know how to command. They
are not able, because they do not have troops that could be friendly
and faithful to them. Furthermore, states that come about suddenly,
like all other things of nature that are born and grow quickly, cannot
develop their roots and branches, with the result that the first adverse
weather eliminates them, unless such men as these, as was stated,
who have thus unexpectedly become princes, are of such virtue that
they know right away how to prepare themselves to keep what fortune
has placed in their laps, and they are able to lay afterward the foundations that others lay in advance of becoming princes.

   Concerning the first and the second of the methods stated for
becoming a prince, by virtue or by fortune, I want to adduce two examples that took place during days that are within our memory, and
these are Francesco Sforza and Cesare Borgia. Francesco was a private man who became duke of Milan by proper means and with great
virtue of his own, and what he acquired with a thousand pains he
maintained with little effort. On the other hand, Cesare Borgia, who
was called Duke Valentino by the people, acquired his state through

---

[1]Darius I, king of Persia (r. 522–485 BCE), installed local tyrants to rule on his
behalf after he conquered the Greek cities of Asia Minor.

his father's fortune, and on the same account he lost it, even though he took every care, and did all those things that ought to have been done by a prudent and virtuous man to put down roots in those states that the arms and fortune of others had granted him. For, as was said above, he who does not lay his foundations in advance may, with great virtue, lay them afterward, although they be laid with pain for the builder and peril for the building. Thus if one will consider all the steps of the duke, one will see that he lay great foundations for his future power. These I do not judge superfluous to discuss, because I would not know what better precepts to give to a new prince than the example of his actions. And if he did not profit by what he established,[2] it was not his fault, because this arose from an extraordinary and extreme malignity of fortune.[3]

Alexander VI, when he wanted to make a great man of the duke, his son, had many difficulties, both present and future. First, he could not see a way to make him the lord of any state that was not a state of the Church. And if he decided to take it from the Church, he knew that the duke of Milan and the Venetians would not allow it to him, because Faenza and Rimini were already under the protection of the Venetians. He saw, beyond this, that the arms of Italy, and especially those of whom he might have made use, were in the hands of those who needed to fear the greatness of the pope, and for that reason he could not trust them, since they were all with the Orsini and Colonna and were their accomplices.[4] Thus it was necessary that those orders should be disturbed, and the states of those men put in disorder, so that he could securely assume the lordship of part of them. This was easy for him, because he found that the Venetians, moved by other reasons, had decided to bring the French again into Italy, which not only did he not prohibit, but which he facilitated by the annulment of the previous marriage of King Louis.[5]

Thus the king came into Italy with the help of the Venetians and the consent of Alexander. No sooner was he in Milan than the pope had troops from him for the invasion of the Romagna, which was permitted him on account of the king's reputation. When, therefore, the duke had acquired the Romagna and defeated the Colonnesi, and he

---

[2]Literally, "by his orders" (*ordini*).

[3]The phrase "malignity of fortune" also appears at the end of M's dedicatory letter.

[4]The Orsini and Colonna were rival noble clans that fought for centuries to control Rome and the papacy.

[5]Previously mentioned in chapter 3.

wanted to maintain it and proceed farther ahead, two things impeded him. One was his own army, which to him did not seem faithful; the other was the will of France. That is, he feared that the Orsini arms of which he had availed himself might fail under him, and not only impede his acquisition, but take away what he had acquired; and that the king might also do the same to him. He had some proof of the Orsini when, after the capture of Faenza, he attacked Bologna, since he saw them go cold in that attack. And as for the king, he understood his spirit when, after taking the duchy of Urbino, Valentino attacked Tuscany and the king made him desist from that undertaking.

Whence it was that the duke decided no longer to depend on the arms and fortune of others. And the first thing he did was weaken the Orsini and Colonna factions in Rome, for he won to himself all of their adherents who were noblemen, making them his own noblemen and giving them great provisions, and he honored them according to their qualities with mercenary contracts and commands, so that within a few months factional attachments were eliminated from their spirits and turned completely to the duke. After this, he waited for the opportunity to eliminate the Orsini leaders, having dispersed those of the Colonna house. It came well to him, and he used it better. For when the Orsini realized, late, that the greatness of the duke and of the Church was their ruin, they held a meeting at Magione, in Perugian territory.[6] From this there arose the rebellion of Urbino and the tumults of the Romagna and infinite dangers for the duke, all of which he overcame with the help of the French. And since he did not trust France or any other outside forces, because he did not want to have to risk using them, when his reputation was restored he turned to deceit. He knew so well how to dissimulate his spirit that the Orsini themselves, through Signor Paolo, were reconciled with him.[7] And in order to secure him the duke did not fail Signor Paolo in any manner of obligation, giving him money,

---

[6]The meeting began on September 24, 1502, and concluded on October 8. Present were the leaders of the Orsini family (Paolo, lord of Mentana; Francesco, duke of Gravina; and Cardinal Giambattista), Vitellozzo Vitelli (lord of Città di Castello), Oliverotto Eufreducci (lord of Fermo), Giampaolo Baglioni (lord of Perugia), Ermes Bentivoglio (representing his father Giovanni, lord of Bologna), Antonio Giordani of Venafro (representing Pandolfo Petrucci, lord of Siena), and a representative of Guidubaldo da Montefeltro (duke of Urbino).

[7]Paolo Orsini, lord of Mentana, signed an accord with Borgia on October 25, 1502, renewing the mercenary contracts of his rebellious captains.

clothing and horses, so that the Orsini's own simplicity led them into his hands at Senigallia.[8]

Thus once these leaders were eliminated, and their partisans had become his friends, the duke had thrown down very good foundations for his power, since he had all of the Romagna and the duchy of Urbino, and it appeared to him that he had especially acquired the friendship of the Romagna and won to himself all of those people because they had begun to savor their own well-being. And because the following point is worthy of notice and should be imitated by others, I do not want to leave it out. After the duke had taken the Romagna, since he found it commanded by impotent lords who preferred to despoil their subjects rather than correct them, and who had given them motive for disunion not unity, so that that province was completely full of robberies, feuds and every other kind of insolence, he judged it necessary, since he wanted to render it peaceful and obedient to the royal power, to give them good government. For this reason he appointed there Messer[9] Remirro de Orco,[10] a cruel and expeditious man, to whom he gave the fullest power. This man rendered the Romagna peaceful and unified in a short time, and had a very great reputation. Then the duke judged that such excessive authority was not necessary, because he worried that it would become hateful. He appointed there a civil tribunal, in the middle of the province, with a most excellent presiding judge, in which each city had its own advocate. And because Valentino knew that the past rigors had generated some hatred toward him, to purge the spirits of those people and to win them wholly to himself, he wanted to show that if any cruelty had taken place, it was not caused by himself, but by the harsh nature of his minister.

---

[8]Returned to the duke's service, the troops of the Orsini and the Vitelli captured the town of Senigallia on December 25, 1501. The duke arrived with his own troops on December 31 and immediately arrested Vitellozzo Vitelli, Liverotto of Fermo, and Paolo and Francesco Orsini. The first two were strangled that night. The two Orsini were put to death on January 18, 1502, after Pope Alexander had arrested the other Orsini leaders in Rome. M witnessed these events while on a Florentine legation to Cesare Borgia, and he later wrote about them in a brief treatise, "A Description of the Method Used by Duke Valentino in Killing Vitellozzo Vitelli, Liverotto of Fermo and Others."

[9]*Messer:* an honorific that indicated noble status, meaning, roughly, "my lord." In the fifteenth and sixteenth centuries it was used principally by men who had been knighted or who were lawyers.

[10]An Italianized form of his Spanish name, Ramiro de Lorqua. He served as Cesare Borgia's majordomo before his appointment as president (governor) of the Romagna in 1502.

And seizing an opportunity for this, in Cesena one morning he had Remirro placed in two pieces in the town-square, with a piece of wood and a bloody knife at his side.[11] The ferocity of that spectacle left those people at once satisfied and stupefied.

But let us return to where we left off. I say that when the duke found himself very powerful and in part secure against present dangers, since he was armed in his own way and had eliminated those arms which, because they were close by, might have harmed him, there remained for him, if he wanted to proceed with his acquisition, his fear of the king of France, because he knew that it would not be tolerated by the king, who had been late to recognize his own error. He began for this reason to look for new alliances, and to vacillate with France about the passage the French were making toward the Kingdom of Naples against the Spanish who were besieging Gaeta. His intention was to secure himself against the French, which he would have succeeded quickly in doing if Alexander had lived. And this was his conduct as regards present things.

But as regards future things, he had to worry, first, that a new successor to the Church might not be his friend, and might try to take away what Alexander had given him. Against this he thought to defend himself in four ways: first, to eliminate all the bloodlines of those lords he had despoiled, in order to take away from a pope that opportunity; second, to win to himself all of the noblemen of Rome, as is said, to be able to hold the pope in check through them; third, to make the College of Cardinals his as much as he could; and fourth, to acquire so much strength[12] before the pope died that he could resist a first assault all by himself. Of these four things he had accomplished three at the death of Alexander; the fourth he had almost accomplished. For of the lords he had despoiled he killed as many as he could reach, and very few saved themselves. The Roman noblemen he had won to himself. And in the College of Cardinals he had a very large faction. As for the new acquisition, he had planned to become lord of Tuscany, and he already possessed Perugia and Piombino, and he had taken up the protection of Pisa. And as soon as he did not have

[11]The "two pieces" were Remirro's head and trunk. According to a local chronicler of the event, which Machiavelli also witnessed, "... on the 25th, the night of the Christmas Feast, in the piazza of Cesena, [Remirro's] head was cut off with a butcher's falchion, and [the body] lay there on a mat all day...."; Giuliano Fantaguzzi, *Caos. Cronache cesenati del sec. XV,* ed. Dino Bazzocchi (Cesena: Bettini, 1915), 167–68 [editor's translation].

[12]Literally, "empire" (*imperio*).

to fear France (although he did not have to fear him any longer, since the French had already been despoiled of the Kingdom of Naples by the Spanish, with the result that both of them had to purchase his friendship), he would have jumped to Pisa. After this, Lucca and Siena would have surrendered immediately, partly out of ill will toward the Florentines, and partly out of fear, and the Florentines would have had no remedy. If this had succeeded for him (it would have happened in the same year that Alexander died), he would have acquired so many forces and such a reputation that he would have been able to stand alone, and he would not have depended any longer on the fortune and forces of others, but on his own power and virtue. But Alexander died five years after Valentino had started to draw his sword. He left the duke with only his state in the Romagna consolidated, and all of the others up in the air, between two very powerful enemy armies, and with the duke himself sick nearly to death. Yet there were such a great ferocity and so much virtue in the duke, and so well did he understand how men are won or lost, and so strong were the foundations that had been made in so little time, that, if he had not had those armies on top of him, or if he had been healthy, he would have stood through every difficulty.

And one could see that his foundations were good, since for more than a month the Romagna waited for him. In Rome, although he was half-alive, he was safe. And although the Baglioni, Vitelli and Orsini came to Rome, against him they had no followers. And if he could not make whomever he wanted pope, at least he could ensure that the pope was not someone he did not want. But if on the death of Alexander he had been healthy, everything would have been easy for him. And he told me, in the days when Julius II was created pope,[13] that he had thought through what might happen if his father died, and for everything he had found a remedy, except that he never thought that at his father's death he too would be close to death.

Thus, having summarized all of the actions of the duke, I would not know how to reproach him. On the contrary, I would like to put him forward, as I have done, as one to be imitated by all those who have risen to rule[14] by fortune and with the arms of others. For, since he had a great spirit, and his intention was high, he could not conduct himself otherwise. And only the brevity of the life of Alexander and

[13]M was in Rome on a Florentine legation during the conclave that elected Pope Julius II on November 1, 1503.

[14]Literally, "empire" (*imperio*).

his own sickness opposed his designs. Thus whoever in his new principality judges it necessary to secure himself against enemies, to gain friends for himself, to win whether by force or by fraud, to make himself loved and feared by his people and followed and revered by his soldiers, to eliminate those who are able or ought to harm you, to renew ancient orders with new modes, to be severe and pleasing, magnanimous and liberal, to eliminate an unfaithful military and create a new one, to maintain the friendships of kings and princes in such a way that they have either to benefit you with grace, or, if they harm you, to do it in fear, can find no fresher examples than the actions of that man.

Only in the creation of Julius as pontiff, since he made a poor choice, may the duke be criticized. For, as is said, although he was not able to make a pope in his own way, he was able to keep anyone from being pope, and he should never have allowed in the papacy any of those cardinals he had offended, or cardinals who, if they became pope, would have to be afraid of him, for men offend out of either fear or hatred. Among all the cardinals, those whom he had offended were St. Peter in Chains, Colonna, St. George and Ascanio Sforza.[15] All the rest, if they became pope, had reason to fear him, except for Rouen and the Spaniards: these last out of kinship and obligation,[16] the former, because of his own power, since he was connected to the Kingdom of France.[17] Therefore the duke, before anything else, should have created a Spaniard as pope. And if he could not, he should have permitted that it be Rouen and not St. Peter in Chains. And whoever believes, in dealing with great personalities, that new benefits make old injuries forgotten deceives himself. Thus the duke erred in this choice, and it was the cause of his final ruin.

[15]The cardinal-priest of the church of St. Peter in Chains in Rome was Giuliano della Rovere, who became Pope Julius II (r. 1503–1513). Giovanni Colonna (d. 1508), cardinal-deacon of Santa Maria in Aquiro, had been forced to flee Rome by Alexander VI. The cardinal-deacon of St. George at Velabrum was Raffaello Riario (1460–1521). Cardinal Ascanio Sforza (1455–1505) was the brother of Duke Ludovico Maria Sforza of Milan.
[16]The Borgia family came from Aragon, in Spain.
[17]Georges d'Amboise, cardinal and archbishop of Rouen, was mentioned in chapter 3.

CHAPTER 8

On those who achieved principalities through wicked deeds

But because a private man may become a prince in two further ways that cannot be attributed wholly to fortune or to virtue, I do not wish to leave them out, although one may be reasoned about more extensively where republics are treated.[1] These ways are when either by some wicked and nefarious way one ascends to the principality, or when a private citizen with the favor of his fellow citizens becomes prince of his fatherland. And to speak of the first way, it will be demonstrated with two examples, one ancient and the other modern, without entering otherwise into the merits of this point, because I judge these examples sufficient[2] for whoever needs to imitate them.

Agathocles the Sicilian, from having a private man's fortune, and one that was most low and abject, became king of Syracuse.[3] This man, who was born of a potter, always led a wicked life through each step of his career. Nonetheless, he accompanied his wicked deeds with such great virtue of spirit and of body that when he dedicated himself to the military he rose through its ranks to be governor of Syracuse. Once he was established in that rank, having decided to become prince, and to hold with violence and without obligation to others what had been granted to him by consent, and having an agreement to this plan of his with Hamilcar the Carthaginian, who was in Sicily fighting with his armies, he assembled the people and the senate of Syracuse one morning, as though he had to decide things pertinent to the republic. And at an arranged signal he had all of the senators and the richest of the people killed by his soldiers. When these persons were dead, he occupied and held the principate of that city without any internal opposition. And although he was twice defeated by the Carthaginians and finally besieged, not only was he able to defend his city, but, having left part of his troops in defense against the siege, with the rest he attacked Africa.[4] And in a short time he freed Syracuse from the siege and brought the Carthaginians to extreme deprivation. And they were forced to come to terms with him, to be content with their possession of Africa, and to leave Sicily to Agathocles.

Thus whoever considers the actions and life of this man will not see things, or will see only a few of them, that he may attribute to fortune, since it is the case, as stated above, that not through anyone's favor, but through the ranks of the military, which he had climbed through a thousand sacrifices and perils, he reached the principate, and he maintained it with so many spirited and very risky decisions.

---

[1] M suggests that the second of these two ways (that is, with the favor of one's fellow citizens) will be treated in the *Discourses*. It is also discussed in the following chapter.

[2] Note that the general discussion resumes after the two examples are related.

[3] Agathocles, tyrant of Syracuse, lived from 361 to 289 BCE.

[4] Thus anticipating the successful strategy used by Scipio Africanus against Carthage in the Second Punic War.

And yet one cannot call it virtue to kill one's fellow citizens, to betray one's friends, to be without faith, without compassion, without religion. These modes may be used to acquire rule[5] but not glory. For if one considers Agathocles' virtue in entering into and escaping dangers, and the greatness of his spirit in enduring and overcoming adverse things, one does not see why he should be judged inferior to any most excellent captain; nonetheless, his bestial cruelty and inhumanity, with infinite wicked deeds, do not allow that he should be celebrated among the most excellent men. One cannot, therefore, attribute to fortune or to virtue what was accomplished by him without either one.

In our times, while Alexander VI was reigning, Liverotto the Fermano,[6] who had lost his father as a small boy several years before, was raised by a maternal uncle of his called Giovanni Fogliani. And in the first years of his youth he was sent to fight under Paolo Vitelli, so that filled with that training he might achieve some excellent military rank. After Paolo was killed,[7] he fought under Paolo's brother, Vitellozzo, and in a very short time, because he was clever and gallant in both his person and his spirit, he became the highest ranking man in Vitellozzo's army. But since it seemed to him a servile thing to follow others, he decided, with the help of some citizens of Fermo to whom serving him was more dear than the liberty of their fatherland, and with the support of Vitellozzo, to occupy Fermo. And he wrote to Giovanni Fogliani that, since he had been many years away from home, he wanted to come to see him and his city, and to inspect some part of his patrimony. And because he had not labored for anything other than to acquire honor, so that his fellow citizens might see how he had not spent his time in vain, he wanted to come in an honorable way, accompanied by one hundred of his friends and servants on horseback. And he begged Giovanni to please order that he should be received honorably by the Fermani, which would bring honor not only to him, but also to Giovanni, since Liverotto was his ward.

And so Giovanni neglected no appropriate ceremonies toward his nephew. And after he had been welcomed honorably by the Fermani, Liverotto stayed in his own houses, where, after few days had passed,

[5]Literally, "empire" (*imperio*).
[6]Oliverotto Euffreducci (ca. 1475–1502) was from the town of Fermo in the Marche region of Italy.
[7]Paolo Vitelli was serving as mercenary captain of the Florentine forces against Pisa when he was accused of intentionally preventing victory and executed in Florence on October 1, 1499. See chapter 12 below.

and intent on secretly arranging that which was necessary for his wicked deed to come, he held a most impressive banquet to which he invited Giovanni Fogliani and all the most prominent men of Fermo. And once the food courses and all the other usual entertainments at similar banquets were finished, Liverotto artfully made certain sensitive statements, speaking of the greatness of Pope Alexander, and of Cesare, his son, and of their undertakings. When Giovanni and the others replied to these statements, Liverotto stood up all at once, telling them that those were things to speak about in a more secret place, and he withdrew to a room where Giovanni and all the other citizens followed him. No sooner were they seated when, from the secret places of the room, there came out soldiers who killed Giovanni and the others. After this homicide Liverotto mounted on horseback, rode through the town, and besieged the highest magistracy in its palace, so that out of fear the magistrates were forced to establish a government of which he made himself prince.[8] And since all those who could have harmed him because they were malcontent were dead, he strengthened himself with new civil and military orders, with the result that in the space of the one year in which he held the principality he was not only secure in the city of Fermo, but he had become frightening to all of his neighbors. And his overthrow would have been as difficult as that of Agathocles, if he had not let himself be deceived by Cesare Borgia, when at Senigallia, as was said above,[9] Valentino took the Orsini and the Vitelli. There Liverotto too was taken, just one year after the parricide[10] he committed, and he was strangled together with Vitellozzo, whom he had had as a teacher in his virtues and his crimes.

Anyone might wonder how it happened that Agathocles, and anyone like him, after infinite betrayals and cruelty, could live for a long time securely in his fatherland, and defend himself from external enemies. And he was never conspired against by his fellow citizens, whereas many others have not been able to maintain their states by means of cruelty, even in peaceful times, not to mention in uncertain times of war. I believe that this comes from cruelties that are badly

---

[8]He seized Fermo on the night of January 8–9, 1502.

[9]In chapter 7.

[10]Technically speaking, Giovanni was not Liverotto's father, although he acted in his place, but in contemporary legal parlance, "parricide" could also refer to the killing of one's relative or one's sovereign ruler. Some scholars have suggested that M was referring to the death of Liverotto's "fatherland" (*patria*), because Fermo was governed as a republic before Liverotto seized power.

used or well used. Cruelties may be called "well used," if it is permitted to speak well of evil, when they are done all at once, out of the necessity of securing oneself, and when afterward they do not persist, but are converted into as much utility for the subjects as possible. Cruelties "badly used" are those, even if at the beginning they are few, which instead grow over time rather than eliminating themselves. Those persons who observe the first mode can have some remedy for their state with God and with men, as Agathocles did. For the others it is impossible to maintain themselves.

Whence it is to be noted that in seizing a state its occupier must run through all of those offenses that it is necessary for him to commit, and commit all of them at once, so as not to have to renew them every day, and to be able, by not renewing them, to secure the men and to win them to himself by benefiting them. Whoever does otherwise, whether out of timidity or out of bad counsel, need always keep his sword in hand. Nor can he ever rely on his subjects, since they, because of their fresh and continuing injuries, can never be sure of him. For this reason injuries ought to be done all together, so that being tasted less, they offend less. Benefits ought to be done little by little, so that they may be tasted better. And above all a prince ought to live with his subjects in such a way that no chance event whatsoever, whether for ill or for good, may make him change it. For when owing to adverse times necessities arise, you[11] have no time to do evil, and the good that you do will not help you, for it is judged to be forced, and you know no gratitude from it whatsoever.

[11] An impersonal *tu*.

CHAPTER 9

On the civil principality

But to come to the other point,[1] when a private citizen, not through wickedness or other intolerable violence, but through the favor of his fellow citizens becomes prince of his fatherland (which may be called a "civil principality"—and to arrive there neither complete virtue nor complete fortune is necessary, but rather a fortunate astuteness), I say that one ascends to this principality either with the favor of the people

[1] Mentioned at the beginning of chapter 8.

or with that of the great. For in every city these two different humors are found, whence it arises that the people desire to be neither commanded nor oppressed by the great, and the great desire both to command and to oppress the people. From these two different appetites there arises in the city one of three effects: principality, or liberty, or license. The principality is caused either by the people or the great, according as the one or the other of these factions has the opportunity for it. For, since the great see that they cannot resist the people, they begin to polish[2] the reputation of one of their own, and they make him prince so as to be able, under his shadow, to satisfy their appetite. The people, too, when they see that they cannot resist the great, polish the reputation of one man, and they make him prince in order to be defended by means of his authority.

He who comes to the principality with the help of the great maintains himself with more difficulty than he who becomes prince with the help of the people, because he finds himself prince with many persons about him who think they are his equals, and for this reason he can neither command nor manage them in his own way. But he who arrives at the principality with popular favor finds himself alone, and he has around him either no one or very few who are not prepared to obey. Beyond this, one cannot in honesty satisfy the great without injury to others, but one may so satisfy the people, for the end of the people is more honest than that of the great, since the latter want to oppress and the former want not to be oppressed. Moreover, a prince can never secure himself against a hostile people since they are too many, but against the great he may secure himself, since they are few. The worst thing that a prince may expect from a hostile people is to be abandoned by it. But from the great who are hostile he must fear not only being abandoned but also that they may come against him, for, since these have more awareness and more astuteness, they leave time to save themselves, and they try to ingratiate themselves with the one they hope will win. Further, the prince always necessarily lives with the same people, but indeed he can do without those same great men, since he is able to make some of them and unmake some of them every day, and take away from them and give them reputation at his pleasure.

To clarify this point better, I say that the great should be considered principally in two ways: either they conduct themselves in such a way in their proceedings that they bind themselves wholly to your fortune, or not. Those who bind themselves, and are not rapacious, ought

---

[2]Literally, "to turn" (*voltare*), as with a lathe or potter's wheel.

to be honored and loved. Those who do not bind themselves have to be examined in two ways. If they do this out of pusillanimity and natural want of spirit, then you[3] should make use of them, especially those who are of good counsel, because in prosperous times it brings you honor and you do not have to fear from them in adverse times. But when out of cleverness and for ambitious cause they do not bind themselves, it is a sign that they think more of themselves than of you; and from those men the prince must guard himself, and fear them as though they had been revealed as enemies, because in adversities they will always help to ruin him.

Therefore one who becomes prince through the favor of the people ought to keep them friendly to him, which will be easy for him, since they ask only not to be oppressed. But one who becomes prince against the people, with the favor of the great, ought, before anything else, to try to win the people to himself, which will be easy for him if he takes up their protection. And since men, when they receive good from someone from whom they were believing they would receive evil, are more obliged to their benefactor, the people become immediately more benevolent toward him than if he had been brought to the principality through their favors. The prince may win them to himself in many ways, although, because they vary according to the circumstances, a certain rule cannot be given for them, and for this reason they will be left out. I shall conclude only that for a prince it is necessary to have his people as a friend, otherwise, in adversities, he has no remedy. Nabis, prince of the Spartans,[4] withstood a siege by all Greece and by a most victorious Roman army, and he defended his fatherland and his state against them. And it sufficed for him, when the danger was coming upon him, only to secure for himself a few men, whereas, if he had had the people as his enemy, this would not have been enough.

And let there be no one who strikes back at this opinion of mine with that trite proverb that "He who builds on the people builds on mud." For that is true when a private citizen builds a foundation on the people and allows himself to think that the people will free him if he is oppressed by his enemies or by the authorities. In this case he could find himself often deceived, as happened at Rome to the Gracchi[5] and

---

[3]The impersonal *tu*.
[4]Nabis ruled Sparta from 205 to 192 BCE. See also *Discourses* 1.10 (where he is called a "tyrant") and 3.6.
[5]The brothers Tiberius Sempronius Gracchus and Gaius Sempronius Gracchus were tribunes of the plebs who promoted agrarian reform. Opposition by the propertied classes resulted in their assassination. Tiberius died in 133 BCE, Gaius in 121 BCE.

at Florence to Messer Giorgio Scali.[6] But if he is a prince who builds on the people, who is able to command, and if he is a man of heart, who does not take fright in adversities, and does not fail in his other preparations, and who with his spirit and his orders keeps the populace inspired, he will never find himself deceived by the people, and he will judge that he has built good foundations.

These principalities are usually imperiled when they are about to ascend from a civil to an absolute order. For these princes command either by themselves or by the means of magistracies. In the latter case their standing is weaker and more dangerous, because they stand completely through the will of those citizens who preside in the magistracies, and these, especially in adverse times, may take the state away from a prince with great ease, either by going against him or by not obeying. And amid dangers the prince has no time to seize absolute authority, for the citizens and subjects who are used to receiving commands from the magistracies are not about to obey his commands in these emergencies. And always in uncertain times he will have a shortage of those in whom he can trust. For a prince of this kind cannot found himself on what he sees in peaceful times, when the citizens have need of his state, because then everyone runs to him, everyone promises, and each is willing to die for him when death is far off. But in adverse times, when his state needs its citizens, few of them are to be found. This experience is so much more dangerous inasmuch as one may go through it one time only. For this reason a wise prince must think of a way by which his citizens, always and in every kind of circumstance, have need of his state and of himself, and then they will always be faithful to him.

---

[6]Giorgio Scali was one of the leaders of the Ciompi regime in Florence from 1378 to 1382. In 1382 he was executed on orders of the Signoria. The episode is recounted in M's *Florentine Histories*, 3.20. A cruder version of the proverb above, "He who builds on the people ... builds on shit," is attributed to him by Piero Vaglienti, *Storia dei suoi tempi, 1494–1514* (Pisa: Nistri-Lischi, 1982), 174.

CHAPTER 10

In what ways the strengths of all principalities should be measured

It is appropriate in examining the qualities of these principalities to consider another thing, that is, whether a prince has a state sufficient that he may stand by himself if he needs to, or if instead he always needs to be defended by others. To clarify this point better I say I judge that the ones who can stand by themselves are those who are able, whether through abundance of men or of money, to put together a proper army and to fight a battle in the field with whoever comes to attack them. And similarly I judge that the ones who always need others are those who cannot appear on the field against the enemy, but must flee within their walls and guard them. As to the first case, it has been discussed,[1] and in what is coming we shall say about it what is needed.[2] As to the second case, nothing else can be said, save to advise such princes to fortify and supply their own town, and to pay no attention to the countryside. Whoever has fortified his town well, and managed himself concerning the other affairs of his subjects, as stated above[3] and as will be said below,[4] will be attacked always with great circumspection. For men are always enemies of undertakings that appear difficult, and it cannot seem easy to attack a man who holds his own town gallantly and is not hated by his people.

The cities of Germany[5] are very free, they have little countryside, they obey the emperor when they want to, and they do not fear him nor any other nearby power. For they are fortified in such a way that each power thinks that taking them would be tedious and difficult. For they all have suitable moats and walls; they have sufficient artillery; they always keep in their public storehouses enough to drink, to eat and to burn for a year. And beyond this, so to be able to keep the plebs fed without loss to the public treasury, they always store with the town government the raw materials needed to be able to give the plebs work for a year in those trades that are the sinews and the life of that city and in the industries from which the plebs feeds itself. They still hold military training in repute, and, in this regard, they have many institutions[6] for maintaining it.

Thus a prince who has a strong city and does not make himself hated cannot be attacked. And even if there were someone who attacked him, the attacker would depart in shame, since the things of

---

[1] In chapter 6.
[2] In chapters 12–14.
[3] In chapters 7–9.
[4] In chapters 15–19.
[5] Elsewhere, M discusses the German cities in the *Discourses,* 1.55 and 2.19, and in a small work entitled *Report on Things in Germany.*
[6] Literally, "orders" (*ordini*).

the world are so changeable that it is almost impossible that someone could stand idle with his armies for a year to besiege him. And if anyone should reply, "If the people have their farmlands outside, and they see them burn, they will have no patience, and the long siege and self-interest[7] will make them forget the prince," I answer that a powerful and spirited prince will always overcome all of those difficulties, sometimes by giving his subjects hope that the evil will not be for long, sometimes by fear of the enemy's cruelty, sometimes by skillfully restraining those he thinks are too bold.[8] Beyond this, the enemy reasonably ought to burn and ruin the countryside upon his arrival, which is also during the time when the spirits of the prince's men are still warm and willing to fight in defense. For this reason the prince should worry even less, because after some days, when spirits cool, the damages are already done, the evils are perceived, and there is no longer a remedy. Then, even more, his men come to unite with their prince, because he seems to have an obligation toward them, since for his defense their houses have been burned and their farmlands ruined, and the nature of men is to obligate themselves for benefits given, just as for those received. Therefore, if everything is considered well, it will not be difficult for a prudent prince first to keep and then to confirm the spirits of his citizens in the siege, so long as he does not lack what is required for living or for their defense.

[7] Literally, "self-charity" (*la carità propria*).
[8] *too bold:* too eager to go out to fight.

CHAPTER 11

On ecclesiastical principalities

At present it remains only for us to reason about ecclesiastical principalities. All of the difficulties concerning these arise before they are possessed, since they are acquired either by virtue or by fortune, and they are maintained without the one or the other. For they are sustained by orders that have become ancient in religion, which have been so powerful, and of a such a quality, that they keep their princes in their states no matter how they proceed and live. Those men alone have states and do not defend them. They have subjects and do not govern them. And their states, although they are not defended, are not taken from them. And the subjects, although they are not governed, do not care, and they do not think of freeing themselves from their princes, nor are they able to. Thus only these principalities are secure and happy. But since they are ruled by superior causes that the human mind is unable to reach, I shall leave out speaking about them, for since they are exalted and maintained by God, it would be the office of a presumptuous and rash man to discuss them.[1] Nonetheless, in case anyone should inquire of me why it happens that the Church has come to such greatness in temporal affairs, despite the fact that, before Alexander,[2] the Italian powers (and not only those that called themselves powers, but every baron and lord, even the least of them) esteemed her little in temporal affairs—and now a king of France trembles at her, and she has been able to remove him from Italy and to ruin the Venetians[3]—although it is known, it does not seem to me to be superfluous to recall it in good part to memory.

Before Charles, the king of France, came into Italy,[4] this province was under the control[5] of the pope, the Venetians, the king of Naples, the duke of Milan and the Florentines. These powers had to have two principal cares: the one being that an outsider should not enter into Italy with arms; the other being that none of them should increase his state.[6]

Those about whom they had the most concern were the pope and the Venetians. To keep the Venetians back, the unity of all the others was needed, as happened in the defense of Ferrara.[7] To keep the pope down, they used the barons of Rome. Since these barons were divided into two factions, the Orsini and Colonna, there was always a cause for scandal among them. And, since they stood with arms in their hands in the sight of the pontiff, they kept the pontificate weak and unstable. Although sometimes there emerged a spirited pope, as Sixtus was,[8] nevertheless fortune or wisdom could never disoblige him of these inconveniences. And the brevity of their lives was the reason for this, for, in the ten years, on average, that a pope lives, he would hardly be able to bring down one of the factions. If, for example, one pope had almost eliminated the Colonna, there sprang up another pope who was

---

[1] For a similar reason, M was reticent about Moses in chapter 6.
[2] Pope Alexander VI.
[3] Pope Julius II achieved these things.
[4] In 1494.
[5] Literally, "empire" (*imperio*).
[6] M describes the diplomatic situation in Italy established by the Peace of Lodi in 1454.
[7] During the war between Venice and Ferrara of 1482–84.
[8] Pope Sixtus IV (r. 1471–1484).

the enemy of the Orsini[9] who permitted the Colonna to rise again, and there was not enough time for the Orsini to eliminate them. This used to make it that the temporal powers[10] of the pope were little valued in Italy.

Then there arose Alexander VI, who, of all those who have ever been pontiff, showed how far a pope with money and armies could prevail. With Duke Valentino as his instrument, and with the opportunity of the arrival of the French, he did all of those things that I discuss above[11] concerning the actions of the duke. Although his intent was not to make the Church great, but the duke, nonetheless what he did resulted in the greatness of the Church, which after his death, when the duke was eliminated, was the heir to his labors.

Then came Pope Julius.[12] He found the Church great, since it possessed all of the Romagna; and the barons of Rome were eliminated, since Alexander's blows had annihilated those factions. He also found the road clear for accumulating money[13] in ways that had never been practiced before Alexander. These things Julius not only continued, but increased. And he thought to win Bologna, to eliminate the Venetians, and to chase the French out of Italy. He succeeded in all of these undertakings, and with so much greater honor for himself inasmuch as he did everything for the increase of the Church and not for any private person. He also kept the factions of the Orsini and Colonna within the bounds in which he found them. And although there may have been leaders among them who could have tried to make some disturbance, still two things stopped them. One was the greatness of the Church, which frightened them; the other was that they did not have any cardinals, who are the origin of the tumults between them. Nor will these factions ever be at peace whenever they have cardinals, because their cardinals nourish the factions in Rome and outside, and their barons are forced to defend the factions, and thus from the ambition of prelates are born the discords and the tumults among the barons.

Thus His Holiness Pope Leo has found this pontificate most powerful. One hopes, if the former popes made it great with their arms, this one will make it very great and venerable through his goodness and his other infinite virtues.[14]

---

[9]Sixtus IV was an enemy of the Orsini. His successor, Innocent VIII (r. 1484–1492), was friendly to them.

[10]Literally, "forces" (*forze*).

[11]In chapter 7.

[12]Julius II.

[13]With the sale of offices and indulgences.

[14]Giovanni de' Medici (1475–1521) was elected Pope Leo X on March 11, 1513.

CHAPTER 12

How many kinds of military there are, and concerning mercenary soldiers

Since I have discussed point by point all of the qualities of those principalities that I proposed to reason about at the start,[1] and since I have considered to some extent the causes for their well being or illness, and shown the ways in which many have tried to acquire and hold them, it remains for me now to discuss generally the attacks and defenses that may befall each of the aforementioned principalities.

We have said above[2] that it is necessary for a prince to have good foundations, otherwise of necessity he must be ruined. The principal foundations that all states must have, whether new or old or mixed, are good laws and good arms. And because good laws cannot exist where there are not good arms, and where there are good arms there should be good laws, I shall leave out the reasoning of laws and I shall speak of arms.

I say, therefore, that the arms with which a prince defends his state are either his own or they are mercenary, either auxiliary or mixed. Mercenary and auxiliary arms are useless and dangerous, and if a prince keeps his state founded on mercenary arms, he will never stand firm nor secure. For they are disunited, ambitious, without discipline, and unfaithful. They are gallant among friends, but cowardly among enemies. They have no fear of God, and no faith with men. And ruin is deferred only so long as the attack is deferred. In peace you[3] are despoiled by them, and in war you are despoiled by your enemies. The reason for this is that they have no other love nor other reason that keeps them in the field save a small stipend, and this is not sufficient to make them want to die for you. They very much want to be your soldiers so long as you do not make war, but when war comes, they want to flee or to go away.

I should not expend much labor in persuasion on this point, because the ruin of Italy now is caused by nothing other than her having relied, for the space of many years, on mercenary arms. These arms once made some advances for some men, and they seemed gallant when they fought among themselves, but when the outsider came they showed what they really were, so that Charles, the king of

---

[1] In chapter 1.
[2] In chapters 7 and 9.
[3] The impersonal *tu,* here and in the following two sentences.

France, was able to seize Italy with a piece of chalk.[4] He who used to say that the cause of this was our sins was telling the truth, although the sins were not the ones he believed they were,[5] but these I have narrated. And, since these were sins of the princes, they, too, have suffered punishment for them.

I want to demonstrate better the infelicity of these arms. Mercenary captains are either men excellent in arms, or not. If they are, you cannot trust them, because they will always aspire to their own greatness, whether by oppressing you who are their patron, or by oppressing others beyond your intention. But if the captain is not virtuous, he ruins you in the ordinary way. And if it is answered that whoever has arms in his hands will do this, whether he is a mercenary or not, I would reply that arms have to be employed either by a prince or by a republic. The prince should go in person, and himself assume the office of captain. The republic has to send its citizens, and if it sends one who does not prove a worthy man, it should exchange him, and when he is worthy, it should restrain him with laws so that he does not cross the line. From experience it is seen that very great strides are made by princes who are by themselves, and by armed republics, and never anything but harm is done by mercenary arms. And with more difficulty does a republic armed with its own arms fall into servitude under one of its own citizens than a republic armed with external arms.

Rome and Sparta stood armed and free for many centuries. The Swiss are highly armed and very free. Among the examples of ancient mercenary arms are the Carthaginians, who were almost undone by their mercenary soldiers after the first war with the Romans was finished, even though the Carthaginians had their own citizens as captains.[6] After the death of Epaminondas[7] the Thebans made Philip the Macedonian the captain of their troops, and after their victory he took away their liberty.[8]

---

[4]Philippe de Commynes, *Mémoires,* 7.14, attributed to Pope Alexander VI this remark: "The French came in with . . . chalk in the hands of their quartermasters to mark their lodgings, without any other hardship."

[5]Fra Girolamo Savonarola, who preached that Charles VIII's invasion was retribution for sins like fornication and usury.

[6]The Mercenary War (241–237 BCE), which followed the First Punic War, is described by Polybius, 1.65–88.

[7]The Theban general Epaminondas died in 362 BCE at the battle of Mantinea.

[8]As a teenager, Philip II of Macedon (359–336 BCE), the father of Alexander the Great, was sent as a hostage to Thebes, where he was instructed by Epaminondas. In 346 BCE, Philip was invited by Thebes to lead allied forces in destroying Phocis in the Third Sacred War. In 338 BCE, however, he crushed the Thebans at the battle of Chaeronea and subjected their city to his rule.

The Milanese, after the death of Duke Filippo,[9] hired Francesco Sforza against the Venetians. Once the enemy was defeated at Caravaggio, he joined with them to undo his patrons the Milanese.[10] Sforza, his father, when hired by Queen Giovanna of Naples, suddenly left her disarmed, so that she, in order not to lose the kingdom, was forced to throw herself in the lap of the king of Aragon.[11]

And if the Venetians and Florentines have in the past increased their empire with these arms, and their captains have not made themselves their princes, but defended them, I answer that the Florentines in this case were favored by chance, for of the virtuous captains whom they might have feared, some did not win, some had opposition, and some turned their ambition elsewhere. The one who did not win was John Hawkwood, whose faithfulness could not be known because he did not win; but everyone will admit that, if he had won, the Florentines would have been at his discretion.[12] Sforza always had the Bracceschi against him, so that each watched the other.[13] Francesco turned his ambition toward Lombardy,[14] Braccio against the Church and the Kingdom of Naples.[15]

But let us come to what happened a little while ago. The Florentines made Paolo Vitelli their captain: he was a most prudent man, and

[9]Duke Filippo Maria Visconti of Milan died without legitimate male heirs in 1447, and the Milanese seized the occasion to establish the Ambrosian Republic.

[10]At the battle of Caravaggio (September 14, 1448) the Milanese forces commanded by Francesco Sforza defeated the Venetians. After the battle, he switched sides, signing a secret agreement with Venice, and in 1450 he suppressed the Ambrosian Republic and entered Milan claiming the ducal title.

[11]Muzio Attendolo, called Sforza (1369–1424), was Francesco Sforza's father. The episode involving Queen Giovanna II of Naples (1371–1435) took place in 1420. See also *Florentine Histories,* 1.38, and *Art of War,* 1. For a more accurate account, see *Dizionario biografico degli italiani,* 49: 544.

[12]John Hawkwood (c. 1320–1394) was an English mercenary captain who entered Italy in 1361. In the employ of Pisa, he was defeated by Florence at the great battle of Cascina (1364). Employed by the Florentine Republic in the 1390s, he was famous for his skillful retreats from the Milanese.

[13]Sforza (i.e., Muzio Attendolo) was employed from 1400 until 1411 by the Florentine Republic during its wars against Milan, Pisa, and King Ladislaus of Naples. The Bracceschi were mercenaries commanded by Andrea Fortebracci, also known as Braccio da Montone (1368–1424), who served Florence between 1409 and 1411, when the two captains were rivals but on the same side. From 1412 they were constantly on opposing sides. In 1420, when Sforza briefly abandoned Giovanna II, he returned to Florentine service, but soon he was called back by Giovanna and sent to oppose Braccio. Sforza and Braccio died within three days of each other in 1424 in a battle for the city of L'Aquila.

[14]Francesco Sforza entered Florentine service in 1436 as commander of a league against the visconti of Milan, and in 1437 he besieged Lucca unsuccessfully for Florence, but afterward his career took him elsewhere.

[15]Between 1412 and 1424, Braccio's troops enabled him to command a sizable area in central Italy that was known as the "*Stato di Braccio.*"

one who from private fortune had won a very great reputation. If he had taken Pisa, there is no one who could deny that it would have been necessary for the Florentines to stay with him, for if he had gone into the pay of their enemies they would have had no remedy, and if they kept him they would have had to obey him.[16]

If one considers the steps of the Venetians, one sees that they advanced securely and gloriously so long as their own people made war (which was before they turned to their enterprises on land), when with their nobles and their plebs under arms they advanced most virtuously. But when they began to fight on land, they left this virtue behind and followed the customs of wars in Italy. And in the beginning of their expansion on land, because they did not have much state there, and because they had a great reputation, they did not have much to fear from their captains. But when they grew, which was under Carmagnola,[17] they had a taste of this error. For when they saw that he was very virtuous, since under his command they defeated the duke of Milan, and since they knew on the other hand that he was cool toward the war, they judged that with him they could not win anymore, because he did not want to, nor could they dismiss him, because they did not want to lose what they had acquired. So, in order to secure themselves against him, it was necessary for them to kill him.

Afterward they had as their captains Bartolomeo of Bergamo,[18] Roberto da Sanseverino,[19] the Count of Pitigliano,[20] and other similar men. With them they had to fear their losing rather than their winning, as then happened at Vailate, where, in one day's battle, they lost what they had acquired with so much trouble over eight hundred

[16]Vitelli did not take Pisa, and he was executed by the Florentines. (See chapter 8.)

[17]Francesco Bussone, called Il Carmagnola (ca. 1385–1432), served Duke Filippo Maria Visconti of Milan with great success from 1412 to 1424, when he lost the duke's favor. In 1425 he was hired by the Venetians, and he quickly conquered Bergamo and Brescia from Milan. However, his failure to prosecute the war aggressively, his continued contacts with Milan (where he maintained properties), and his desire to create a state for himself caused the Venetians to execute him for treason.

[18]Bartolomeo Colleoni of Bergamo (c. 1400–1475), after years of switching service between Venice and Milan, was given command of Venice's forces in 1455, although the Peace of Lodi (1454) meant that there were few opportunities for military action. His one major campaign resulted in the indecisive battle of Molinella in 1467.

[19]Roberto da Sanseverino, count of Caiazzo (1418–1487) commanded Venice's troops in the unsuccessful war against Ferrara of 1482–84, left temporarily to fight in Naples, and returned in 1486 only to die in a battle of Calliano that was lost to the Austrians in 1487.

[20]Niccolò Orsini, count of Pitigliano (1442–1510), entered Venetian service in 1495. Along with Bartolomeo d'Alviano, he was in charge of the Venetian forces during their disastrous defeat at the battle of Vailate in 1509.

years.[21] For these arms bear only slow, weak and late acquisitions, and the losses are sudden and astonishing.

And because I have offered these examples from Italy, which has been governed by mercenary arms for many years, I want to discuss them from a higher perspective, so that having seen the origin and progresses of them, one may better correct them. You[22] have to understand, therefore, that in these latter times, as soon as the Empire began to be cast off in Italy, and the pope seized more reputation there in temporal affairs, Italy was divided into many states. For many of the large cities took up arms against their nobles, who, with the favor of the emperor, had previously kept them oppressed. The Church favored the cities as a way of gaining reputation for itself in temporal affairs. In many other cities their own citizens became their princes. Hence, since Italy had almost fallen into the hands of the Church and of a few republics, and since those priests and the other citizens customarily did not know about arms, they began to hire outsiders. The first who gave reputation to this military was Alberico of Cunio, a Romagnol.[23] From the school of this man were descended, among others, Braccio and Sforza, who in their times were the arbiters of Italy. After these came all the others who down to our times have governed these arms. And the result of their virtue was that Italy was overrun by Charles, plundered by Louis, forced by Ferdinand, and insulted by the Swiss.

The order they followed was, first, in order to give themselves reputation, to strip their infantry of its reputation. They did this because, being without a state and in need of work, a few infantrymen did not give them reputation, and they could not feed a great number. For this reason they resorted to horses, with which they were both supported and honored in tolerable numbers. And things were reduced to the point that in an army of twenty thousand soldiers there were not even two thousand foot infantry. Beyond this, they had used every craft to relieve themselves and their soldiers from labor and fear, since they did not kill one another in their battles, but took prisoners without asking ransom. They did not shoot[24] at night into the towns; those in the towns did not shoot at night at the tents. They made neither a

---

[21]Venice's mainland empire was created more recently, in the early 1400s; M refers instead to Venice's reputation as being built over such a long period.

[22]*voi.*

[23]Alberico da Barbiano, count of Cunio (1348–1409), was said to have established the first Italian mercenary company. Compare *Florentine Histories,* 1.34.

[24]With arrows or other projectiles.

stockade nor a ditch around their camp. They did not campaign in winter. And all of these things were permitted in their military orders, and invented by them, as has been said, in order to flee labor and dangers, so much so that they have conducted[25] Italy into slavery and shame.

[25]Mansfield indicates a pun in the use of *condurre,* which also has the specific meaning "to hire soldiers." The chapter's theme is that those whom Italy has hired (*condotto*) have "conducted" (*condotto*) Italy into shame.

CHAPTER 13

On auxiliary troops, mixed troops, and one's own

Auxiliary arms, which are the other useless ones, are when one calls on a powerful person who with his arms comes to help and defend you,[1] as Pope Julius did in recent times. Julius, after he witnessed the failure of his mercenary arms in his invasion of Ferrara, turned to auxiliary arms, and made an agreement with Ferdinand, the king of Spain, that with his troops and armies Ferdinand would help him. These arms may be useful and good in themselves, but for whoever calls on them they are almost always harmful. For if they lose, you remain defeated, and if they win, you are left their prisoner. And although the ancient histories are full of examples of this, I do not want to leave out this fresh example of Pope Julius II, whose decision could not have been less considered, when, because he wanted Ferrara, he put himself entirely in the hands of an outsider. But his good fortune made a third thing happen, so that he did not have to harvest the fruit of his bad choice: for after his auxiliaries were routed at Ravenna,[2] the Swiss rose up, and beyond all expectation, whether of others or his own, they chased away the victors, and he became the prisoner neither of his enemies, who had fled, nor of his auxiliaries, since he had won with arms other than theirs. The Florentines, when they were completely unarmed, brought ten thousand French troops to Pisa to take it, and in this decision they bore more danger than in any other time of their troubles.[3] The Emperor of Constantinople, to

[1]The impersonal *tu.*
[2]April 11, 1512.
[3]This happened in 1498. The danger was that the French would turn on Florence. The "time of their troubles" refers either to Florence's war with Pisa (1494–1509) or to the entire period of popular government in Florence (1494–1512).

oppose his neighbors, brought ten thousand Turks into Greece, who, when the war was over, did not want to leave.[4] This was the beginning of the servitude of Greece to the infidels.

Whoever, therefore, wants not to be able to win should avail himself of these arms, since they are much more dangerous than mercenary arms. For in auxiliary arms one's ruin is already prepared: they are all united, all directed toward the obedience of others. But with mercenary arms, after they have won, more time is needed, and a greater opportunity, before they offend you, since they are not one body, and since they were found and paid by you, and a third party whom you make their leader cannot immediately seize so much authority among them as to offend you. In sum, in mercenary arms cowardice is more dangerous, in auxiliary arms virtue is. A wise prince, therefore, has always avoided these arms and relied on his own; and he has wanted rather to lose with his own men than to win with others, judging it not a true victory if it was acquired with the arms of others.

I shall never hesitate to cite Cesare Borgia and his actions. This duke entered the Romagna with auxiliary arms, bringing in troops that were all French. And with these he took Imola and Forlì. But since he did not think such arms were safe, he turned to mercenary arms, since he judged there was less danger in them. And he engaged the Orsini and the Vitelli, whose arms, when he later discovered them to be doubtful and faithless and dangerous to manage, he eliminated, and he relied on his own. And one can easily see what difference there is between the one and the other of these kinds of arms, if one considers what a difference there was in the reputation of the Duke from when he had only the French, to when he had the Orsini and the Vitelli, to when he remained with his own soldiers with himself on top. And one will find that his reputation always increased, and he was never esteemed so much as when everyone saw that he was completely in possession of his own arms.

I did not want to depart from my examples, which are Italian and fresh, nevertheless, I do not want to leave out Hiero the Syracusan, since he was one of those who were named by me above.[5] That man, as I said, when he had been made head of the armies by the Syracusans, knew immediately that the mercenary military was not useful, because their commanders were made like our Italians, and since he

---

[4]Emperor John Cantacuzene, in 1353–54, brought in Ottoman soldiers. Sonnino suggests Cantacuzene's *Histories,* 4.34, as the likely source.
[5]In chapter 6.

decided he could neither keep them nor let them go, he had them all cut to pieces, and afterward he made war with his own arms, and not those of others. I want also to recall to memory a figure[6] of the Old Testament suited to this purpose. When David offered himself to Saul to go to combat Goliath, the Philistine challenger, Saul, in order to give David spirit, armed him with his own arms. But David, once he had put them on, refused, saying that with those arms he could not make good use of himself, and for that reason he wanted to find the enemy with his sling and his sword.[7] In the end, the arms of others fall off your back, or they weigh you down, or they constrict you.

After Charles VII, the father of King Louis XI, had, with his fortune and virtue freed France from the English,[8] he understood this necessity of arming oneself with one's own arms, and he decreed in his kingdom the ordering of men-at-arms and of infantry. Afterward King Louis, his son,[9] eliminated the ordering of infantrymen and began to hire the Swiss. This error, which was followed by the other kings, is, as in fact one now sees, the cause of that kingdom's dangers, because while it gave reputation to the Swiss it degraded the king's own arms. For he has completely eliminated the infantry, and obligated his men-at-arms to the arms of others, for because they are accustomed to fight along with the Swiss they do not think they can win without them. From this it arises that the French are wanting against the Swiss, and without the Swiss they do not try against others. Thus the armies of France have been mixed, part mercenary and part their own, and both of these arms together are much better than simple auxiliary or simple mercenary troops. Let the example mentioned be sufficient, for the Kingdom of France would be unconquerable if Charles's order had been expanded or preserved. But the small prudence of men begins a thing because it tastes good for the time being, while it does not notice

[6]The Italian *figura* has a specific meaning as "parable" or "example." The sentence is typical of contemporary treatises on the so-called art of memory.

[7]In the biblical account (1 Samuel 17:40, 50–51), David was armed not with a sword, but with a sling and a staff. After felling Goliath, David used Goliath's own sword to cut off his head. M's mistake must have been prompted by familiarity with Andrea del Verrocchio's statue *David* (now in the Bargello Museum in Florence), who holds a small sword that might easily be assumed to be David's rather than Goliath's. For many years M passed this statue, then situated in the Palace of the Signoria, on the way to work in the chancery.

[8]Note that Charles VII (r. 1422–1461) receives all of the credit for this military success, and there is no mention of Joan of Arc. In *The Art of War*, 4, M praises Charles VII's manipulation of Joan as a successful ruse.

[9]Louis XI ruled France from 1461 to 1483.

the poison that lies beneath, as I said above concerning consumptive fevers.[10] Thus he who in a principality does not recognize evils when they arise is not truly wise, and this ability is given to few. And if the first cause of the ruin of the Roman Empire is considered, it will be found that it was in the beginning to hire the Goths, for from that beginning the forces of the Roman Empire began to be enervated, and all of the virtue that was taken from it was given to the Goths.[11]

Thus I conclude that unless it has its own arms, no principality is secure. Instead it is completely dependent on fortune, since it does not have the virtue reliably to defend itself in adversities. And it was always the opinion and judgment of wise men "that nothing is so weak and unstable as a reputation for power not founded on its own strength."[12] And one's own arms are those that are composed of your subjects, your citizens, or your dependents: all the others are either mercenary or auxiliary. And the way to order one's own arms is easy to find, if one goes over the orders of the four men named by me above,[13] and if one sees how Philip, the father of Alexander the Great, and how many republics and princes have armed and ordered themselves. In these orders I have complete trust.

[10]In chapter 3.
[11]Compare Ammianus Marcellinus, *History,* 31.16.
[12]Tacitus, *Annals,* 13.19, here quoted in Latin, probably from memory, with a slight change in meaning. Tacitus wrote "Nothing is so unstable and fleeting in mortal affairs as the reputation of a power that is not founded on its own strength" [editor's translation].
[13]Probably the four are Cesare Borgia, Hiero II of Syracuse, Charles VII of France, and David, although some commentators have thought that M intended the four to be Moses, Cyrus, Theseus, and Romulus (see chapter 6).

CHAPTER 14

What the prince should do concerning the military

Thus a prince must have no other object or thought, nor take any thing as his art save warfare and its institutions[1] and training. For that is the only art that is expected of one who commands, and it is an art of such virtue that it not only maintains those who are born princes, but many times it makes men of private fortune rise to that rank. On the contrary, one sees that princes, when they have thought more about delicate things than arms, have lost their state. The first reason

[1]Literally, "orders" (*ordini*).

that makes you lose it is the neglect of this art; and the reason that makes you acquire it is your being proficient in this art. Francesco Sforza, because he was armed, from being a private man became duke of Milan. His sons, because they fled the hardships of arms, from being dukes became private men.[2] For, among the other reasons that being unarmed does you evil, it makes you contemptible, which is one of the infamies against which the prince should guard himself, as will be said below.[3] For between an armed and an unarmed man there is no harmony whatsoever, and it is not reasonable that a man who is armed should willingly obey a man who is unarmed, and that the unarmed should be secure among servants who are armed, because since there is disdain in the armed man and suspicion in the unarmed man, it is not possible for them to work well together. And therefore a prince who does not understand the military, beyond his other unhappinesses, as was said, cannot be esteemed by his soldiers nor trust them.

Therefore he ought never to lift his thought from the exercise of war, and in peace he should train more than in wartime. This he may do in two ways: one is with his deeds, the other is with his mind. And as to his deeds, beyond keeping his men ordered and trained, he must be frequently on hunts, and through these accustom his body to hardships, and meanwhile learn the nature of terrains, and to recognize how mountains rise, how valleys open up, how plains lie, and to understand the nature of rivers and marshes, and in this take very great care. This knowledge is useful in two ways: first, one learns to recognize one's own country and the prince can better understand its defenses; afterward, through the recognition and use of those terrains, he can easily understand any other new terrain that it may be necessary for him to study. For the ridges, the valleys, the plains, the rivers, the marshes that are in Tuscany, for example, have a certain similarity with those of other provinces, so that from the knowledge of

[2]Francesco Sforza's eldest son and heir, Galeazzo Maria, was assassinated in 1476. Galeazzo Maria's son, Gian Galeazzo, was next in line, but because he suffered from debilitating disease (possibly tuberculosis), his uncle, Ludovico (who was a son of Francesco), ruled as regent until Gian Galeazzo's death, in 1494, when Ludovico became the first in the Sforza line to assume the ducal title with imperial recognition. Ludovico (see chapter 3) was captured by the French in April 1500 and died in 1508 as a prisoner. The word "sons" here probably encompasses Ludovico and his brother, Cardinal Ascanio Sforza. During Ludovico's brief return to power, on February 2, 1500, Ascanio took charge of Milan in Ludovico's name. When the French re-took Milan, both were taken prisoner.
[3]In chapter 19.

the terrain in one province, one can easily arrive at the knowledge of other provinces. And the prince who lacks this skill lacks the first part of what a captain should have, because this part teaches how to find the enemy, select encampments, conduct armies, order battlefields, and besiege towns to your advantage.

Among the other praises that writers have given Philopoemen, prince of the Achaeans, is that in times of peace he thought only of the ways of war.[4] And when he was in the countryside with his friends, he used often to stop and reason with them: "If your enemies were on top of that hill, and we found ourselves here with our army, which of us would have the advantage? How could one go to meet them while preserving order? If we wanted to retreat, what would we have to do? If they retreated, how would we have to follow them?" And as he went he used to propose to them all of the cases that may happen in an army. He used to listen to their opinion, he used to say his own, and he used to strengthen it with his reasons, so that because of these continuous cogitations there could never arise any accident when he was leading armies for which he did not have the remedy.

But as for the exercise of his mind, the prince ought to read histories, and in them consider the actions of the excellent men. He should see how they governed themselves in war, and examine the causes of their victories and losses, so as to be able to avoid the latter and imitate the former. And, above all, he must do as some excellent men did in the past, who chose some man from before their time who had been praised and glorified to imitate, and they always kept a book with his deeds and actions close by themselves, as it is said that Alexander the Great imitated Achilles; Caesar, Alexander; and Scipio, Cyrus. And whoever reads the life of Cyrus written by Xenophon recognizes afterward in the life of Scipio how much that imitation brought him glory, and how much, in his chastity,[5] affability, humanity and liberality, Scipio conformed with those things that had been written by Xenophon about Cyrus.[6]

A wise prince should observe modes such as these, and never in peaceful times remain idle, but industriously make capital of them so as to be able to avail himself of them in adversities, so that when fortune changes she finds him prepared to resist adversities.[7]

---

[4]Philopoemen of Megalopolis (252–184 BCE) was commander of the Achaean League. The passage that follows is based on Livy, 35.28.

[5]On Scipio's chastity, see *Discourses*, 3.20.

[6]Xenophon's *Education of Cyrus*. Publius Cornelius Scipio Africanus (235–183 BCE) is discussed less positively in chapter 17.

[7]This passage anticipates chapter 25.

CHAPTER 15

On those things for which men and especially princes are praised or criticized

It remains therefore to see what should be the ways and conduct of a prince, whether with his subjects or with his allies.[1] And because I know that many people have written about this, I worry in writing about it too that I shall be held presumptuous, especially since in debating this material I shall depart from the orders of the others. But since my intent is to write a thing that is useful for whoever understands it, it seemed to me more appropriate to go after the effectual truth of the thing than the imagination of it. And many have imagined republics and principalities that have never been seen or known to exist in truth.[2] For there is such a distance from how one lives to how one ought to live that he who abandons what is done for what ought to be done learns what will ruin him rather than what will save him, since a man who would wish to make a career of being good in every detail must come to ruin among so many who are not good. Hence it is necessary for a prince, if he wishes to maintain himself, to learn to be able to be not good, and to use this faculty and not to use it according to necessity.

Thus, leaving behind the things that have been imagined about a prince, and discussing those that are true, I say that all men, when they are spoken about, and especially princes, because they are placed higher, are noted for some of the following qualities, which bring them either blame or praise. That is to say that one man is held liberal, one a miser (I use a Tuscan word because in our tongue an "avaricious"[3] man is still he who desires to take through robbery; we call a "miser"[4] the man who refrains excessively from using his own wealth); one is held a giver, one rapacious; one cruel, one compassionate.[5] The one is held a breaker of faith, the other faithful; the one

---

[1] Relations with subjects are discussed in chapters 16–17, relations with allies in chapter 18. In Italian, *amici* generally means "friends," but in *The Prince* it usually means "allies."

[2] Plato's *Republic* is certainly intended, and the imagined principalities probably include Xenophon's *Education of Cyrus,* and any number of medieval mirrors of princes. Compare also Livy, 26.22: "If there were a city of philosophers, such as learned men imagine rather than know from experience. . . ." When Thomas More's *Utopia* was published in December 1516, *The Prince* had already begun to circulate in manuscript in Florence.

[3] *avaro.*

[4] *misero.*

[5] The adjective *pietoso,* like the noun *pietà,* has a range of meanings, from "compassionate" to "merciful" to "pitiable."

effeminate and pusillanimous, the other fierce and spirited; the one humane, the other proud; the one lascivious, the other chaste; the one honest, the other crafty; the one hard, the other easygoing; the one serious, the other light; the one religious, the other unbelieving; and similar things. And I know that everyone will admit that it would be a most praiseworthy thing, among all the qualities listed above, for there to be found in a prince those that are held to be good. But because they cannot be had, nor wholly observed, since human conditions do not allow it, it is necessary for the prince to be so prudent that he knows how to flee the infamy of those vices that might take the state away from him. And as for those that would not take the state away from him, he should guard himself against them if possible, but, if he cannot, here he may let himself proceed with less caution. Indeed, let him not worry about incurring the infamy of those vices without which it is difficult for him to save the state. For, if everything be well considered, something will be found that will appear a virtue, but will lead to his ruin if adopted; and something else that will appear a vice, if adopted, will result in his security and well-being.

CHAPTER 16

On liberality and parsimony

If I am to begin, therefore, with the first of the qualities stated above, I say that it would be good to be held liberal. Nonetheless, liberality, used in such a way that you are held to be liberal, harms you, for if it is used virtuously and as it should be used, it will not be recognized, and you will not shed the infamy of its contrary. And for this reason, out of wanting to retain among men the name of a liberal man, it is necessary not to leave out any quality of sumptuousness, so that always a prince of this kind will consume all of his means in works such as these. And he will be required, in the end, if he wishes to maintain the name of a liberal man, to burden his people extraordinarily, to tax heavily, and to do all those things that can be done to get money. This will begin to make him hateful to his subjects, or little esteemed by anyone because he becomes poor. So that, by means of this liberality of his, since he has offended the many and rewarded the few, he feels every new hardship, and with any new danger he is imperiled. And if he recognizes this, and wishes to retreat from it, he immediately incurs the infamy of the miser. Thus, since a prince cannot use this virtue of the liberal man in such a way that it is recognized without harm to himself, he ought, if he is prudent, not to worry about the name of the miser. For with time he will be thought ever more liberal, seeing as, on account of his parsimony, his revenues are sufficient for him, he can defend himself from whoever makes war on him, and he can make campaigns without burdening his peoples. So much so that he arrives at using "liberality" toward all those from whom he does not take, who are infinite, and "miserliness" toward all those to whom he does not give, who are few.

In our times we have not seen great things done except by those who have been thought misers; the others were eliminated. Pope Julius II, although he used the name of a liberal man to reach the papacy,[1] afterward did not think to maintain it for himself when he wanted to be able to make war. The present king of France[2] has made so many wars without imposing an extraordinary tax on his subjects only because his long parsimony has subsidized his superfluous expenses. If the present king of Spain had been thought liberal, he would neither have made nor won so many campaigns.[3] Therefore a prince ought to care little—if he wishes not to have to rob his subjects, to be able to defend himself, not to become poor and contemptible, and not to be forced to become rapacious—about incurring the name of miser. For this is one of those vices that let him rule. And if someone should say, "Caesar arrived at the empire through liberality, and many others, because they were, and were held, liberal, achieved the highest ranks," I answer that either you[4] already are a prince, or you are on the way to acquiring a principality. In the first case, this liberality is harmful; in the second, it is indeed necessary to be and to be held liberal. And Caesar was one of those who wanted to achieve the principality of Rome. But if, after he had achieved it, he had survived,[5] and he had not refrained from those expenditures, he would have destroyed that empire.

And if someone should reply, "Many have been princes and have done great things with their armies who were held very liberal," I respond to you that either the prince spends what belongs to himself and his subjects, or what belongs to others. In the first case, he ought

---

[1] By making generous promises.

[2] Louis XII, who died the night of December 31, 1514–January 1, 1515.

[3] Ferdinand the Catholic, who died January 23, 1516. In a private letter to Francesco Vettori, dated August 26, 1513, M called Ferdinand "stingy and avaricious." For Ferdinand's campaigns, see chapter 21.

[4] A hypothetical *tu,* here and in the remainder of the chapter.

[5] Julius Caesar was assassinated in 44 BCE.

to be sparing. In the other, he ought not leave out any part of liberality. And as to the prince who goes with his armies, who feeds himself with spoils, with sackings and with ransoms, and manages on what belongs to others, for him this liberality is necessary: otherwise he would not be followed by his soldiers. And of what is not yours or your subjects' one may give more broadly, as did Cyrus, Caesar and Alexander. For spending what belongs to others does not strip you of reputation but adds to it; the spending of what is yours is what hurts you. There is nothing that consumes itself so much as liberality, since as you use it you lose the ability to use it, and either you become poor and contemptible or, in order to avoid poverty, rapacious and hateful. Among all the things that a prince ought to guard himself against is being contemptible and hateful,[6] and liberality leads you to both things. Therefore there is more wisdom in keeping for oneself the name of miser, which bears an infamy without hatred, than, out of wishing for the name of liberal, to be required to incur the name of rapacious, which bears an infamy coupled with hatred.

[6]Compare chapter 19.

CHAPTER 17

On cruelty and compassion, and whether it is better to be loved than to be feared, or the contrary

Descending next to the other qualities mentioned before,[1] I say that each prince ought to desire to be believed compassionate and not cruel, nonetheless he must be alert not to use this compassion badly. Cesare Borgia was believed cruel; nonetheless, that cruelty of his restored the Romagna, unified it, and led it back to peace and to faith. If one considers this well, one will see that he was much more compassionate than the Florentine people,[2] who, to avoid the name of cruelty, allowed the destruction of Pistoia.[3] A prince, therefore, must not

[1]In chapter 15.
[2]*Florentine people:* a criticism of the *governo popolare* that ruled Florence from 1494–1512—and also employed M.
[3]Pistoia was a town subject to Florence and only twenty miles distant. Between 1499 and 1502 Pistoia was convulsed by a factional war in which more than three thousand persons died. In 1500 and 1501, M was sent on five missions to Pistoia, and in March 1502 he wrote a small work, *On Pistoiese Affairs*. On Pistoia, see also chapter 20, and *Discourses*, 3.27.

care about the infamy of cruelty in keeping his subjects united and faithful, because if he makes a very few examples, he will be more compassionate than those who, through too much compassion, allow disorders to occur from which arise killings or robberies. For the latter usually harm an entire population, but those executions that come from the prince harm a particular person. Among all the kinds of princes, it is impossible for the new prince to avoid the reputation of cruelty because new states are full of perils. And Virgil, in the mouth of Dido, says

> The harshness and the newness of my kingdom drive me to make such exertions, and to protect my borders far and wide with guards.[4]

Nonetheless, the new prince must be weighty in giving credence and taking action, and he should not create fear of himself, but proceed in a manner tempered with prudence and humanity, lest too much confidence make him incautious, and too much distrust render him intolerable.

From the above a debate arises whether it is better to be loved than feared or the contrary. The answer is that one would want to be both the one and the other, but because it is difficult to join them together, it is much safer to be feared than loved, if one has to do without one of the two. For the following may be said generally about men: that they are ungrateful, changeable, pretenders and dissemblers, avoiders of dangers, and desirous of gain, and while you[5] do them good they are wholly yours, offering you their blood, their property, their life, and their children, as I said above,[6] when the need is far off, but when it comes close to you they revolt. And that prince who has founded himself wholly on their words, because he finds himself naked of other preparations, is ruined. For the friendships that are acquired at a price, and not with greatness and nobility of spirit, are paid for but they are not possessed, and when they come due they cannot be used. Men have less fear of offending one who makes himself loved than one who makes himself feared, since love is held in place by a bond of obligation which, because men are wretched, is broken at every opportunity for utility to oneself, but fear is held in place by a fear of punishment that never abandons you.

---

[4]Virgil, *Aeneid,* 1.563–4, in which Dido, queen of Carthage, assures the newly arrived Trojans of her goodwill.
[5]An impersonal *tu* throughout the paragraph.
[6]Chapter 9.

Nonetheless, the prince must make himself feared in such a way that, although he does not acquire love, he avoids hatred. For being feared and being not hated may exist together very well. And this he will always do if he abstains from the property of his citizens and his subjects, and from their women.[7] And if he must proceed against someone's life,[8] he should do it when there is appropriate justification and manifest cause. But above all he should abstain from the property of others, for men sooner forget the death of their father than the loss of their patrimony. Furthermore, reasons for taking property are never lacking, and he who begins to live through robbery always finds a reason for occupying what belongs to others, and, on the contrary, the reasons for bloodshed are more rare and sooner disappear.

But when the prince is with his armies, and has command of a multitude of soldiers, then it is wholly necessary not to care about the reputation of cruelty, because without this reputation no army ever was kept united and disposed to any feat of arms. Numbered among the admirable actions of Hannibal is the following, that, while he led a very great army, mixed with infinite kinds of men, to fight in foreign lands, there never arose any dissension, neither among themselves, nor against the prince, in bad as well as in his good fortune. This could not have arisen from anything other than his inhuman cruelty, which, together with his other infinite virtues, made him always venerable and terrible in the sight of his soldiers; and without it, his other virtues would not have sufficed for him to achieve that effect. In this regard the writers have understood little, for on the one hand they have admired this action of his, and on the other they condemned the principal cause of it.[9]

And that it is true that Hannibal's other virtues would not have sufficed may be understood in Scipio, who was very rare, not only in his own times but in all the memory of things that are known, but against whom his armies in Spain rebelled.[10] This did not arise from anything other than his compassion, which had given more license to his soldiers than is appropriate to military discipline. His compassion was reproved in the Senate by Fabius Maximus, who called him the corrupter of the

---

[7]See also *Discourses,* 3.26, and Aristotle, *Politics,* 1311a.
[8]Literally, "blood."
[9]See Livy, 21.4.9.
[10]Livy, 28.24–29. The mutiny broke out in 206 BCE, when there was a rumor that Scipio was ill. He put down the revolt in blood.

Roman military.[11] When the Locrians had been destroyed by a legate of Scipio's,[12] they were not avenged by him, nor was the insolence of that legate corrected. And it all arose from his easy nature; so much so that when someone wanted to excuse him in the Senate, he said that there were many men who knew better how not to err than to correct errors.[13] This nature of his would, with time, have dishonored the fame and glory of Scipio, if in his command he had persevered in it, but, since he lived under the direction of the Senate, this harmful quality of his not only was hidden, indeed it brought him glory.[14]

I conclude, therefore, returning to being feared and loved, that since men love at their own pleasure, and fear at the pleasure of the prince, a wise prince must found himself on that which is his, and not on that which belongs to others: he must only contrive to avoid hatred, as was said.

[11]Quintus Fabius Maximus Cunctator (275–203 BCE) criticized Scipio not only for indulging his troops, but also for his cruelty in putting down the revolt (Livy, 29.19.4).

[12]Locris was a Greek city in Calabria. The city was traditionally loyal to Rome, but it was taken by Hannibal. When Scipio's legate, Quintus Pleminius, retook the city for Rome in 205 BCE, he plundered the treasury of Persephone. Scipio held his own inquiry, which left Pleminius in command; but as Pleminius' crimes continued, the Locrians appealed to the senate, which had Pleminius arrested and imprisoned. The episode is in Livy, 29.8–9.

[13]Livy, 29.21.11.

[14]On Hannibal and Scipio, see also *Discourses,* 3.19–21.

CHAPTER 18

In what way faith should be kept by princes

How laudable it is in a prince to maintain faith and to live with integrity and not with cleverness, everyone understands. Nonetheless, one sees from experience in our own times that those princes have done great things who have held faith of small account, and who have known how, with their cleverness, to trick men's brains, and at the end they have surpassed those who founded themselves on sincerity.[1]

You[2] should know, therefore, that there are two kinds of combat: one with laws, the other with force. The first one is proper to man, the second is proper to beasts. But because many times the first is not

[1]*sincerity:* some manuscripts give "loyalty" (*lealtà*).
[2]*voi.*

enough, one must have recourse to the second. For a prince, therefore, it is necessary to know well how to use both the beast and the man. This point has been taught covertly[3] to princes by the ancient writers,[4] who write how Achilles and many others of those ancient princes were given to Chiron the centaur to raise, so that under his instruction he would look after them. This having as preceptor a half-beast and half-man, means nothing other than that it is necessary for a prince to know how to use the one and the other nature; and the one without the other does not endure.

Thus, since it is necessary for a prince to know well how to use the beast, from among the beasts he should choose the fox and the lion, for the lion does not defend himself from traps, and the fox does not defend himself from wolves.[5] He must, therefore, be a fox to recognize traps, and a lion to awe the wolves. Those who simply stick with the methods of the lion do not understand this. Therefore a prudent lord cannot, nor should he, observe faith when such observance turns against himself, and when the reasons that made him promise it are eliminated. And if men were all good, this precept would not be good; but because they are wicked, and they would not observe faith for you, you too do not have to observe it for them. Nor does a prince ever lack legitimate reasons for painting over his inobservance. Of this one could give infinite modern examples, and show how many peaces, how many promises have been made void and vain by the faithlessness of princes. And the one who has known better how to use the fox has come out better. But it is necessary to know how to color this nature well, and to be a great pretender and dissembler, and men are so very simple, and they so well obey present necessities, that he who deceives will always find someone who will allow himself to be deceived.

I do not want to be silent about one of the fresh examples. Alexander VI never did anything, never thought about anything, other than deceiving men, and he always found a subject to whom he could do it. Never was there a man who had greater efficacy in his assertions; and

---

[3] In the form of an allegory.

[4] See especially Statius, *Achilleid,* 1.105–97. An image of Chiron appears in the frontispiece of the first edition of M's play, *Mandragola*. In Xenophon, *Education of Cyrus,* 4.3.17, the centaur is described as possessing a man's intelligence and his ability to make things with his hands, but the speed and force of a horse. Because centaurs were famous in classical mythology for their violence and lust, Dante, *Inferno,* 12, describes them as a race of subordinate devils in hell.

[5] Compare Cicero, *De officiis,* 1.11.34 and 1.13.41. Note also that M was an admirer of *Aesop's Fables.* There are also lions and foxes in the fourteenth-century vernacular poetry of Antonio Pucci.

the greater the oaths with which he affirmed something, the less he observed it. Nonetheless, his deceits always fell out for him according to his desires, because he knew well this side of the world.

Thus it is not necessary for a prince actually to have all the above written qualities, but it is very necessary to seem to have them. Indeed, I shall dare to say the following: that when these qualities are possessed and always observed they are harmful. And when they seem to be possessed, they are useful. So that it is useful to seem compassionate, faithful, humane, honest, religious—and to be so, but to stay so constructed in your spirit that if it is necessary not to be these things, you[6] are able and know how to become the contrary. And one must understand the following: that a prince, and especially a new prince cannot observe all of those things for which men are believed good, since to maintain his state he is often required to act against faith, against charity, against humaneness, and against religion. And for this reason he needs to have a spirit disposed to change as the winds of fortune and the variation of things command him, and, as I said above, not to depart from the good if he is able, but to know how to enter into evil when he needs to.

Thus a prince must take great care that nothing ever leave his mouth that is not full of the five qualities stated above, and that he appear, to hear him and to look at him, all compassion, all faith, all integrity, all humaneness, all religion—and there is nothing more necessary to appear to have than this last quality. And men as a whole judge more with their eyes than their hands, because everyone is permitted to see, but few are permitted to touch. Everyone sees what you seem to be, few feel what you are—and those few do not dare to oppose the opinion of the many, who have the majesty of the state that defends them. And in the actions of all men, and especially of princes (where there is no judge to whom to protest), one looks to the end.[7] Therefore let a prince act so as to win and maintain his state; the means will always be judged honorable and praised by everyone. For the masses[8] are always captivated by appearances, and by the outcome of the thing,[9] and in the world there are only the masses, and the few have no standing when the many have someone to support

---

[6]The impersonal *tu,* here and in the following paragraph.

[7]*end:* outcome. In a letter dated October, 28, 1503, M wrote that Cardinal Riario said, "of all things men watch the end more than the means."

[8]The Italian is *vulgo.*

[9]Compare Ovid, *Heroides,* 2.85: "The outcome judges the deeds."

them.[10] A certain prince of present times, whom it is best not to name, never preaches anything but peace and faith, and he is a great enemy of both; and if he had observed both, either his reputation or his state would have been taken from him many times.[11]

[10]Some manuscripts read: "... the few *have* standing" (literally, "a place"), but compare the advice in chapter 9.
[11]Probably Ferdinand the Catholic. On Ferdinand, see especially chapter 21.

CHAPTER 19

On avoiding contempt and hatred

But because I have spoken concerning the most important of the qualities that are mentioned above,[1] I want briefly to discuss the others under the following general terms: that the prince should think, as is said in part above,[2] to avoid those things that could make him hateful and contemptible, and whenever he will avoid this thing, he will have fulfilled his duties and he will not find any peril at all in the other infamies. It makes him hateful, above all, as I said,[3] if he is rapacious and the usurper of the property and women of his subjects, from which he should abstain. And whenever he does not take away property or honor from the generality of men they live content. One has only to combat the ambition of the few, which is checked in many ways and with facility. It makes him contemptible if he is believed to be changeable, light, effeminate, pusillanimous, irresolute: from this a prince ought to guard himself as from a reef, and contrive that in his actions are recognized greatness, spiritedness, weightiness, and strength. With regard to private dealings among his subjects, he should want his pronouncements to be irrevocable. And he should maintain a reputation such that no one thinks either to deceive or to get around him.

That prince who creates this opinion of himself has a very great reputation; and against anyone who has a reputation it is difficult to conspire, and with difficulty is he attacked, so long as it is understood that he is excellent and revered by his people. For a prince must have two fears: one inside, on account of his subjects, the other outside, on account of external powers. From the latter he is defended by good arms and good allies; and always, if he has good arms, he will have

[1]In chapter 15.
[2]In chapters 16 and 17.
[3]In chapter 17.

good allies. And internal things will always stand firm when external ones stand firm, unless they have already been disturbed by a conspiracy. And even if external things should be in motion, if he is composed and has lived as I have said, provided he does not abandon himself, he will always withstand every thrust, as I said Nabis the Spartan did.[4]

But as to his subjects, if external things are not in motion, he has to fear that they may conspire secretly, against which the prince secures himself very well if he avoids being hated and despised and keeps the people satisfied with him, which it is necessary to achieve, as I said above at length.[5] And one of the most powerful remedies a prince has against conspiracies is to be not hated by his people. For whoever conspires always believes he satisfies the people with the death of their prince, but if he believes he offends them, he does not find the spirit to make such a decision. For the difficulties that exist on the side of the conspirators are infinite, and from experience one sees that conspiracies have been many, but few have had a good end. For whoever conspires cannot be alone, nor can he take partners but from those he believes to be malcontent. And as soon as you have revealed your intention to a malcontent, you give him the stuff with which to make himself content, because plainly he can hope for every advantage from it: so that when he sees the sure gain on this side and he sees that it is doubtful and full of peril on the other side, he must be either a rare friend or a completely obstinate enemy of the prince to observe faith with you. And to reduce the thing to brief terms, I say that on the side of the conspirator there is only fear, apprehension and worry about a punishment that frightens him; but on the side of prince there is the majesty of the principality, the laws, the defenses of his friends and of his state that defend him. So that when popular benevolence is added to all these things, it is impossible that anyone should be so foolhardy as to conspire, because where a conspirator ordinarily has to be afraid before the execution of the evil, in this case he must also fear after the crime has happened, since he has the people as his enemy, and for this reason he can hope for no refuge whatsoever.[6]

One could give infinite examples of this matter, but I want to be content with only one, which happened within the memory of our fathers. When Messer Annibale Bentivoglio, grandfather of the present Messer Annibale, who was prince in Bologna, had been killed by the

---

[4]In chapter 9. But Nabis was killed in a conspiracy.

[5]In chapters 9, 16, and 17.

[6]Shortly before he wrote *The Prince*, M was himself arrested and tortured on an unproven charge of conspiracy. This passage probably presents his sincere views, however, it may also be an effort to clear his name. See also *Discourses*, 3.6.

Canneschi,[7] who conspired against him, and no others survived him save Messer Giovanni, who was still in swaddling clothes, the people rose up immediately after such a homicide and killed all of the Canneschi. This arose from the popular benevolence that the house of the Bentivoglio used to have in those times. This benevolence was so great that although no one of the house remained in Bologna who could rule the state, when the Bolognese had information that in Florence there was someone born of the Bentivoglio who was believed until then to be the son of a blacksmith, the Bolognese came for him in Florence, and they gave him the government of their city, which was governed by him until Messer Giovanni reached an age appropriate for governing.[8]

I conclude therefore that a prince must hold conspiracies of little account, if the people are benevolent to him. But if they are his enemy, and they have hatred for him, he must fear everything and everyone. And well-ordered states and wise princes have with all diligence taken care not to make the great desperate and to satisfy the people and keep them content, because this is one of the most important matters that concern a prince.

Among the kingdoms that are ordered and governed well in our times is the Kingdom of France. In it are found infinite good institutions on which the liberty and the security of the king depend, of which the first is the Parlement[9] and its authority. For the person who ordered that Kingdom[10] recognized the ambition of the powerful and their insolence, and he judged that a bit in their mouth was necessary to correct them; and, on the other hand, he recognized that the hatred of the populace against the great was founded on fear. And although he wanted to secure the populace, he did not want that this fear should be the particular care of the king, in order to take away from himself that blame that he might have had with the great if he favored the popular side, and with the popular side if he favored the great. And for this reason he established a third judge who should be one who, without blame for the king, would beat down the great and favor the lesser folk. And this order could not have been better or more prudent, nor could

[7]The Canetoli family of Bologna and their followers were also known as "Caneschi," or "dogs" (after *cane*), although M calls them the "Canneschi."
[8]The episode, which took place in 1445, is also recounted in *Florentine Histories,* 6.9–10. For what really happened, see Cecilia M. Ady, *The Bentivoglio of Bologna* (Oxford: Oxford University Press, 1937), 28–30.
[9]The Parlement of Paris was the highest judicial court in France.
[10]Perhaps King Louis IX (1214–1270).

there be a greater cause for the security of the king and the kingdom. From this one may extract another notable thing: that princes must have administered by others the things that bring blame, but keep for themselves the things that bring favor. Again I conclude that a prince must esteem the great, but not make himself hated by the people.

It would appear perhaps to many, if the life and death of some Roman emperor is considered, that these emperors were examples contrary to this opinion of mine, since they could find some emperor who always lived excellently and showed great virtue of spirit, but nonetheless lost his empire, or indeed was killed by his own men who had plotted against him. Since I want, therefore, to respond to these objections, I shall, on the one hand, discuss the qualities of certain emperors, showing that the causes of their ruin were not dissimilar to what has been advanced by me; and, on the other hand, I shall put under consideration those things that are notable to whoever reads the actions of those times. And I want it to suffice for me to select all of those emperors who succeeded to the empire from Marcus the philosopher down to Maximinus: these were Marcus, his son Commodus, Pertinax, Julianus, Severus, his son Antoninus Caracalla, Macrinus, Heliogabalus, Alexander, and Maximinus.[11] And first it is to be noted that where in other principalities it is only necessary to contend with the ambition of the great and the insolence of the people, the Roman emperors had a third difficulty: to have to endure the cruelty and avarice of their soldiers. This thing was so difficult that it was the cause of the ruin of many emperors, since it was difficult to satisfy the soldiers and the people. For the people loved quiet, and for this reason they loved modest princes; and the soldiers loved the prince of military spirit, and that he should be insolent, cruel, and rapacious. They wanted him to practice these things among the people, so as to have their pay doubled and to vent their avarice and cruelty. These things brought it about that those emperors who, whether by nature or by art, did not have a great reputation, such that with it they might hold the one and the other in check, were always ruined. And most of them, especially those who came to the principality as new men, once

---

[11] The chief source for what follows is Herodian's *History of the Empire from the Time of Marcus Aurelius,* translated from Greek into Latin by Angelo Poliziano and published in 1493. "Marcus the philosopher" is Marcus Aurelius (r. 161–180 CE). The emperors who follow are Commodus (r. 180–192), Pertinax (r. January 1–March 28, 193), Didius Julianus (r. March 28–June 2, 193), Septimius Severus (r. 193–211), Caracalla (r. 211–217), Macrinus (r. 217–218), Heliogabalus (r. 218–222), Alexander Severus (r. 222–235), and Maximinus (r. 235–238).

they recognized the difficulty of these two different humors, turned to satisfying their soldiers, while they cared little about injuring the people. This choice was necessary, because, since princes cannot fail to be hated by someone, they must first try not to be hated by collectivities,[12] and when they cannot achieve this, they must contrive with all industry to avoid the hatred of those collectivities that are more powerful. For this reason, those emperors who, because of their newness, had need of extraordinary favors, adhered to the soldiers rather than the people. This turned out to be useful or not for them depending on whether that prince knew how to maintain his reputation with them.

From these causes mentioned above it happened that Marcus, Pertinax and Alexander, who were all of modest life, lovers of justice, enemies to cruelty, humane and benign, all, except for Marcus, had a bad end. Marcus alone lived and died a most honored man, because he succeeded to the empire by hereditary right, and he did not have to acknowledge it from either the soldiers or the people. Afterward, since he was accompanied by many virtues that made him venerable, he always kept the one and the other order within its bounds, and he was never hated nor despised. But Pertinax was created emperor against the will of the soldiers, who, being accustomed to live licentiously under Commodus, could not tolerate that honest life to which Pertinax wished to bring them back. So that having created hatred of himself, and to this hatred having added disdain, since he was old, he was ruined in the first beginnings of his administration. And here one must note that hatred is acquired by means of good works as well as wicked ones; and for this reason, as I said above,[13] a prince who wants to maintain his state is often forced not to be good. For when that collectivity, whether it be the people, the soldiers or the great, that you[14] judge you need most to maintain yourself, is corrupt, to satisfy it you must follow its humor, and then good works are your enemies.

But let us come to Alexander, who was of such goodness that among the other praises that are attributed to him there is this: that in the fourteen years he held the empire no one was killed by him without a trial. Nonetheless, since he was held to be effeminate, and a man who allowed himself to be governed by his mother, and on this account he came into disdain, the army conspired against him and killed him.

---

[12]*collectivities: università.* M refers to groups in society that have shared or collective interests.

[13]In chapters 15 and 18.

[14]The impersonal *tu.*

Now, on the other side, reviewing the qualities of Commodus, of Severus, of Antoninus Caracalla and Maximinus, you[15] will find them most cruel and rapacious. These, to satisfy the soldiers, did not spare any kind of injury that could be committed against the people. And all had a wretched end except Severus. For in Severus there was such virtue that, by maintaining the soldiers as his friends, although the people were burdened by him, he was able always to rule happily. For those virtues of his made him so marvelous in the sight of the soldiers and the people that the latter remained somehow stupefied and astonished, and the former reverent and satisfied. And because the actions of that man were great and noteworthy in a new prince, I want briefly to show to what extent he knew well how to use the person of the lion and of the fox, whose natures, I say above,[16] are necessary for a prince to imitate.

Since Severus knew the sloth of the emperor Julianus,[17] he persuaded his army, of which he was captain in Slavonia,[18] that it would be good to go to Rome to avenge the death of Pertinax, who had been killed by the praetorian soldiers. And under this color, without showing that he aspired to the empire, he moved his army against Rome, and he was in Italy before his departure was known. When he arrived at Rome, the Senate, out of fear, elected him emperor and put Julianus to death. After this beginning there remained for Severus two difficulties, since he wanted to become lord of all the state: one in Asia, where Pescennius Niger, the head of the Asian armies, had had himself proclaimed emperor; and the other in the West, where there was Albinus, who also aspired to the empire. And because he judged it dangerous to reveal himself the enemy of both, he decided to attack Niger and deceive Albinus. To the latter he wrote that, now that he was elected emperor by the Senate, he wanted to share with him that dignity, and he sent him the title of Caesar and by decision of the Senate he joined him as a colleague, which things were accepted by Albinus as true. But after Severus had defeated and killed Niger and pacified eastern things, when he returned to Rome he complained in the Senate that Albinus, little cognizant of the benefits received from him, had tried treacherously to kill him: and for this reason it was necessary to go and punish his ingratitude. Then he went to meet him in France, and

[15]*voi.*
[16]In chapter 18.
[17]Didius Julianus was chosen emperor after a mock auction held by the Praetorian Guard.
[18]In Roman times the province was known as Pannonia.

took from him his state and his life. And whoever will examine minutely the actions of this man will discover him a most ferocious lion and a most clever fox, and he will see him feared and revered by everyone, and by the army not hated, and he will not marvel that Severus, a new man, will have been able to hold so great an empire, because his very great reputation always defended him from that hatred which, on account of his robberies, people could have been able to conceive.

But his son Antoninus was also a man of most excellent parts, which made him marvelous in the sight of the people and welcome to the soldiers, for he was a military man, most ready to endure any labor, a disdainer of all delicate food and of any other comforts, and this made him loved by all the armies. Nonetheless his ferocity and cruelty were so great and so unheard of—since after infinite single murders he had killed a great part of the people of Rome and all that of Alexandria—that he became most hateful to all the world. And he began to be feared even by those he had around him: so that he was killed by a centurion in the midst of his army. Here it is to be noted that deaths such as these, which result from the deliberation of an obstinate spirit, cannot be avoided by princes, since anyone who does not care about dying is able to harm him. But still the prince ought to fear these deaths less, for they are very rare. Only he should guard himself against doing serious injury to any of those whom he uses and that he has around in the service of his principality, as Antoninus had done, who had disgraced and killed a brother of that centurion, and used to menace the centurion every day, yet kept him as his bodyguard, which was a reckless decision, apt to bring ruin, as happened to him.

But let us come to Commodus, who had great facility in holding his empire because he had it by hereditary right, since he was the child of Marcus. And he needed only to follow in the footsteps of his father, and he would have satisfied both the soldiers and the people. But since he was of a cruel and bestial spirit, in order to practice his rapacity on the people, he turned to indulging the armies and making them licentious. On the other hand, by not maintaining his dignity, by descending often into the arenas to fight with gladiators, and by doing other things most vile and little worthy of his imperial majesty, he became contemptible in the sight of his soldiers. And since he was hated by one side and despised by the other, there was a conspiracy against him and he was killed.

It remains for us to narrate the qualities of Maximinus. He was a most warlike man, and since the armies were disgusted with the softnesses of Alexander, of whom I discoursed above, after Alexander's death they elected him to the empire. This he possessed for not very long, because two things made him hateful and contemptible. The one was that he was most vile because he had formerly herded sheep in Thrace, which thing was very well known everywhere, and used to bring him great disdain in the sight of everybody. The other was because, by having deferred his going to Rome and entering into possession of the imperial seat at the beginning of his principality, he had created an opinion of himself as a very cruel man, since through his prefects in Rome, and in every part of the empire, he had practiced many cruelties. So, when all the world was stirred up with disdain for the vileness of his blood, and with hatred for fear of his ferocity, first Africa revolted, and then the Senate conspired against him with all of the people of Rome and of all Italy; to which was added his own army, which, since it was besieging Aquileia and was finding difficulty in capturing it, became disgusted with his cruelty. And since they feared him less, because they saw he had so many enemies, they killed him.

I do not want to reason about Heliogabalus or Macrinus or Julianus, who were immediately eliminated because they were entirely contemptible, so I shall come to the conclusion of this discourse. And I say that the princes of our own times, in their conduct, have less of this difficulty of satisfying their soldiers extraordinarily: because, notwithstanding that some consideration has to be given to them, still the difficulty is quickly resolved, for none of these princes keeps together armies that are experienced in the government and administration of provinces, as were the armies of the Roman empire. And for this reason, if then it was more necessary to satisfy the soldiers than the people, because the soldiers could do more than the people, today, for all princes except for the Turk[19] and the Sultan,[20] it is more necessary to satisfy the people than the soldiers, because the people can do more than the soldiers. From this I except the Turk, because he continually keeps together around him twelve thousand infantry[21] and fifteen thousand cavalry, on which the security and strength of his kingdom depend; and it is necessary for that lord to put aside any

[19]Selim I, sultan of the Ottoman Turks (r. 1512–1520).

[20]Egypt was controlled by a military caste, known as the Mamelukes, who elected one of their own as sultan. In 1517 the Ottomans defeated the Mamelukes and annexed Egypt.

[21]The janissaries were an elite corps made up mostly of Christians and non-Muslims who were forced into service as boys, sworn to celibacy, encouraged to convert to Islam, and followed only the Turkish sultan's orders.

other consideration and keep them his friends. Similarly, since the
kingdom of the Sultan is entirely in the hands of his soldiers, it is
appropriate that he, too, without regard for the people, should maintain them as his friends. And you[22] should notice that this state of the
Sultan is unlike all the other principalities, because it is similar to the
Christian pontificate, which cannot be called either a hereditary principality or a new principality. For the children of the old prince are not
the heirs, and they do not remain the lords, but rather he who is
elected to that rank by those who have authority over it. And since
this order is ancient, it cannot be called a new principality, since there
are not any of those difficulties in it that there are in new ones. For
even if the prince is new, the orders of that state are old, and they are
established to welcome him as though he were their hereditary lord.[23]

But let us return to our matter. I say that whoever will consider the
above-written discourse will see that either hatred or contempt has
been the cause of the ruin of those emperors named above. And he will
recognize, too, whence it arises that, with part of them proceeding in
one way and part in the contrary way, in each of these ways one of
them had a happy end and the others unhappy ends. Because for Pertinax and Alexander, since they were new princes, it was useless and
harmful to want to imitate Marcus, who was in the principality by
hereditary right. And similarly for Caracalla, Commodus and Maximinus it was a pernicious thing to imitate Severus, because they did not
have virtue such as would be sufficient to follow in his footsteps.
Therefore a new prince in a new principality cannot imitate the actions
of Marcus, nor again is it necessary for him to follow those of Severus.
But he must choose from Severus those parts that are necessary to
found his state, and from Marcus those that are appropriate and glori-
ous for preserving a state that is already established and firm.

[22]*voi.*
[23]Note that M speaks of the papacy obliquely rather than directly as in chapter 11.

CHAPTER 20

**Whether fortresses and many other things made or done by
princes every day are useful or useless**

Some princes, to hold their states securely, have disarmed their subjects; some others have kept their subject towns divided. Some have
fed hatreds against themselves; some others have turned themselves

to winning over those who were suspect to them at the beginning of their states. Some have built fortresses; some have ruined and destroyed them. And although on all of these things I cannot pass definitive sentence without coming to the particulars of those states where any decision like this has to be made, nonetheless I shall speak in the broad way that the matter by itself allows.

Thus it never happened that a new prince disarmed his subjects; on the contrary, when he has found them unarmed he has always armed them. For in arming them those arms become yours:[1] those who are suspect to you become faithful, and those who were faithful remain so, and from subjects they are all made into your partisans. And because all of your subjects cannot be armed, if the ones you arm are benefited, the others are dealt with more securely. And that difference in treatment, which they recognize among themselves, makes them obligated to you. And those others excuse you, since they judge it necessary that the ones who have greater danger and duty should have greater reward. But if you disarm them, you begin to offend them: you show that you have diffidence toward them, whether for cowardice or lack of faith, and the one and the other of these opinions generate hatred against you. And because you cannot stay unarmed, you must turn to a mercenary military, which is of that quality as is said above,[2] and even if it were good, it cannot be large enough to defend you against powerful enemies and subjects who are suspect. For this reason, as I have said, a new prince in a new principality has always ordered the arms there. Of these examples the histories are full. But when a prince acquires a new state, which like a limb is attached to his old state, then it is necessary to disarm that state, except for those who were your partisans in acquiring it; and these, too, it is necessary to render soft and effeminate, with time and with opportunities, and to order things so that the arms of all of your state belong only to your own soldiers who used to live with you in your old state.

Our own ancients, including those who were esteemed wise, used to say that it was necessary to hold Pistoia with factions and Pisa with fortresses.[3] And because of this they nourished the differences in

---

[1]The impersonal *tu,* here and throughout the paragraph.

[2]In chapter 12.

[3]A Venetian ambassador, Marco Foscari, describing Florence in 1527, said he was told that Lorenzo de' Medici the Magnificent (1449–1492) used to say "it was necessary to hold Pistoia with her factions, Pisa with poverty, Volterra with force, Arezzo with her countryside and Cortona with favors." See *Relazioni degli ambasciatori veneti,* ed. Eugenio Alberi, ser. 2, vol. 1 (Florence: Società editrice fiorentina, 1839), 73.

certain towns that were subject to them in order to possess them more easily. This, in those times when Italy was in a certain way balanced,[4] must have been a good feat; but indeed I do not believe it can be given as a precept today, for I do not believe that divisions ever did any good whatsoever. On the contrary, divided cities, when the enemy approaches, are necessarily lost, because the weaker party always joins with the outside forces and the other will not be able to stay in power.

The Venetians, moved, as I believe, by the reasons stated above, used to nourish the Guelf and Ghibelline sects[5] in the cities subject to them. And although they never let them come to bloodshed, nevertheless they used to nourish these disagreements among them so that, since those citizens were occupied with those differences of theirs, they could not unite against the Venetians. This, as was seen later, did not turn to their advantage, since when they were defeated at Vailate, immediately one of these factions became bold and took away from them all of their state.[6] Measures like these are therefore evidence of weakness in the prince, because in a strong principality such divisions will never be permitted. For they are profitable only in peacetime, since by their means the prince may manage his subjects more easily, but when war comes such an order shows its own fallacy.

Without doubt princes become great when they overcome the difficulties and the oppositions that are made against them. And for this reason fortune—most of all when she wants to make a new prince great, since he has greater need of acquiring reputation than a hereditary one—makes enemies arise for him and makes them make undertakings against him, so that he should have reason to overcome them, and to climb higher by means of the ladder that his enemies have brought for him. For this reason, many judge that a wise prince, when he has the opportunity, must cleverly nourish some enmity, so that, when it is defeated, his greatness results increased.

Princes, and especially those who are new, have found more faith and more usefulness in those men who were held suspect at the beginning of their states than in those of whom they were confident

[4]See chapter 11 on the Italian balance of power during the period 1454–94.

[5]During the Middle Ages, the Guelfs were the papal faction and the Ghibellines the imperial faction. In the early sixteenth century, the Guelfs supported the French and the Ghibellines supported emperor-elect Maximilian. As used here, "sects" (*sètte*) has no religious connotation, apart from a certain disdain for what M considers an irrational system of social allegiances.

[6]The pro-French Guelfs moved immediately to revolt from Venice and give their cities over to the French. The Ghibellines were less swift.

at the beginning. Pandolfo Petrucci, prince of Siena,[7] ruled his state more through those who were suspect to him than through the rest. But of this thing one cannot speak broadly, because it varies according to the subject. I shall say only this, that the prince can always win to himself with the greatest facility those men who had been enemies in the beginning of a principate, and who are of a quality such that to maintain themselves they must rely on others.[8] And they are forced all the more to serve him with faith, inasmuch as they recognize that it is more necessary for them to cancel with deeds the sinister opinion that was had of them. And thus the prince always extracts more utility from them than from those who, because they serve him with too much security, neglect his affairs.

And since the matter requires it, I do not want to neglect to remind the princes who have taken a state anew, by means of favors from within it, that they should consider well what cause moved those who favored him to favor him. And, if there is not natural affection toward them, but if it was only because those men were not content with the former state, he will be able to maintain them as friends only with hardship and great difficulty, because it would be impossible for him to be able to content them. And if he goes over the cause of this well, with those examples that are drawn from ancient and modern affairs, he will see that it is much more easy for him to win to himself as friends those men who used to be content under the previous state than those who, because they were not content with it, became his friends and favored him in occupying it.

It has been the custom of princes, in order to hold their states more securely, to build fortresses, so that they may be the bridle and the bit of those who design to act against them, and to have a secure refuge from sudden attack. I praise this mode, because it has been practiced since ancient times. Nonetheless, Messer Niccolò Vitelli, in our own times, was seen to destroy two fortresses in Città di Castello in order to hold that state.[9] Guidubaldo, duke of Urbino, when he returned to his dominion,[10] from which he had been chased out by Cesare Borgia, razed to the foundations all of the fortresses of that province, and he judged that without them it would be more difficult to lose that state

---

[7]Here as in chapter 22, Pandolfo Petrucci (1450–1512) is called "prince of Siena." But in *Discourses*, 3.6, Petrucci is called "tyrant of Siena."

[8]M has in mind his personal situation, as an employee of the former regime.

[9]In 1482. Niccolò Vitelli (1414–1486), mercenary captain and lord of Città di Castello, was the father of Paolo and Vitellozzo Vitelli.

[10]In 1503.

again. The Bentivoglio, when they returned to Bologna, used similar measures.[11] Fortresses, therefore, are useful or not according to the times; and if in one respect they do well for you,[12] in another they harm you. And this point may be discussed as follows: that prince who has more fear of the people than of outsiders should make fortresses, but he who has more fear of outsiders than of the people should do without them. The castle of Milan that was built there by Francesco Sforza has brought more harm to the house of Sforza than any other disorder of that state. For this reason the best fortress there is is not to be hated by the people. For even if you have fortresses, if the people hold you in hatred, the fortresses do not save you, since outsiders who will help them are never lacking for the people once they have taken up arms. In our own times, it is not evident that fortresses have profited any prince at all, except the countess of Forlì, after Count Girolamo, her consort, was killed, since by means of her fortress she could flee the popular attack, wait for help from Milan, and recover her state.[13] And the conditions then were such that the outsider was not able to help the people. But afterward, for her, too, the fortresses were of little value when Cesare Borgia attacked her, and her hostile people joined together with the outsider.[14] For that reason, both then and earlier, it would have been safer for her not to be hated by the people than to have her fortresses. Therefore, having considered all of these things, I shall praise whoever will make fortresses, and whoever will not make them, and I shall blame anyone who, because he trusts in fortresses, will think little of being hated by the people.

[11] In 1511.
[12] The impersonal *tu,* here and in the rest of the paragraph.
[13] On Caterina Sforza Riario, see also *Discourses,* 3.6. This took place in 1488.
[14] In 1499–1500.

CHAPTER 21

What the prince should do to be thought outstanding

Nothing makes a prince so greatly esteemed as do great campaigns and giving rare examples of himself. We have in our own times Ferdinand of Aragon, the present king of Spain. This man can be called almost a new prince, since from being a weak king he has become by fame and by glory the first king of the Christians; and if you will consider his actions, you will find them all very great and some you will find extraordinary. He attacked Granada[1] in the beginning of his reign, and that campaign was the foundation of his state. First of all, he did it privately and without fear of being impeded.[2] He kept occupied in the campaign the spirits of those barons of Castile, who, while they were thinking of that war, did not think of innovating; and by this means he acquired reputation and command over them that they did not notice. He was able to supply armies with money from the Church and the people, and through that long war to make a foundation for his military that afterward brought him honor. Beyond this, so as to be able to undertake greater campaigns, ever making use of religion, he resorted to an act of pious cruelty by chasing the Marranos[3] from his kingdom and despoiling them: nor could this example be more wretched or more rare. He attacked Africa under this same cloak;[4] he made his campaign in Italy;[5] lately he has attacked France.[6] And so he has always done and ordered great things, which have always kept the spirits of his subjects suspended and wondering and occupied with their outcome. And these actions of his have originated the one from the other in a way that has never given space, between the one action and the next, for men to be able to work quietly against him.

It also helps a prince very much to give rare examples of himself concerning internal government (similar to those that are told about Messer Bernabò of Milan[7]) when the opportunity occurs of someone who does something extraordinary in civil life, whether for good or evil, and to choose a way for rewarding or punishing him that will be very much talked about. And above all a prince must contrive, in each of his actions, to give himself the fame of a great man and of an excellent talent.

---

[1]The Muslim kingdom in the south of Spain, conquered in 1492.

[2]By other European powers.

[3]Jews and Muslims were officially expelled from Spain in 1492. *Marranos,* Spanish for "pigs," was an insulting name, given to Jewish and Muslim converts, that referred to the dietary prohibition in both Judaism and Islam against eating pork. In Italy, *Marrano* was often applied, as here, to the Jews and Muslims who were forced to flee Spain, rather than to converts to Christianity.

[4]Under the pretext of religion—a crusade. Ferdinand took Oran in 1509 and Tripoli in 1511.

[5]The Kingdom of Naples was definitively seized in 1503.

[6]In May–December 1512.

[7]Bernabò Visconti (1323–1385) came to power in 1355 as coruler of Milan with his two brothers, Matteo II and Galeazzo II. Matteo was poisoned by the other two, who shared power until Galeazzo's death in 1378. Galeazzo was succeeded as coruler by his son, Giangaleazzo, who in 1385 deposed Bernabò, imprisoned him, and may have put him to death. Bernabò was largely responsible for the creation of a Milanese territorial state at the expense of local feudatories. Franco Sacchetti, *Trecentonovelle,* 4, wrote, "however cruel he was, still, in his cruelties, he had very much justice."

A prince is still esteemed when he is a true friend and a true enemy; that is, when without any hesitation he reveals himself in favor of one person against another. This decision will always be more useful than staying neutral. For if two powerful neighbors of yours[8] come to blows, either they are of a quality that if one of them wins you have to fear the victor, or not. In each of these two cases, it will always be more useful for you to reveal yourself and wage open war. For, in the first case, if you do not reveal yourself, you will always be the prey of whoever wins, to the pleasure and satisfaction of the one who was defeated, and you do not have justice or anything at all that defends you or gives you refuge. For he who wins does not want friends who are suspect, and who do not help him in adversities; and he who loses does not give you refuge, because you did not want to take up arms to share in his fortune.

Antiochus had passed into Greece, having been brought there by the Aetolians in order to chase out the Romans.[9] Antiochus sent orators to the Achaeans, who were allies of the Romans, to encourage them to remain neutral; and, on the other side, the Romans were trying to persuade them to take up arms for them. This matter came to be decided in the council of the Achaeans, where Antiochus' legate tried to persuade them to stay neutral, to which the Roman legate replied: "As to what they say, moreover, about your not intervening in the war, nothing is farther from your interests: you will be the prize of the victor, without thanks and without dignity."[10] It will always happen that he who is not an ally will ask for neutrality from you, and the one who is your ally will ask that you come out with your arms. Irresolute princes, to avoid present dangers, follow that neutral way most of the time, and most of the time they are ruined.

But when the prince reveals himself strongly in favor of one side, if the one to whom you adhere wins, although he is powerful and you remain at his discretion, he is obliged to you, and there is a contract of love; and men are never so dishonest that in a very great example of ingratitude they would oppress you. And then victories are never so clear that the victor does not have to have some regard, and for justice most of all. But if the one to whom you adhere loses, he gives you refuge; and so long as he can he helps you, and you become a partner in a fortune that can rise again.

[8]The impersonal *tu*, here and in the following three paragraphs.
[9]In 192 BCE. See also chapter 3.
[10]Livy, 35.49.13, quoted imprecisely, possibly from memory. The Roman legate was Titus Quinctius Flamininus (229–174 BCE). The passage also appears in a letter from Marcello Virgilio Adriani to M dated August 29, 1510, and in two letters from M to Francesco Vettori, both dated December 20, 1514.

In the second case, when those who fight each other are of a quality such that you do not have to fear the one who wins, it is even greater prudence to ally oneself, because you go to the destruction of one with the help of the one who, if he were wise, ought to save him. And if he wins, he remains at your discretion; and it is impossible, with your help, that he not win. And here it should be noted that a prince must be careful never to make a partnership with one who is more powerful than himself in order to harm others, unless necessity compels him, as is said above, because if you win you remain his prisoner, and as much as they can princes should avoid being at the discretion of others. The Venetians became partners of France against the duke of Milan,[11] and they could have avoided making that partnership from which their ruin resulted. But when one cannot avoid it (as happened to the Florentines when the pope and Spain went with their armies to attack Lombardy[12]), then the prince must ally himself for the reasons said above. Nor let any state ever believe that it can always make safe choices. On the contrary, let it think that it has to take them all as doubtful. Because we find this, in the order of things, that one never tries to avoid one inconvenience without incurring another one. But prudence consists in knowing how to recognize the qualities of the inconveniences and choosing the less bad as if it were good.

A prince must also show himself to be a lover of the virtues by giving hospitality to virtuous men, and he must honor those who are excellent in an art. Next, he must encourage his citizens to be able quietly to practice their trades, in commerce, in agriculture and in every other human occupation, so that one man is not afraid to improve his properties for fear they will be taken from him, and another is not afraid to open a business for fear of taxes. But he must prepare rewards for whoever wants to do these things, and for whoever thinks to increase his city or his state in whatever way. Beyond this, at the appropriate times of the year he should keep his people occupied with feast-days and spectacles. And because every city is divided into guilds or wards,[13] he should take account of those collectivities, meet with them sometimes, and offer himself as an example of humanity and munificence, while nonetheless always keeping firm his dignity's majesty, for he does not want this ever to be lacking in anything.[14]

---

[11] In 1499.

[12] In 1512.

[13] *wards:* literally, "tribes" (*tribù*), but with the sense of "neighborhoods."

[14] In this paragraph M probably has in mind Lorenzo de' Medici the Magnificent (d. 1492). Compare *Florentine Histories,* 8.36.

CHAPTER 22

On those whom princes have in their service for secret matters[1]

The choice of his ministers is not of small importance to a prince. These are good, or not, depending on the prudence of the prince. And the first conjecture that is made about the mind of a lord is in seeing the men that he has around him. And if they are capable and faithful one may always reckon him wise, since he has known how to recognize that they are capable and to maintain them as faithful. But if they are otherwise, always one may come to a judgment of him that is not good, because the first error that he makes, he makes in this choice.

There was no one, if he knew Messer Antonio of Venafro[2] when he was the minister of Pandolfo Petrucci, prince of Siena, who could not have judged Pandolfo to be a most worthy man, since he had that man as his minister. And because minds are of three kinds—one that understands by itself; another that discerns what others understand; and a third that understands neither itself nor others: the first is most excellent, the second is excellent, and the third useless[3]—it must be, therefore, of necessity, that if Pandolfo was not in the first rank, he must have been in the second. For whenever someone has the judgment to recognize the good or the evil that one does and says, although he does not have the inventiveness by himself, he does recognize the good works and the wicked ones of his minister, and he exalts the former and he corrects the others; and the minister cannot hope to deceive him, and he remains good.

But as for how a prince may know his minister, there exists the following way that never fails: when you[4] see the minister think more of himself than of you, and that in all of his actions he seeks some profit for himself, a man of this kind, made in this way, will never make a good minister, and never will you be able to trust him. For the man who has someone's state in his hand should never think of himself,

---

[1]A manuscript with Italian rather than Latin chapter titles is more succinct: "On the secretaries that princes have in their service."

[2]Messer Antonio Giordani (1459–1530) came from the town of Venafro, near the abbey of Montecassino, in the Molise region of Italy. He made his career in Siena, where he was a professor of law and the minister of Pandolfo Petrucci. On Giordani, see also Francesco Guicciardini, *Ricordi,* C.112.

[3]M probably has in mind Livy, 22.29, although similar statements appear in Hesiod, Aristotle, Leon Battista Alberti, and Matteo Palmieri.

[4]An impersonal use of *tu.*

but of the prince, and he should never bring to the prince's attention anything that does not pertain to the prince. And on the other side, the prince, in order to keep him good, ought to think of the minister by honoring him, making him rich, obligating him to himself, and sharing with him his honors and offices; so that he sees that he cannot stand without him, and that his many honors do not make him desire more honors, his many riches do not make him desire more riches, and his many offices make him fear revolutions. Thus when ministers and princes are made in this way, they are able to trust one another; and when otherwise, the end will always be harmful, either for one or for the other.

CHAPTER 23

In what way flatterers are to be avoided

I do not want to leave out one important point, and an error from which princes defend themselves with difficulty, if they are not very prudent, or if they do not make good choices. And these are the flatterers, of whom the courts are full; because men so take pleasure in their own things, and in a way they deceive themselves with them, that with difficulty they defend themselves from this plague. And in wanting to defend themselves against them, they run the danger of becoming contemptible. For there is no way to guard against flatteries, other than for men to understand that they do not offend you[1] when they tell you the truth; but when everyone can tell you the truth, you lack their reverence.

Therefore a prudent prince must keep to a third way, by choosing wise men in his state, and only to them should he give free access[2] to speak the truth to him, and only concerning those things that he asks, and nothing else. Yet he should ask them about everything, and hear their opinions, and afterward he should choose by himself, in his own way. And in these councils, and with each of their members, he should conduct himself in such a way that everyone knows that the more freely he speaks the more welcome he will be. Outside of those councils he should not want to hear anyone; he should follow what has been decided, and be obstinate in his decisions. Whoever does otherwise

---

[1]The impersonal *tu*.
[2]Some manuscripts have "free will."

either falls headlong because of flatterers, or often changes his mind because of the changeability of their opinions, from which arises a low reputation for himself.

I want in this regard to bring forth a modern example. Priest Luca,[3] a man of Maximilian, the present Roman emperor,[4] when he spoke of His Majesty, said that he used to take counsel with no one and that he used never to do anything in his own way. This arose from his holding to a pattern contrary to the one stated above. For the emperor is a secretive man, he does not communicate his plans, and he does not seek out opinions about them. But once his plans start to be recognized and to be revealed as he puts them in motion, they begin to be contradicted by the persons he has around him, and he, like a simpleton, discards them.[5] From here it arises that the things that he does in one day he destroys the next, it is never understood what he wants, or what he plans to do, and one cannot found oneself on his decisions.

A prince therefore must always take counsel, but when he wants, and not when others want: to the contrary, he must discourage everyone from counseling him about anything if he does not ask him about it. But yet he must be a broad questioner, and then, concerning the things asked about, a patient listener for the truth; indeed, when he understands that anyone, out of whatever regard, does not tell him the truth, he must become upset about it. And because many reckon that any prince who creates for himself a reputation as prudent is held thus, not because of his nature, but because of the good counselors that he has about him, I say without doubt they are deceived. For the following is a general rule that never fails: a prince who is not wise by himself cannot be counseled well, unless by chance he has already entrusted himself to one person alone, who is a most prudent man, to govern him in everything. In this case it could even happen that he would be counseled well, but it would not last long, because that governor, in a brief time, would take his state away from him. But if he takes counsel with more than one person, a prince who is not wise will never have unified coun-

---

[3]Luca Rinaldi, bishop of Trieste, was known as "Pre' (Priest) Luca." He served as an ambassador of Maximilian, and M met him on a legation to the court of the emperor in the Tyrol, December 1507–June 1508.

[4]Maximilian of Habsburg (1459–1519), was elected king of the Romans in 1486, sharing the administration of the Holy Roman Empire with his father, Emperor Frederick III. When Frederick III died in 1493, Maximilian became sole ruler of the empire and head of the house of Habsburg. The full title of emperor required coronation in Rome, however, and Maximilian never achieved this. In 1508, with the consent of Pope Julius II, Maximilian assumed the title of emperor-elect.

[5]There is a similar judgment in M's *Report on Things in Germany*.

sels, nor will he know how to bring them together by himself. Among the counselors, each will think of his own affairs; he will not know how to correct them or understand them; and they cannot be found otherwise. For men will always turn out wicked for you[6] if they are not made by some necessity to be good. For this reason one concludes that good counsels, wherever they come from, must arise out of the prudence of the prince, and not the prudence of the prince from good counsels.

[6]The impersonal *tu*.

CHAPTER 24

Why the princes of Italy have lost their kingdom[1]

The things set forth above, if observed prudently, make a new prince appear ancient, and they make him immediately more secure and more firm in his state, as though he had grown old in it. For a new prince is observed with much more interest in his actions than a hereditary one; and when these actions are recognized to be virtuous, they grip men much more, and they obligate them much more than does ancient blood. For men are taken with present things much more than with past ones, and when they find good in present things, they enjoy it there and do not look for anything else; indeed, they will take up every defense for a prince, if he himself is not lacking in the other things. In this way he will have doubled his glory, by having given a beginning to a principality, and by having adorned it and strengthened it with good laws, with good arms and good examples; just as a man has doubled his shame if, although born a prince, he has lost his principality through his lack of prudence.

And if one considers those lords who in Italy have lost their states in our own times, such as the king of Naples, the duke of Milan and others, he will find in them, first, a common defect as regards their arms, for the causes that have been discussed at length above. Next, one will see either that some of them had their people as enemies, or, if they had their people as an ally, they did not know how to assure themselves of the great. For without these defects states that have enough

[1]The word *kingdom* (*regnum*) possibly echoes medieval usage and the practice of the Holy Roman Empire, according to which northern and central Italy was referred to as "the Italian Kingdom" (*Regnum Italicum*). The Italian version of the chapter title that appears in some of the manuscripts reads: "For what cause the princes of Italy have lost their states (*stati*)."

sinews that they can keep an army in the field are not lost. Philip the Macedonian, not the father of Alexander, but the one who was defeated by Titus Quinctius,[2] had a state that was not very large with respect to the greatness of the Romans and of Greece, who attacked him. Nonetheless, because he was a military man, and one who knew how to please the people and to assure himself of the great, he supported a war for many years against them; and if, in the end, he lost his dominion over certain cities, nonetheless he kept his kingdom.

Therefore these princes of ours, who were in their principalities for many years, ought not to accuse fortune for having lost them, but their own laziness. For they never during quiet times thought that the times could change—which is a common defect of men, to not think of storms during a calm. Then, when adverse times did come, they decided to flee, not to defend themselves; and they hoped that the people, when they were disgusted with the insolence of the victors, would call them back. This decision, when others do not exist, is good; but it is surely bad to have abandoned the other remedies for this one. For one should never fall down because of the belief that you[3] will find someone to catch you. Either this does not happen, or, if it happens, it is not to your safety. For that defense was cowardly, and it did not depend on you; and the only defenses that are good, certain, and enduring are those that depend upon yourself and your own virtue.

---

[2] Philip V of Macedon, not Philip II (the father of Alexander the Great). Philip V was defeated by the Roman general Titus Quincius Flamininus in 197 BCE.
[3] *tu:* here and in the following two sentences.

CHAPTER 25

How much fortune is able to do in human things, and by what means she may be opposed

It is not unknown to me that many persons have held, and hold, the opinion that the things of the world are governed by fortune and by God, that men, with their prudence, cannot correct them, and that instead they have no remedy for them whatsoever. For this reason they might judge that there would be no point in sweating much in the things of this world, but let themselves be governed by chance. This opinion has been more believed in our own times on account of the great variety of things that have been seen, and are seen every day, beyond all human conjecture. Sometimes, when I think of this, I am inclined in some part toward their opinion. Nonetheless, so that our free will may not be eliminated, I judge that it may be true that fortune is the arbiter of half of our actions, but that she indeed allows us to govern the other half of them, or almost that much. And I liken her to one of these ruinous rivers that, when they become angry, flood the plains, ruin the trees and the buildings, and lift earth from one side and place it on the other. Each person flees before them; everyone surrenders to their attack without being able, under these circumstances, to block them at any point. Although they really happen this way, it does not follow from this that men, when there are quiet times, are not able to make provision for it with both dikes and embankments, so that, if later the rivers rise, either they would go into a canal, or their attack would be neither so boundless nor so harmful. It happens similarly with fortune. She shows her power where virtue is not prepared to resist her; and she turns her rushing current here where she knows that embankments and dikes have not been made to hold her. And if you[1] will consider Italy, which is the seat of these changes and the one who has put them in motion, you will see that this is a landscape without embankments and without any dikes. For, if she had been diked by appropriate virtue, like Germany, Spain and France, either this flood would not have made the great changes that it has, or it would not have come here. And, in general terms,[2] I want it to suffice to have said this concerning opposing fortune.

Yet, narrowing myself more to the particulars, I say that one sees today a certain prince is happy, and tomorrow ruined, without having seen him change in nature or any quality. This I believe arises first from the causes that are reviewed at length earlier, that is, that the prince who relies completely on fortune is ruined when she changes. I believe, too, that the man who conforms his way of proceeding to the quality of the times is happy, and similarly that he whose proceedings the times disagree with is unhappy. For one sees men, in the things that drive them toward the end that each has before him (that is, glories and riches), proceeding in it differently: one with caution, another with impetuosity; one with violence, another with art; one with patience, another with its opposite. And each one, by these different ways, is able to arrive there. One also sees that of two cautious men, one arrives as he planned, but the other not. Likewise, two men are equally happy but from different inclinations, since the one is cautious and the other

[1] *voi.*
[2] Literally, "in universals" (*universali*).

is impetuous. This arises from nothing but the quality of the times, to which they conform in their proceedings, or not. From this arises what I said, that two people, although they operate differently, obtain the same effect; and of two operating equally, one achieves his end and the other not. From this too depends the variation in outcomes. For one who governs himself with caution and patience, if the times and his circumstances run in such a way that this course of action is good, becomes happy. But if the times and his circumstances change, he is ruined, because he does not change his way of proceeding. Nor is a man to be found who is so prudent that he knows how to accommodate himself to this: both because he cannot deviate from that toward which his nature inclines him, and, moreover, because when a man has always prospered by walking in one path, he cannot be persuaded to depart from it. For this reason the cautious man, when it is time to become impetuous, does not know how to do it, whence he is ruined; although, if he could change his nature with the times and with the circumstances, he would not change in his fortune.

Pope Julius II proceeded impetuously in all his affairs, and he found that the times and the circumstances so conformed to his way of proceeding that he always pulled out a happy ending. Consider the first undertaking he accomplished, against Bologna, while Messer Giovanni Bentivoglio was still living.[3] The Venetians were not happy with it; the king of Spain was the same; with France Julius was still holding negotiations about such an undertaking; nonetheless, because of his ferocity and impetuousness, he pushed himself personally into the expedition. This move made Spain and the Venetians stand still and suspended; the latter out of fear, and the other because of the desire he had to recover all of the Kingdom of Naples. On the other side, Julius pulled in the king of France behind him. For, when that king had seen him move, since the king desired to make the pope his friend in order to bring down the Venetians, he judged that he could not deny him his troops without manifestly injuring him. Thus Julius brought about, by his impetuous movement, what another pope, with all human prudence, could never have brought about. For if he had waited to depart from Rome with firm conclusions and all his affairs ordered, as any other pontiff would have done, it would never have succeeded for him, because the king of France would have had a thousand excuses, and the others would have put into him a thousand

---

[3] In 1506, Julius II, who had been bishop of Bologna, attacked the city, drove out the ruling Bentivoglio family, and put Bologna under direct papal rule.

fears. I want to omit his other actions, which were all similar, and all succeeded well for him. And the brevity of his life did not allow him to experience the contrary. For if there had come times in which it was necessary to proceed with caution, his ruin would have followed, for he would never have deviated from those ways toward which his nature inclined him.

I conclude, therefore, that since fortune varies, and since men are obstinate in their ways, they are happy so long as together they agree, and when they disagree, they are unhappy. Yet, I judge the following: that it is better to be impetuous than cautious, for fortune is a lady, and it is necessary, if one wants to hold her down, to beat her and to dash her. And one sees that she lets herself be won more by these men, than by those who proceed coldly. For this reason, as a lady, she is always the friend of the young, because they are less cautious, more ferocious, and they command her with more audacity.[4]

[4]In Italian (as in Latin and Greek), "fortune" is a feminine noun, and in English we speak of "Lady Luck." According to Cicero, *Tusculan Disputations,* 2.4.11, the phrase "fortune favors the strong" is proverbial—although here M gives the expression extra force. Similar ideas are stated in M's earlier *Capitolo on Fortune* (1506), and his later play, *Clizia* (1525), act 4, scene 1. See also Document 1. Passages M may have had in mind, from two poets he was reading in 1513 are Ovid, *Art of Love,* 1.665–6, 673–8, and Tibullus, 1.2.16–17. For medieval representations, see Howard R. Patch, *The Goddess Fortuna in Mediaeval Literature* (Cambridge, Mass.: Harvard University Press, 1927).

CHAPTER 26

An exhortation to seize Italy, and to set her free from the barbarians[1]

Having considered, therefore, all the things discussed above, while thinking to myself whether at present in Italy the times were running so as to honor a new prince, and whether there would be material that could give opportunity to someone who was prudent and virtuous, so that by introducing form to the material, it would do honor to him and good to the collectivity of its inhabitants, it seems to me that so many things are coming together to the benefit of a new prince that I do not know what time for this has ever been more appropriate. And if, as I

[1]A feeling of Italian cultural superiority, combined with the ravages Italy suffered from the armies from France, Spain, and Germany that marched through the peninsula in the decades after 1494, led Italians to apply the term *barbari* to the invading nations.

said,[2] it was necessary, if one wanted to see the virtue of Moses, that the people of Israel should be enslaved in Egypt; and to recognize the greatness of the spirit of Cyrus, that the Persians should have been oppressed by the Medes; and for the excellence of Theseus, that the Athenians should have been dispersed; so, at present, in order to recognize the virtue of an Italian spirit, it was necessary that Italy should be reduced to its present circumstances, and that she should be more enslaved than the Hebrews, more servile than the Persians, and more dispersed than the Athenians: without a head, without order, beaten, despoiled, torn, pillaged, and having suffered ruin of every sort.

Although before now there was visible in a certain person[3] a flickering light such that one could judge that he was ordained by God for Italy's redemption, nevertheless it was seen afterward how, at the very peak of his exertions, he was rejected by fortune, with the result that, remaining as though lifeless, Italy awaits whoever it could be who can heal her wounds, and put an end to the sackings of Lombardy and to the ransoms demanded from Naples and Tuscany, and cure her of the sores with which she has been infested for so long. One sees how she prays to God that he send someone to redeem her from these cruelties and barbaric insolences. One sees her still completely ready and disposed to follow a banner, provided there be someone who takes it up. Nor is there to be seen at present anyone in whom she could hope more than in your[4] illustrious house, which, with its fortune and virtue favored by God and by the Church of which it is now the prince,[5] can make itself the leader of this redemption. Thus it will not be very difficult, if you will keep in mind the actions and lives of the men named above. Although such men are rare and marvelous, nonetheless they were men, and each of them had a lesser opportunity than the present one, for their undertakings were not more just than this, nor easier, nor was God more a friend to them than to you. Here there is great justice: "[F]or war is just for those for whom it is necessary, and arms are pious where there is no hope save in arms."[6] Here there is a greatest

---

[2]In chapter 6.
[3]Probably Cesare Borgia.
[4]*voi.*
[5]Under Pope Leo X (Giovanni de' Medici).
[6]The quotation in Latin (probably from memory) is from Livy, 9.1.10, who writes: "War is just for those for whom it is necessary, and arms are pious for those for whom no hope remains save in arms" [editor's translation]. M also quotes the passage in *Discourses,* 3.12, and *Florentine Histories,* 5.8. Livy's speaker, a Samnite general, is responding to religious objections to his campaign against the Romans. He triumphed in the battle that followed.

readiness, and where there is great readiness there cannot be great difficulty, provided that your house takes up the institutions of those persons whom I have proposed for your aim. Beyond this, see here the extraordinary things, without precedent, conducted by God: the sea has opened; a cloud has shown you the way, the stone has poured forth water; here the manna has rained down.[7] All things have come together for your greatness. The remainder you have to do yourselves. God does not want to do all things, so as not to take away our free will[8] or any part of that glory that belongs to us.

And it is no wonder if none of the aforenamed Italians has been able to do that which it can be hoped your illustrious house may do; and if, in so many revolutions of Italy and in so many maneuvers of war, it seems always that military virtue is extinguished in Italy. This arose from her former orders not being good ones, and from there not being anyone who knew how to find new ones. And nothing confers so much honor on a man who rises anew as do new laws and the new orders he invents. These things, when they are well established and have greatness in them, make him worthy of reverence and admirable. And in Italy there is no want of material into which every form may be introduced; here there is great virtue in the limbs, provided she does not lack leaders. Reflect on the duels and engagements of small groups, and how much superior are the Italians in their force, their skill, and their intelligence, but when it comes to armies they do not compare. All proceeds from the weakness of the leaders, because those who know how are not obeyed, and everyone thinks he knows how, since until now there has been no one who stood out in virtue and fortune such that the others would yield.

Whence it arose that, over so much time, in so many wars waged in the past twenty years, whenever there has been an army that was entirely Italian it always has failed the test. To this stands witness, first, the battle of the Taro, then Alessandria, Capua, Genoa, Vailate, Bologna and Mestre.[9]

If your illustrious house wishes to follow these excellent men who redeemed their provinces, it is necessary, before all other things, as

---

[7]These were signs received by the Hebrews during their years in the desert: the opening of the Red Sea (Exodus 14:21), the cloud that led the Israelites by day (13:21), the rock that gave forth water (17:6), and the manna that fed them (16:15).

[8]*free will:* compare chapter 25.

[9]The battles are: Fornovo on the Taro River, 1495; Alessandria, 1499; Capua, 1501; Genoa, 1507; Vailate, 1509; Bologna, 1511; and Mestre, 1513. M's "twenty years" led Hans Baron to suggest that this chapter was written in 1515 (twenty years after Fornovo), and that it must therefore have been added to what was written in 1513–14.

the true foundation of every undertaking, that you provide yourself with your own arms. For you cannot have more faithful, more true or better soldiers. Even if each one of them is good, all of them together will become better when they are seen to be commanded by their prince, and honored and treated warmly by him. It is necessary, therefore, to prepare these arms so as to be able, with Italian virtue, to defend against outsiders. And although the Swiss and Spanish infantry are regarded with fear, nonetheless there is weakness in both of them, such that a third order could not only oppose them but be confident in overcoming them. For the Spanish are not able to sustain a cavalry charge; and the Swiss must have fear of infantry troops when they meet those who are as obstinate as themselves in fighting. Whence it has been seen, and will be seen, by experience, that the Spanish are not able to resist a French cavalry charge, and the Swiss are ruined by a Spanish infantry charge. And although of this last point complete experience may not have been seen, nevertheless a taste has been seen in the battle of Ravenna,[10] when the Spanish infantry met the German companies that observe the same order as the Swiss. There, the Spanish, with their bodily agility and the help of their bucklers,[11] had entered below among the Germans' pikes; and they were secure in attacking them without the Germans having remedy against it; and if it were not for the cavalry that charged them, they would have finished them all. It is possible, therefore, knowing the defect of the one and the other of these infantries, to order anew an infantry that resists horses and does not fear footsoldiers. The kind of arms and the changed placement of the ranks will accomplish this. And these are among those things which, when ordered anew, give reputation and greatness to a new prince.

This opportunity, therefore, should not be allowed to pass, so that Italy, after so much time, may see a redeemer for herself. Nor can I express with what love he would be received in all those provinces that have suffered from these foreign floods; with what thirst for revenge, with what obstinate faith, with what piety, with what tears. What gates would be closed to him? What peoples would deny him their obedience? What envy would oppose him? What Italian would deny him homage? This barbarian domination stinks to everyone. Let your illustrious house therefore take up this enterprise with that spirit

[10] April 11, 1512. See also chapter 13.
[11] Small, round shields with a point at the center.

and that hope with which just undertakings are taken up, so that under its insignia this fatherland may be ennobled, and under its auspices that saying of Petrarch may be realized:

> Virtue against fury
> Will take up arms, and may the struggle be short;
> since the ancient valor
> in Italian hearts is not yet dead.[12]

---

[12]The verses are from Petrarch's famous poem, "Italia mia," in his *Rime,* no. 128 (lines 93–96).

PART THREE

Related Documents

1

NICCOLÒ MACHIAVELLI

Draft of a Letter to Giovan Battista Soderini

September 13–27, 1506

A large number of personal letters exchanged by Machiavelli and his friends have survived. They offer an unusually detailed picture of Machiavelli's private life, and they also tell us a great deal about his state of mind; he was often expansive in discussing his thoughts, his worries, and his ambitions. The letters' style is figuratively and rhetorically complex, but they nonetheless give the reader a feeling for Machiavelli's personal "voice," which is quite different from the formal one he used in much of The Prince. *A letter that Machiavelli wrote in 1506 to Giovan Battista Soderini, translated here, anticipates some of the important themes of* The Prince, *which Machiavelli composed seven years later, in 1513–14.*

Giovan Battista Soderini (1484–1528) was the eighteen-year-old nephew of the Florentine head of state, Pier Soderini. In 1506, while Machiavelli was in Perugia on a mission to the court of Pope Julius II for the Florentine Republic, he received a personal letter from the young Soderini, dated

Niccolò Machiavelli, *Lettere,* ed. Franco Gaeta, in Machiavelli, *Opere,* 3: 239–45. Translated from the Italian by William J. Connell.

September 12.[1] *Soderini spoke of his affection for Machiavelli, wrote that he was sticking to "a plan of doing infinite things aimlessly," and discussed a possible trip with a mutual friend, Filippo Casavecchia (1472–d. after 1520), to the port of Piombino. There they hoped to witness the arrival of the Spanish general, Gonzalvo de Cordoba, and King Ferdinand II of Spain.*

Machiavelli's much longer, undated response to Soderini's letter, possibly never sent, survives only in a draft, written sometime between September 13 and September 27, 1506. In this period Machiavelli also dedicated a poem to Giovan Battista, the Capitolo on Fortune, *which treats themes present in* The Prince.[2]

In the opening passage of his letter Machiavelli distinguishes the outlook of the young Soderini, who seeks always to do what is prudent, from his own. Machiavelli admits that he could never condemn the young man's prudence, because it has brought him much success, but he praises this prudence only because of its successful outcome. To judge a person's character by its results is an approach that Machiavelli believes he shares with "the many," who "judge the end of things as they are done." This is unlike the approach of the few, evidently including the young Soderini, who instead judge "the means by which they are done." The letter was one of the earliest occasions in Machiavelli's career when he assumed the role of a teacher who claimed to instruct young potential statesmen. In its emphasis on ends as opposed to means, in its examples from Roman and contemporary history, and in its discussion of the role of fortune, Machiavelli's letter looks ahead to The Prince, *which evidently went through a long gestation period.*

Interesting notations that Machiavelli inserted in the margins when returning to his written draft appear in the margins on pages 127–28.

A letter of yours[3] presented itself to me in disguise; yet, after ten words, I recognized it.[4] And truly I believe that there will be many people at Piombino who will know you. And as to what is holding you back, and what is holding Filippo, I am certain, because I know that one of you is affected by too little light, and the other by too much.[5] January doesn't

---

[1] Soderini to Machiavelli, September 12, 1506, in Niccolò Machiavelli, *Lettere,* ed. Gaeta, in Machiavelli, *Opere,* 3: 237–38.

[2] Published in Niccolò Machiavelli, *Capitoli,* ed. Giorgio Inglese (Rome: Bulzoni, 1981), 113–24; with an English translation in *Lust and Liberty: The Poems of Machiavelli,* trans. Joseph Tusiani (New York: Obolensky, 1963), 111–19.

[3] The *voi* form is used throughout.

[4] The address on the outside of Giovan Battista's letter was not in his own hand, but in the hand of Machiavelli's chancery colleague, Biagio Buonaccorsi, hence "in disguise."

[5] Possibly there is an astrological reference here. Gaeta (p. 240 n. 3) suggests Machiavelli meant that Filippo had too little wisdom (light) and Giovan Battista too much.

bother me, so long as February remains under my control.[6] I am sorry to learn about Filippo's suspicion, and in suspense I await the end of it. Your letter was brief, and I, as I reread it, made it long.

A man who does not know how to fence is confusing to one who knows fencing![7]

It was welcome to me, because it gave me the opportunity to do what I was hesitating to do and what you remind me not to do.[8] And only this last point did I think was without cause. Which would amaze me, if my career had not shown me so many and such diverse things that I am little moved to wonder, or to admit not to have tasted, whether through reading or in practice, the actions of men and their ways of behaving. I know you, and the compass[9] by which you sail; and if it could be condemned, which it cannot, I would not condemn it, since I see to what ports it has guided you,[10] and with what hope it is able to sustain you. Hence I am looking not through your glass, in which nothing is seen but prudence, but through the glass of the many, who have to judge the end of things as they are done, and not the means by which they are done. And I see that with different courses of conduct the same thing happens, just as by different paths one arrives at the same place, and many persons, although they act differently, get the same end.[11] And whatever evidence was lacking for this opinion has been supplied by the actions of the present pope and their effects. So it was with Hannibal and Scipio, apart from their military discipline, which was equally excellent in both of them. The one, with cruelty, perfidy and irreligion, kept his armies united in Italy, and made himself admired by the people, who, to follow him, rebelled against the Romans; the other, with compassion, faith and religion, achieved the same outcome in Spain from those people; and both had infinite victories. But because it is not usual to trot out the Romans: Lorenzo de' Medici disarmed the people to control Florence; Messer Giovanni Bentivoglio, in order to control Bologna, armed the people; the Vitelli in Città di Castello and the present Duke of

Do not counsel anyone nor take counsel with anyone, save one general counsel: let everyone do what his spirit dictates, and with boldness.

---

[6]Machiavelli would have to remain at Perugia until January 1507. In February he was planning to begin work on a new Florentine militia.

[7]Machiavelli jestingly accuses Soderini of not knowing how to write a proper letter, and thus of confusing him.

[8]Soderini had written in his letter of September 12, 1506, "I do not want you to write anything back to me." Machiavelli thinks this unjustified.

[9]That is, the "moral compass."

[10]Machiavelli's first draft read instead: "with what ranks it has honored you."

[11]Compare *Prince,* chapter 25.

Urbino tore down their fortresses in order to control those states;[12] Count Francesco and many others built them in their states in order to defend themselves. The Emperor Titus used to believe that he would lose his state the day he did not benefit someone,[13] others thought they would lose theirs the day they did someone a favor. Many achieve their designs by weighing and measuring everything. The present Pope, who has in his house neither scales nor yardstick, achieves by chance, and unarmed, what even with order and arms ought to have come his way only with difficulty.[14] *Test fortune, since she is the friend of the young. But one cannot have fortresses and not have them, be cruel and also compassionate.*

All of the men mentioned above, and infinite others who could be suggested to be like them with regard to this subject matter, have been seen, and are seen, to acquire kingdoms and dominions, or to fall, according to accidental things. And sometimes that way of proceeding, which was praised when they were acquiring, is blamed when they are losing; and, sometimes when, after a lengthy prosperity, they are losing, no quality of their own is blamed at all, but heaven is accused, and the disposition of the Fates. But why it is, that operations that are different sometimes do equal help or equal harm, I do not know; yet I would very much like to know it, so, in order to learn your opinion, I shall be presumptuous and tell you mine. *When fortune grows weary, a man, a family, a city are ruined. Each has its own fortune, founded on its own way of proceeding, and each of these fortunes grows weary, and when fortune is weary it is necessary to win her back in a new way.*

I believe that just as nature has made different faces for man, so she has made different geniuses and characters for him. And because, on the other hand, the times are changeable, and the orders of things are diverse, that man is happy, and his desires are met according to his wishes, who measures his way of proceeding with the times, and the man is unhappy who, on the contrary, in his actions goes against the times and the order of things. From this it may very well be that two people, acting differently, reach the same end, because each of them is able to conform to his own standard, for there are as many orders of things as there are provinces and states. But because the times and all things, both in their universals and particulars, change themselves frequently, and men do not change their characters nor their ways of proceeding, it happens that a man at one time *Comparison of the horse and bit concerning fortresses.*

---

[12]The same examples appear in the discussions of fortresses in *Prince,* chapter 20, and *Discourses,* 2.24.

[13]Titus was Roman emperor from 79 to 81 CE. On Titus, see also *Discourses,* 1.10.

[14]Compare especially *Discourses,* 1.27, describing Julius II's entrance into Perugia, which M had witnessed shortly before writing this letter.

has good fortune, but at another time ill fortune. And truly whoever could be so wise that he knew the times and the order of things, and could accommodate himself to them, would always have good fortune, or he would always defend himself against ill fortune, and it would come to be true that the wise man commands the stars and the fates.[15] But because none of these wise men are to be found, since, first, men are shortsighted, and since they cannot command their own nature, it follows that fortune varies and commands men, and keeps them under her yoke. And to prove this opinion, I would like the above-written examples, on which I have based it, to suffice, and thus I desire that the one support the other.

To give reputation to a new dominator, cruelty, perfidy and irreligion are helpful in that province where humaneness, faith and religion have been abundant for a long time, no less than humanity, faith, and religion are helpful where cruelty, perfidy and irreligion have reigned for a while. For, as bitter things disturb the taste and sweet ones disgust it, so too men become disgusted with the good and complain of evil. These causes, among others, opened Italy to Hannibal, and Spain to Scipio, and thus each encountered times and affairs in accordance with his own order of proceeding. And in those same times a man like Scipio could not have done so well in Italy, nor could a man like Hannibal have done so well in Spain, as each did in his own province.

[15]Alluding to a maxim of Ptolemy of Alexandria: "The wise man will control the stars."

2

FRANCESCO VETTORI

Letter to Niccolò Machiavelli

November 23, 1513

On March 11, 1513, Cardinal Giovanni de' Medici became the first Florentine ever elected as pope, and he chose the name Leo X. The Medici family thus controlled both the papacy and the government of Florence simultaneously. In conjunction with the festivities in Florence, the

Machiavelli, *Lettere,* ed. Gaeta, in Machiavelli, *Opere,* 3: 419–23. Translated from the Italian by William J. Connell.

government announced a pardon of prisoners. Machiavelli, who a few weeks before had been accused of participating in a plot against the Medici, arrested, tortured, and sentenced to life imprisonment, was suddenly freed. Only the terms imposed on November 10, 1512, when Machiavelli lost his chancery job, remained in effect, and one of these required that Machiavelli remain within Florentine jurisdiction for one year.

Meanwhile, one of Machiavelli's closest friends, Francesco Vettori, also a friend of the Medici family, was appointed as Florence's ambassador to the papal court in Rome. After Machiavelli's release from prison, he and Vettori began an intense exchange of letters. They discussed the international situation, the prospect that Machiavelli might find employment with the Medici, and their personal affairs and mutual friends. The correspondence broke off at the end of August 1513, when Vettori failed to reply to a letter of Machiavelli's, as Vettori acknowledges in the letter translated here. Vettori now resumes the correspondence with a letter that describes his situation in Rome. Vettori wrote this letter shortly after the prohibition on Machiavelli's travel expired, so he does not fail to include a warm invitation to Machiavelli to stay with him in Rome.

To the honorable man, Niccolò di Messer Bernardo Machiavelli. In Florence.

My dear *compare:*[1] I have practiced toward you[2] such "sobriety of the pen," as Cristofano Sernigi says, that it slipped my mind where I was. If I remember rightly, the last letter I had from you began with the story of the lion and the fox.[3] I looked for it a little among my letters, but when I could not find it right away I decided not to look anymore. For in truth I did not reply to you then because I worried that to me and you might happen what once happened to me and Panzano:[4] we began playing with cards that were old and worn out, so we sent for new ones, but by the time the servant returned with these one of us had lost his money. Similarly, we were speaking about getting princes to come to terms, but all along they were still playing, so I worried that while we were using up letters about getting them to

---

[1]The word *compare* (cofather) is used in Italian when addressing a man who has stood as godfather to one's own child, or whose child is one's godchild.

[2]*voi:* used throughout.

[3]Machiavelli's letter was dated August 26, 1513. The allusion is to one of *Aesop's Fables,* in which a fox is first frightened by a lion, then takes courage, then approaches the lion and converses with it.

[4]Fruosino da Panzano, also mentioned in Document 3.

come to terms one of them might lose his money. And after we stopped writing certain things have been seen to happen; furthermore, the party is not over, although it seems to have stopped for a while, and I believe it is good not to speak about the party until it is done.

In this letter I have decided to write to tell you how my life in Rome is. It seems fitting, first things first, to let you know where I live, because I have moved, and I am no longer near so many courtesans as I was this summer. My lodging is in a place called San Michele in Borgo,[5] which is very close to the palace and piazza of St. Peter's. But it is in a place that is a little solitary, because it is towards the hill the ancients called the Janiculum. The house is very good, and has many apartments, although small ones; and it is open to the north wind, so there is a perfect breeze.

From the house one enters the church, which, because I am a religious person, as you know, is quite useful for me. It is true that the church is used more for walking through than for anything else, because mass is never said there, nor any other divine office, save once in the whole year. From the church one enters a garden that once was clean and beautiful but now is ruined in large part, although it is continually being repaired. From the garden one climbs up the Janiculum hill, where one can go for pleasure among the paths and vineyards without being seen by anyone. And in this place, according to the ancients, were the gardens of Nero, of which one sees the remains. In this house I have nine servants, and in addition to them I have Il Brancaccio,[6] a chaplain, a scribe, and seven horses, and I spend liberally all of my salary. In the beginning, when I arrived, I started by wanting to live in splendor and refinement, inviting outsiders, serving three or four courses, eating with silver and similar things. Then I realized that I was spending too much and was no better off, so I decided to invite no one and to live at a good, ordinary rate. The silver I gave back to the people who had loaned it to me, both so I wouldn't have to look after it, and also because they often asked me to speak with Our Holiness concerning some need of theirs. I would do it, but their need was not met. So I determined to rid myself of this business, giving bother and blame to no one so that these could not be imputed to me.

In the morning, in this season, I rise at nine o'clock, and when I am dressed I go to the palace; not every morning, that is, but once every

---

[5]The church is now known as SS. Michele e Magno, in Borgo Santo Spirito.
[6]Giuliano Brancacci of Florence.

two or three days. Here, sometimes, I say twenty words to the Pope, ten to Cardinal de' Medici,[7] six to the magnificent Giuliano[8] (and if I cannot speak with him, I speak with Piero Ardinghelli[9]), and then I speak with whatever ambassador happens to be in those chambers. I learn some small thing, albeit of little importance. Having done this, I return home, save that sometimes I lunch with Cardinal de' Medici. Once back, I eat with my own people, and, sometimes, an outsider or two who come on their own, say Ser Sano, or that Ser Tommaso who was in Trent, Giovanni Rucellai or Giovanni Girolami. After eating I play cards, if I have someone to do it with, but if I don't have anyone, I walk through the church and the garden. Then I ride a little bit outside of Rome, when the weather is fine. At night I return home; and I have arranged to have many history books here, especially by Roman writers, which is to say Livy, with the epitome by Lucius Florus, Sallust, Plutarch, Appian of Alexandria, Cornelius Tacitus, Suetonius, Lampridius and Spartianus, and those others who wrote about the emperors: Herodian, Ammianus Marcellinus and Procopius. And with these I pass my time. I consider what emperors this poor Rome, who once caused the world to tremble, has suffered, and reflect that it is no great wonder that Rome could further tolerate two pontiffs of the kind that these last ones were. I write a letter once every four days to my lords the Ten,[10] and I tell some weary news of no importance, since I have nothing else to write for the reasons that you yourself understand. Then I go off to sleep, after I have dined and told some short story with Brancaccio and Messer Giovambatista Nasi, who often stays with me. On feast-days I hear mass, and I do not do as you, who often skip it. If you were to ask me whether I have any courtesan, I should reply that at the beginning, when I arrived, I had some as I wrote you. Then, frightened by the summer's air, I abstained. Nonetheless, I spoiled one of them, so that often she comes all by herself. She is quite reasonably beautiful, and her speech is charming. I have also in this place, although it is solitary, a neighbor woman who would not displease you, and although she is of noble family, she does business on the side.

[7] Giulio de' Medici (1478–1534), archbishop of Florence and illegitimate son of Giuliano di Piero de' Medici, was elevated to cardinal by Pope Leo X on September 23, 1513. In 1523 he was elected Pope Clement VII.

[8] Giuliano de' Medici (1479–1516), was the younger brother of Pope Leo X.

[9] Piero di Niccolò Ardinghelli (1470–1526) of Florence was the secretary of Pope Leo X. He is also mentioned in Document 3.

[10] The Ten of Liberty and Peace was the Florentine magistracy in charge of military and foreign affairs.

My Niccolò, I invite you to share this life! If you come here you will give me great pleasure, and then we shall return back there[11] together. Here you will have no other business save to go about looking, then return home, trade jokes and laugh. Nor do I want you to believe that I live like an ambassador, for I wanted always to be a free man. I dress sometimes in long robes and sometimes short ones; I ride alone, with servants on foot, and sometimes with them on horseback. I never go to the houses of cardinals because I have none to visit, except Medici[12] and sometimes Bibbiena[13] when he is healthy. Let everyone say what they like: if I don't satisfy them, let them recall me. For, in the end, I want to go home after a year and to have made some money after selling my robes and horses, and, if possible, I don't want to spend any of my own.

And I want you to believe this one thing for me, and I say it without flattery. Although I haven't labored much here, nonetheless the commotion is so great that one can't help but have dealings with very many men. In reality few of them satisfy me, and I have found no man of better judgment than yourself. "But we are dragged along by the Fates."[14] So that when I speak at length to certain persons, when I read their letters, I wonder to myself that they have achieved any rank at all, since their speech and letters are nothing but ceremonious displays, lies, and fables, and there are few of them who rise above mediocrity. Bernardo of Bibbiena, who is now a cardinal, has in truth a noble genius, and he is a man both facetious and discreet, and in his time he exerted himself in great labors. Nonetheless, now he is ill; he has been this way for three months, and I do not know whether he will again be what he once was. Often we exert ourselves in order to relax, but it doesn't work. For this reason, therefore, let's be happy, come what may. Remember that I am at our pleasure, and that I commend myself to you, to Filippo [Casavecchia] and Giovanni Machiavelli, to Donato, and to Messer Ciaio. Nothing more. May Christ watch over you.

> Franciscus Victorius, ambassador.
> The twenty-third day of November, 1513. Rome.

---

[11]To Florence.

[12]Cardinal Giulio de' Medici.

[13]Bernardo Dovizi da Bibbiena (1470–1520) was made cardinal-deacon of Santa Maria in Pórtico by Leo X in 1513.

[14]Vettori quotes Seneca, *Moral Letters,* 197. Machiavelli disagrees with this kind of fatalism in *Prince,* chapter 25.

3

NICCOLÒ MACHIAVELLI

Letter to Francesco Vettori

December 10, 1513

Machiavelli's letter to Francesco Vettori of December 10, 1513, in which he announces that he is writing a work On Principalities, *is the most famous private letter in the Western literary tradition. To his friend Vettori, Machiavelli offers an often moving and sometimes humorous account of how he spends his days and evenings on his farm at Sant'Andrea in Percussina, outside of Florence, while also describing his hopes for employment by the Medici family.*

Readers should understand the letter in the context of Machiavelli's lengthy and intense correspondence with Francesco Vettori, who was the Florentine ambassador to the court of Leo X in Rome. Machiavelli wrote the description of his day at Sant'Andrea in direct response to a letter from Vettori recounting his busy life in Rome (Document 2). Machiavelli thus did everything he could to highlight the contrast between his friend's situation and his own. There was also a good chance that Vettori would show or read from Machiavelli's letter to other persons in Rome. The letter's highly polished tone, with its frequent literary allusions and the writer's charming portrayal of himself as someone who has handled disappointment admirably ("my recent accidents"), probably reflect Machiavelli's wish that his letter will find an audience beyond Vettori. Possibly Machiavelli hoped that Vettori would pass this highly polished literary creation to Giuliano de' Medici himself, who, as the letter declares, is the intended dedicatee of On Principalities.

Although the letter is poignant—it splendidly communicates Machiavelli's feelings of isolation, and his unhappiness at the abrupt termination of his career in government—one should not accept everything in it at face value. To begin with, the reader needs to understand the letter in the context of Machiavelli's material situation in 1513. Machiavelli certainly experienced intense anguish as a consequence of losing his job in November 1512, and his arrest and torture before his release in March 1513. Machiavelli seems to have been just getting by on the proceeds

Machiavelli, *Lettere*, ed. Gaeta, in Machiavelli, *Opere*, 3: 423–28. Translated from the Italian by William J. Connell.

from his farm, and the Sant'Andrea farm had not been very profitable in the previous generation either, as we know from a record book kept by Machiavelli's father, Bernardo.[1] *Machiavelli was fortunate to have a farm to which to retreat during his political difficulties; it meant that he and his family would be provided for. In November 1512, when he was fired, Machiavelli was required to leave a security deposit of one thousand gold florins with the government, and presumably the government had recently restored those funds to him at the time he wrote this letter. Thus there is a certain exaggeration of Machiavelli's hardships in the letter of December 10.*

Moreover, although scholars often refer to Machiavelli's time at Sant' Andrea as a period of "exile," this is not quite accurate, inasmuch as Machiavelli was not required to stay at his farm. By the terms of his removal from office, he was allowed to move freely both in the city of Florence and outside, although for one year he was not permitted to enter his former workplace, the Palace of the Signoria, and he was not allowed to leave Florentine territory. On November 10, 1513, after a year of this restriction, Machiavelli was permitted to travel: hence Vettori's invitation to Rome in the previous letter (Document 2), and the discussion in this letter of a possible visit. Furthermore, Machiavelli was not quite as isolated at Sant'Andrea as some have thought, and as his letter at times seems to intimate. Sant'Andrea was only about six and a half kilometers from Florence, which meant that Machiavelli was able to go to and from the city without much difficulty. His farm was situated at a convenient spot along the principal road, known as the "Royal Roman Road" (strada regia romana), which connected Florence with Rome. The many ambassadors, messengers, merchants, and pilgrims who traveled between Rome and Florence all would have passed by Machiavelli's farm, and some would have dined or lodged at the local inn, the Albergaccio, which was partly owned by the Machiavelli family. Thus, even at his farm, Machiavelli was able to stay apprised of events in the political world he so sorely missed.[2]

---

[1] The country property was studied on the basis of this record book by Ildebrando Imberciadori, "I due poderi di Bernardo Machiavelli, ovvero mezzadria poderale nel '400," in *Studi in onore di Armando Sapori*, 2 vols. (Milan: Cisalpino, 1957), 2: 833–46.

[2] On the manuscript tradition of the letter, see Cecil H. Clough, "Machiavelli's 'Epistolario' and Again What Did Machiavelli Wear in the Country?" *Bulletin of the Society for Renaissance Studies*, 1, no. 3 (October 1983): 7–18. The original letter is lost, as is a draft Machiavelli appears to have retained. The text is based on a copy of Machiavelli's lost draft that was included in a manuscript compiled by Machiavelli's grandson, Giuliano de' Ricci, probably in the 1570s, known as the "Apografo Ricci." M uses *voi* and its forms throughout.

To the magnificent Florentine ambassador to the Highest Pontiff, my patron and benefactor. In Rome.

Magnificent ambassador: "Divine favors were never late."[3] I say this because it appeared to me not that I had lost your favor, but that I had misplaced it, since you had gone a long time without writing to me, and I was worrying how the cause could have arisen. And I took little account of all the causes that came to my mind, except for when I was worrying that you had pulled yourself back from writing to me because it had been written to you that I was not a good manager of your letters; and I knew that, apart from Filippo[4] and Paolo,[5] no others had seen them on my account.

I have had your favor restored in the latest letter of yours of the twenty-third of last month,[6] for which I remain most content to see how regularly and calmly you exercise that public office, and I counsel you to continue in this way, because I know how whoever abandons his own advantages for the advantages of others loses his own, and for him there is not the slightest acknowledgment. And since fortune wants to do everything, one should let her do it, stay calm and not give her trouble, and wait for a time that allows her to do something for men. And then will be the time for you to try harder, to survey matters better, and for me to leave my country house and say "Here I am." For this reason, since I want to make equal return of your favors, in this letter of mine I cannot say to you anything other than how my life is, and if you judge that it should be traded for yours, I shall be happy to exchange it.

I am staying in my country house, and since those latest accidents of mine happened,[7] I have not been in Florence twenty days if I count them all together. Until now I have been hunting thrushes by myself.[8]

---

[3]Petrarch, *Triumph of Eternity,* 13, in Francesco Petrarca, *Rime, Trionfi, e poesie latine,* ed. Ferdinando Neri, Guido Martellotti, Enrico Bianchi, and Natalino Sapegno (Milan and Naples: Ricciardi, 1951), 554. In a poem, *Serenade,* Machiavelli changed only one of the words in this Petrarchan line, writing: "Amorous favors never came late."

[4]Filippo Casavecchia. See Document 1.

[5]Paolo Vettori, Francesco's brother.

[6]Document 2.

[7]Machiavelli refers to his arrest and torture on a charge of conspiring against the Medici rulers of Florence, and to his unexpected release from prison.

[8]According to the terms of a late fifteenth-century lease on Machiavelli's farm, the tenants were prohibited from netting birds; Imberciadori, "I due poderi," 839. Presumably the privilege was reserved for the owners. Dante, *Purgatorio,* 23.3–6, criticizes those "who lose their lives chasing small birds," without realizing that "time should be spent more usefully."

I would rise before dawn, I would set the basket-traps, and, further, I would go out with a band of cages on my back, so that I seemed like Geta, when he was returning from the port with the books of Amphitryon,[9] and I would take at least two, and at most six thrushes. And thus I remained all September.[10] Afterward, to my displeasure, this diversion, although unseemly and strange, ended. How my life is now I shall tell you. I rise in the morning with the sun and I go out into a wood of mine that I am having cut, where I stay two hours to review the work of the previous day, and to pass time with those woodcutters, who always have some disaster at hand, either among themselves or with their neighbors. Concerning this wood I could have a thousand beautiful things to tell you that have befallen me, both with Fruosino da Panzano and with others who wanted some of this firewood. Fruosino in particular sent for certain cords without saying anything to me, and at payment time he wanted to hold back ten lire that he says he has been owed by me for four years, since he beat me at *cricca*[11] in the house of Antonio Guicciardini. I began to raise the devil; I wanted to accuse the carter who had gone there for the woodpiles as a thief; however Giovanni Machiavelli then intervened and set us in agreement. Batista Guicciardini, Filippo Ginori, Tommaso del Bene and certain other citizens, when that north wind was blowing,[12] each took a cord from me. I promised some to everyone; and I sent one of the cords to Tommaso, which was counted in Florence as a half-cord, because to stack it there were Tommaso, his wife, his servants, and his children, and they looked like Gabburra on a Thursday, when with those apprentices of his, he clubs an ox.[13] The result was, when I saw

---

[9]The reference is to a popular fifteenth-century verse novella, *Geta and Birria*. Amphitryon, who has returned from studying philosophy in Athens, gives his servant Geta a great load of books to carry. In a humorous passage, Geta, loaded down by the books, attempts to persuade a second servant, Birria, to carry them for him. John M. Najemy, *Between Friends: Discourses of Power and Desire in the Machiavelli Letter of 1513–1515* (Princeton: Princeton University Press, 1993), 225–30, suggests that Machiavelli likens himself to Geta, Vettori to Birria, and *The Prince* to the load of books.

[10]This appears to conflict with the phrase "Until now," which appears a few lines earlier. Ridolfi proposed changing this to "November," when the migration of birds through Tuscany comes to an end. Gaeta points out that Machiavelli could have made the mistake.

[11]*cricca:* a card game.

[12]Machiavelli refers to his recent political troubles as a cold "north wind."

[13]"Gabburra" was in all probability a butcher. Typically a butcher and his assistants would club the legs of an ox to bring it to a kneeling position for slaughtering. The image Machiavelli means to convey is of a team of people swinging clubs. He suggests that Tommaso and his family beat down the firewood in order to turn their full cartload of wood into half a cartload.

to whose profit it was, that I said to the others that I have no more firewood. And they all have made a big point of it, especially Batista, who numbers this among the other disasters of Prato.[14]

When I have left the wood, I go out to a spring, and from there to a birding site of mine. I have a book under my cloak, either Dante or Petrarch, or one of these minor poets: Tibullus, Ovid and ones like them. I read of those amorous passions of theirs and of their loves, I remember my own, and I delight for a while in these thoughts. Then I put myself on the road to the inn, I speak with those who pass by, I ask for news of their countries, I learn various things, and I note the varying tastes and diverse characters of men. During this the hour for dinner comes, when with my family I eat of those foods that this poor villa and very small patrimony permit. When I have eaten, I return to the inn; here is the host, and ordinarily a butcher, a miller and two brickmakers. With these men I loaf about the whole day, playing *cricca* and backgammon, and so forth, whence arise a thousand disputes and infinite insults with injurious words, and most of the time a *quattrino*[15] is being fought over, and nonetheless we are heard to be shouting by San Casciano.[16] In this way, folded up with these lice, I shake the mold from my brain, and I vent the malignity of this fate of mine, since I am glad that she should trample me in this way in order that I may see whether she feels any shame about it.

When evening comes, I return home, and I enter into my study; and at the door I take off my everyday dress, full of mud and of dirt, and I put on royal and courtly clothes; and decently dressed I enter into the ancient courts of ancient men, where, received lovingly by them, I eat the only food which is mine, and for which I was born. There I am not ashamed to speak with them, and to ask them the reason for their actions; and they, in their humanity, answer me. And for four hours at a time I feel no boredom. I forget all trouble, I do not fear poverty, death does not frighten me. I put myself completely at their disposal. And because Dante says that what has been learned does not become knowledge unless it is retained,[17] I have noted down what I have capitalized

---

[14]Battista di Braccio Guicciardini was *podestà* (governor) and commissioner of Prato when Spanish troops sacked the city on August 29, 1512. With the city lost, Battista attempted to flee, but was captured and put in irons by the Spanish, who put a ransom of 1,000 florins on his head; see Francesco Guicciardini, *Le lettere,* ed. Pierre Jodogne, 1 (Rome: Istituto Storico Italiano per l'Età Moderna e Contemporanea, 1986), 226.

[15]*quattrino:* a coin of small worth, like a penny.

[16]A town approximately five kilometers to the south on the road to Rome.

[17]Dante, *Paradiso,* 5. 41–42.

through my conversation with them, and composed a small work *On Principalities,* in which I immerse myself as much as I can in the understandings of this subject, discussing what a principality is, of what kinds they are, how they are acquired, how they are maintained, why they are lost. And if ever any fantasy of mine did please you, this one should not displease you; and for a prince, and especially for a new prince, it should be welcome. For this reason I am addressing it to the magnificence of Giuliano. Filippo Casavecchia has seen it; he will be able to inform you in part of both the thing in itself and the reasonings that I have had with him, although I am still adding to it and cleaning it.

You would like, magnificent Ambassador, that I should leave this life and come to enjoy yours with you. I shall do it any case, but what tempt me now are certain affairs of mine that I shall have completed within six weeks. What makes me remain doubtful is that those Soderini are there,[18] since I would be forced, if I come there, to visit and to speak with them. I would worry that on my return I could not believe I would dismount at home and I would dismount in the Bargello,[19] because although this state has the greatest foundations and great security, nevertheless it is new, and for this reason suspicious, nor is there a lack of wiseacres who, to appear like Paolo Bertini, would turn others into boarders[20] and would leave the reckoning to me. I beg you to forgive me on account of this fear, and afterward I shall come within the stated time to visit you in any case.

I have reasoned with Filippo about this small work of mine, whether it were well to give it or not to give it; and if it is well to give it, whether it were well that I should bring it, or that I should send it to you. What was making me not give it was the worry that it would not be read by Giuliano, apart from anyone else, and that this Ardinghelli[21] would get himself honor from this latest labor of mine. What was making me give it was the necessity that hounds me, because I am consuming myself, and I cannot stay this way for a long time lest through poverty I become contemptible, and further the desire I would have that these Medici lords should begin to make use of me,

---

[18]Pier Soderini, the former Florentine head of state, and his brother, Cardinal Francesco Soderini, were not viewed favorably by the Medici, but they had been close associates and patrons of Machiavelli until 1512, and he would have felt obligated to call upon them.

[19]The Florentine Palace of Justice, where criminals were tried.

[20]In other words, into prisoners.

[21]Pietro Ardinghelli, also mentioned in Document 2. Machiavelli is afraid that Ardinghelli will plagiarize *The Prince.* See also p. 18 above.

even if they should begin by having me roll a stone;[22] because, if then I do not win them over to me, I would complain of myself; and as for this thing, once it were read, it would be seen that the fifteen years I spent studying[23] the art of the state were neither slept through nor gambled away; and everyone should hold it dear to make use of one who at the expense of others is full of experience. And of my faith one should not doubt, because, since I have always observed faith, I do not need to learn now how to break it; and whoever has been faithful and good for forty-three years,[24] as I have, does not have to change his nature; and to my faith and goodness my poverty is witness.

I would therefore desire that you too write me what you think about this matter, and to you I commend myself. Be happy.

> 10 December 1513.
> Niccolò Machiavelli, at my country house.

[22]Like Sisyphus.
[23]Literally, "at university in."
[24]Machiavelli was forty-four at the time of the letter, but he was forty-three when he lost his job in 1512.

4

NICCOLÒ MACHIAVELLI

The Thrushes

1513

It has been argued that Machiavelli wrote the following poem as a dedicatory sonnet to accompany The Prince, *the first version of which Machiavelli wrote for Giuliano de' Medici,[1] as we know from his letter to Vettori of December 10, 1513 (Document 3). The poem announces a gift of thrushes Machiavelli sent to Giuliano. Sending birds from the country*

[1]Hugo Jaeckel, "I 'tordi' e il 'principe nuovo.' Note sulle dediche del 'Principe' di Machiavelli a Giuliano e a Lorenzo de' Medici," *Archivio storico italiano*, 156 (1998), 73–92. The argument is endorsed and finds further support in Riccardo Fubini, "Postilla ai 'Tordi'," ibid., 93ff.

Niccolò Machiavelli, *Lust and Liberty: The Poems of Machiavelli*, trans. Joseph Tusiani (New York: Obolensky, 1963), 46.

(to be eaten as delicacies) was a common way of paying homage, win-
ning favor, or expressing thanks in Renaissance Italy.[2] *But since these*
thrushes, as Machiavelli describes them, are "neither good nor fat at all,"
it is possible that they are a conceit for The Prince, *the work that Machi-*
avelli hoped would redeem his reputation and stop the men around Giu-
liano from "rending" his "name and right."

I'm sending you, Giuliano, if I might,
Several thrushes — a small gift, I guess,
But good to make Your Lordship think a bit
Of your poor Machiavello in distress.

And if you have around you men who bite,
Into their throats you may soon force all this,
So that, while eating of these birds, who knows!
They may stop rending some man's name and right.

But you will say: "How can these birds achieve
All this, being neither good nor fat at all?
Of touching them my men would not conceive."

Then let me tell you this: As they recall,
I am too thin, yet of my flesh they leave
No inch untried by their teeth's hungry fall.

Oh, answer not the call
Of empty words, my Lord; and judge and see,
Not with your eyes but with your hands, my plea.

---

[2]Thus Roberto Ridolfi, *Vita di Niccolò Machiavelli,* 7th rev. ed. (Florence: Sansoni,
1978), 507 n. 25, argues that the poem really did accompany a gift of thrushes.

5

RICCARDO RICCARDI

Machiavelli's Presentation of The Prince to Lorenzo de' Medici

ca. 1515

Riccardo di Giovanni Riccardi (1558–1612) was a Florentine who gathered information about Machiavelli in the second half of the sixteenth century. In a record book he kept, Riccardi wrote down an anecdote concerning the audience that Machiavelli had with Lorenzo de' Medici when he presented him with a copy of The Prince, *a work dedicated to Lorenzo. Although Riccardi's account was written nearly sixty-five years after the event, most scholars agree that it contains some truth. Riccardi had access to people who had known Machiavelli, and to documents that have since been lost. The story is also consonant with what we know of Lorenzo's character. The young prince, for instance, was keenly interested in hunting. We do not know precisely when Machiavelli presented his work to Lorenzo, although most scholars believe he did it in 1515. The presentation manuscript of* The Prince *is not known to survive.*

Niccolò Machiavelli presented to [Lorenzo di] Piero de' Medici his book on *The Prince*. And it counted against him that he happened to give it to him at the same time that a brace of hunting dogs was given to him, whereupon Lorenzo gave greater thanks and responded in a friendlier way to the man who had given him the dogs, than to [Machiavelli]. Hence [Machiavelli] went away offended. And he had occasion to say, among his friends, that he was the kind of man who could make conspiracies against the prince, but that, all the same, if [the Medici] observed his methods [in *The Prince*], they would see that conspiracies resulted from it, as if he meant to say that his book would get him his revenge.

Cecil H. Clough, *Machiavelli Researches* (Naples: Istituto Universitario Orientale, 1967), 67–68. Translated from the Italian by William J. Connell.

NICCOLÒ GUICCIARDINI

FROM *A Letter to Luigi Guicciardini*
July 29, 1517

In a letter to his father written in 1517 a young Florentine, Niccolò Guicciardini, mentioned The Prince. *The letter, most of which is published below, is one of our earliest solid indications that people were reading the book in manuscript, and it provides a helpful indication of how one of Machiavelli's Florentine contemporaries first interpreted the work. At the time Niccolò wrote his letter he was studying law. His family, the Guicciardini, was one of Florence's most prominent families. An uncle, Francesco Guicciardini, who was then serving as papal governor of Reggio and Modena, would later write a great* History of Italy. *Niccolò's father, Luigi, to whom the letter was addressed, was serving as commissioner general in the subject city of Arezzo, where the residents were of dubious loyalty to Florence. In a letter intended to give the latest news from home, Niccolò mentions the situation in Arezzo, and suggests that one option would be for his father "to do what Machiavelli, in that work of his* On Principalities, *says that Iuriotto of Fermo did when he wanted to become lord of Fermo." The reference is to the discussion in chapter 8 of* The Prince *of Liverotto of Fermo, whom Niccolò probably calls "Iuriotto" because he is writing from memory. As Machiavelli tells it, Liverotto invited the leading citizens of Fermo to a banquet where he had them all killed.* The Prince *describes this as a complete success, because Liverotto became "secure in the city of Fermo" and "frightening to all of his neighbors." Niccolò is not entirely serious in his proposal; as he writes, "even then one could not entirely trust the rest" of the Aretine citizenry. The letter shows that this young Florentine, like readers ever since, was struck by the fact that Machiavelli could discuss a terrible crime as a useful tool of statecraft.*

Honorable father, etc. I learn from a letter of yours recently arrived the judgment you make of these things of the Spaniards: that you think that if no extraordinary case arises, the things should settle themselves

John N. Stephens and Humfrey C. Butters, "New Light on Machiavelli," *English Historical Review*, 97 (1982): 54–69. Translated from the Italian by William J. Connell.

in a good state with the coming of these Swiss, and it seems to me that in the way you discuss them you judge them very well. But then, on the other hand, what I learn here and from Jacopo,[1] who has returned from the countryside, and from Battista[2] and from the others, which is, according to my interpretation, a commonly held small hope for a good outcome, gives me annoyance, and I cannot decide who is deceiving himself. For I presume that you who are there, in its presence, one can say, learn these things directly; yet I think that Jacopo, if it is not his wicked wish to give us annoyance, judges according to what he learns, and it seems reasonable that he is not told things the opposite of what they are. I am half confused, yet I attend to your judgment, because I believe you are better informed than these others; although continually Jacopo and Francesco[3] tell me that you are making a mistake, and that you are not well advised concerning current things. And I believe that if you were here, and could hear what they are deciding on, although it seemed reasonable to you that the opposite should happen, in order to completely satisfy them, and to maintain them in their errors, you would make a show of agreeing with their views, and maybe, on that account, they would also then become more generous in writing than they are, since they see you as being of a different spirit and contrary to theirs. But to me, however, it seems that if our enemies turn toward you, as you show you have some suspicion, you would endure no small trouble in defending yourself, considering the small steadiness and faith of those Aretines toward our city. And it would be needed, if one wanted to secure Arezzo for oneself, to do what Machiavelli in that work of his *On Principalities* says that Iuriotto of Fermo did when he wanted to become lord of Fermo, and even then one could not entirely trust the rest. So may God keep this away from you, and instead send that plague on the backs of others. I am sorry that there is, as you write, such very great heat there, and I would advise you to watch out, if I did not believe that you will do it without further reminders. Your letter was given to Jacopo, and, as for everything you desire, I believe I am responding to you by the bearer. Francesco, unbecomingly, has a bit of business, and, for that reason, if he does not respond to you today, there is nothing to wonder about. . . .

---

[1] Jacopo di Piero di Jacopo Guicciardini was Niccolò's uncle and Luigi's brother.
[2] Battista di Braccio Guicciardini, also mentioned in Document 3.
[3] The historian Francesco Guicciardini.

Nothing else, save that I pray you to write me as you have done. Now I commend myself to you. The 29th day of July.

Your Niccolò Guicciardini, in Florence.
To the magnificent man, Luigi Guicciardini, Florentine Commissioner General, illustrious and honorable father. In Arezzo.

7

Early Prefaces of The Prince

Machiavelli's Prince *was considered a shocking work, and this was probably one of the reasons its author did not publish it in his lifetime. All the same,* The Prince *circulated in manuscript, and a few years after the author's death, the book was published in two competing editions, one in Rome and one in Florence. In view of the work's notoriety, it is interesting to read how the persons responsible for copying the treatise in manuscript and for publishing the first editions justified their part in disseminating it in the prefaces they wrote.*

BIAGIO BUONACCORSI

Prefatory Letter to Pandolfo Bellacci

ca. 1516–1517

Biagio Buonaccorsi, who had been a close friend and collaborator of Machiavelli's in the Florentine chancery, prefaced a manuscript copy of The Prince *that he made for his friend Pandolfo Bellacci with the following letter. Both Buonaccorsi and Machiavelli had been fired from their chancery posts when the Medici family returned to Florence in 1512, although most of their colleagues retained their jobs. At some point there*

Niccolò Machiavelli, *De Principatibus,* ed. Giorgio Inglese (Rome: Istituto Storico Italiano per il Medio Evo, 1994), 47. Translated from the Italian by William J. Connell.

appears to have been a falling out between Machiavelli and Buonac-corsi, and it has been suggested that the opening lines of this letter, which speak of "the little faith of men," refer to Buonaccorsi's disappointment with Machiavelli.[1] *Buonaccorsi must still have thought well of his for-mer friend, however, because he calls on Bellacci to defend* The Prince, *even though he recognizes there are those who may want to criticize it. The letter cannot be dated precisely, but it is probably from 1516–17. Because Buonaccorsi calls* The Prince *"newly composed," it appears that Machiavelli's* Prince *had remained on his desk since the period of its original composition in 1513–14, and that it was only now beginning to circulate.*

Biagio Buonaccorsi to Pandolfo Bellacci, a special friend, greetings.

Among other Greek proverbs, dearest Pandolfo, one reads of one the substance of which is, "Friends hold all things in common."[2] Although, on account of the malignity of the times and the little faith of men, this proverb has failed to achieve that ancient and perfect observance it used to have, that is no reason for it not to be preserved and continued in with the same integrity that is looked for in an action that is so perfect and affectionate. Since at present, as always in the past, I do not wish to depart from this proverb, because you are not only my friend but my protector, I send you the small work, newly composed, *On Principalities,* by our Niccolò Machiavelli. In this you will find written down, with the greatest transparency and brevity, all of the qualities of principalities, all of the ways to preserve them, all of the harms they suffer, with an exact account of the ancient and mod-ern histories and many other most useful documents, so that if you will read with that same attention that you devote to other things, I am most certain that you will draw from it no small utility. Receive it, therefore, with that readiness that it warrants, and prepare yourself to be its keenest defender against all those who, out of malignity or envy, might wish, according to the practice of these times, to bite and to lac-erate it. Be well.

---

[1] Enrico Niccolini makes this suggestion in Biagio Buonaccorsi, *Diario dall'anno 1498 all'anno 1512, e altri scritti,* ed. E. Niccolini (Rome: Istituto Storico Italiano per il Medio Evo, 1999), xviii–xx.
[2] The initial proverb in Erasmus' very popular *Adages,* first published in 1500.

TEOFILO MOCHI
Preface to a Manuscript of The Prince
ca. 1530

Teofilo Mochi was a notary from Siena who made a manuscript copy of The Prince *about 1530. Mochi's brief preface addresses a wide readership, and therefore seems to indicate an intention, never fulfilled, to publish the first printed edition of* The Prince.

Do not hope, o readers, to read a more welcome, more worthy, and more necessary reading than this little work that is given to you, if you want to know what lords who rule have to attend to, and to know those who have the spirit to become lords and to rule. For here you will see written down, with ancient and new examples, all of those things that pertain to princes. However many and of whatever qualities these things may be, there is no one who should not both know and think about them. Farewell.

Teofilo Mochi, "Preface to a Manuscript of *The Prince*," in Niccolò Machiavelli, *De Principatibus*, ed. Giorgio Inglese (Rome: Istituto Storico Italiano per il Medio Evo, 1994), 39. Translated from the Italian by William J. Connell.

ANTONIO BLADO
Dedicatory Letter to Filippo Strozzi
January 4, 1532

The following dedicatory letter, addressed by the printer Antonio Blado (1490–1567) to Filippo Strozzi, appeared in the first edition of Machiavelli's Prince, *which was published in Rome in 1532. Some of the impetus to publish Machiavelli's works, which was done with papal permission, probably derived not from their political content, but from the sixteenth-century*

Antonio Blado, "Dedicatory Letter to Filippo Strozzi," in Niccolò Machiavelli, *De Principatibus*, ed. Rinaldo Rinaldi, in Machiavelli, *Opere*, 1:1, 403–6. Translated from the Italian by William J. Connell.

literary quarrel over the suitability of the Tuscan dialect as the written language to be used by educated Italians. Machiavelli was known as an eminent Tuscan writer, and thus Blado writes that "Machiavelli is easily praised today for speaking well and accurately."

This printed edition was dedicated to the wealthy Florentine banker, Filippo Strozzi (1489–1538), a friend and correspondent of Machiavelli's who reportedly visited him on his deathbed (see Documents 9 and 10). Strozzi was also a close friend and financial backer of Pope Clement VII, so he may have helped secure permission to publish Machiavelli's works in Rome. Furthermore, as Blado points out in his letter, Strozzi was the brother-in-law of Lorenzo de' Medici, now dead, to whom Machiavelli had dedicated The Prince. *Although Lorenzo failed to appreciate* The Prince *(see Document 5), Blado suggests that Strozzi will now give the work its due. The letter contains rhetorical echoes of many passages in* The Prince, *but the printer appears oblivious to the work's harsh political implications and to its unsavory reputation, which was already established in Florence on the basis of manuscript copies.*

TO THE VERY MAGNIFICENT LORD,

MY PATRON,

MESSER FILIPPO STROZZI, A FLORENTINE NOBLEMAN

Since I, most worthy Messer Filippo, in accordance with my lowly ability, have decided to give some luster (for men who are worthy of it) to my everyday trade,[1] which is now in poor condition, I have contrived to act like one who by himself is not sufficient to assume any worthwhile rank, and who approaches a sumptuous prelate, or a powerful prince or a valorous captain, so that, whether through the strength of such a mediator, or through the authority of such a patron, he makes his servile condition less ignominious. And while considering what subject would be apt to satisfy this bold appetite of mine, what occurred to me was what often occurs to the industrious potter, who, with the same clay, makes vessels that are more honorable and less honorable (such that he carries off more honor from the more honorable ones, and less honor from the less honorable ones), when he tries by means of the more honored product to ennoble his craft as much as he can.[2] Not otherwise do I feel has it befallen to me, since a little while ago I, with these small letters of mine[3]

---

[1] As a printer.
[2] The metaphor is taken from Romans, 9:21.
[3] The printer's type.

(which are fighters more for the name of others than for my own name), was accustomed to give to the populace whatever the opportunity for greater gain used to offer; yet I have wished, in the shadow of a man who is valorous and prized, that these small letters might not only find respect, but also be honored by some worthier subject. And I have hoped, through the opportunity to secure another person's praise, to mask my own hitherto inopportune errors, which, through my ignorance of the art I have allowed to occur. Therefore, while I was meandering through the ample and most amenable slopes of Tuscan eloquence, there offered itself to me *The Prince*[4] of Messer Niccolò Machiavelli, your friend, and a Florentine citizen, who, on account of the excellence of his genius and the sagacity of his judgment, is easily praised today for speaking well and accurately. Now that, through another person's[5] industry, I have repaired my own defects, I am persuaded that this honorable ambition of mine has turned out happily, not only in the other things of [Machiavelli's] that I have published,[6] but also in this one. For just as he considered the writing about principalities to be of greater importance than other writings,[7] so he names *The Prince* as his work that treats of the affairs of princes. In it he tried to construct a new prince, one who would acquire the name of prince no less by nature than by fortune. And, since the author addressed this well-ordered work of his to the magnificent Lorenzo de' Medici, your brother-in-law, who possessed the effectual principate,[8] I have decided to address my diligent labor in printing it to you, and so to associate my labor with another imagined prince, one who lacks nothing, save the effectual principate, for him to be called "prince" in truth.[9] Such you certainly are, my most worthy Messer Filippo, for your manners are of a sort that easily we may count you among those who have held the principate, and put you in the company of whomever[10] our author thought should be in the company of his ideal prince. This renders me certain, having attended to your virtue, nobility and outstanding parts, that, if Machiavelli himself had not woven together this little garland for him[11] whom he has adorned with very

---

[4]It was Blado who gave *The Prince* the title it still goes by. Early manuscripts, and Machiavelli himself, usually referred to the book as *On Principalities*.

[5]Machiavelli's.

[6]Blado had previously published Machiavelli's *Discourses on Livy,* on October 18, 1531.

[7]Machiavelli's dedicatory letter, states "I have not found among my valuables anything that I hold more dear or estimate so highly. . . ."

[8]Compare *Prince,* chapter 6, on the "effectual truth"; and chapter 15, on Hiero II of Syracuse.

[9]Machiavelli uses similar words in his dedication of the *Discourses.*

[10]Lorenzo, Machiavelli's dedicatee.

[11]Lorenzo.

sweet flowers, he could easily have placed it on your head. For you are a man who, because of your experience, would have recognized its importance, because of your nobility, would have appreciated it, and, because of your authority, would have given it reputation among those you know and among those who have some sense of your exemplary actions.[12] For these reasons, and for many others that for brevity's sake I omit, I have judged it very well that this gift is appropriate for you. And thus I give it you, both to show you in part how much I owe you, and also, as I have said already, to embellish my work with such names and to defend myself with such a champion against whoever in this might wish wrongly to calumniate me. And thus, bowing, I recommend myself to you. In Rome, the fourth day of January of the year MDXXXII.

At your service,
Antonio Blado of Asola,[13]
printer of books.

[12]Blado implies that in these respects Lorenzo failed Machiavelli.
[13]Asola is a small town near Mantua.

BERNARDO GIUNTA

Dedicatory Letter to Giovanni Gaddi

May 8, 1532

Four months after the publication of The Prince *in Rome, Bernardo Giunta in Florence published a competing edition that, unlike Blado's, had the formal permission of Machiavelli's heirs. Giunta's dedicatory letter shows that he approached the publication of* The Prince *with caution. In Florence, the circulation of manuscript versions had already made* The Prince *a notorious work. Its Florentine printer thus asks his dedicatee, Monsignor Giovanni Gaddi, to defend* The Prince *against persons who, he says, "go about lacerating" the book "harshly, all day long," a phrase that appears to echo Biagio Buonaccorsi's prefatory letter to Pandolfo Bellaci. Gaddi, a Florentine prominent in the Papal Curia, helped to arrange the publication and papal permission for Blado's earlier edition in Rome, and Giunta probably thought it would be helpful to enlist this churchman to fend off the criticism he feared his Florentine edition would encounter. To further deflect accusations of promoting a scandalous work, Giunta takes the unusual step of quoting and directing the reader to Agostino Nifo's earlier* On Skill in Ruling, *which had published large sections of* The Prince *in Latin (Document 8). Because this material already appeared in Nifo's Latin version, Giunta argues, he should bear no personal responsibility for publishing whatever might be found objectionable in* The Prince.

TO THE MOST REVEREND MONSIGNOR
MESSER GIOVANNI GADDI,
CLERIC OF THE APOSTOLIC CHAMBER
AND HIS MOST WORTHY PATRON

Now that we have additionally printed, reverend Monsignor, after the *Discourses* and the *Histories* of your Niccolò Machiavelli, his *Prince,* with a few other small works, and since we would like to publish it, according to our custom, under the name of some honored person, there sprang to mind immediately your reverend lordship, who, although perhaps it is not really worthy of your lordship's greatness, may take it nonetheless willingly, and with that spirit in which I offer it to your lordship. And may your lordship defend it from those persons who, because of its subject, go about lacerating it so harshly, all day long, not knowing that those who teach herbs and medicines equally teach poisons too, only so that we may defend ourselves from them because we know them.[1] Nor yet do they realize that there is no art or science whatsoever that may not be used wickedly by those who are bad. And who would ever say that iron was discovered rather to kill men than to defend ourselves against animals? Certainly, as I believe, no one. For which reason, leaving these persons aside, and to speak instead with those who have more sincere judgment, I say that both they and all those who are yet to come ought to be much obliged and obligated to your most reverend lordship, through whose courtesy and humanity both the *Discourses* and the *Histories* (which have been desired so much, by so many, for so long) have finally come to light;[2] and for the work and diligence of those persons (who are so many and

---

[1] Compare Agostino Nifo's dedication to Charles V of *On Skill in Ruling* (Document 8).
[2] The *Discourses* and the *Florentine Histories* were published before *The Prince.*

Machiavelli, *De Principatibus,* ed. Rinaldi, in Machiavelli, *Opere,* 1:1, 407–9. Translated from the Italian by William J. Connell.

so excellent) that your lordship keeps in his household, through which they were corrected and emended. And, in truth, if there is any-one in this corrupt age who may be likened to that ancient Maecenas,[3] who was so greatly praised, it is really you. For since you delight in all of the virtues, you know all of them; and to all the professors and lovers of the virtues you are no less a friend than the friendliest sup-porter and the readiest donor. But now is not the time, nor is it appro-priate for me to tell of the innumerable merits of your lordship; however, this much I shall say, that in so far as regards the memory of Machiavelli, he is no less obliged to you for this single work than for the other two,[4] even though there have already been those who, after in good part translating it into the Latin language, have sent it out into print as theirs, as anyone will be able easily to see, if he reads the ear-lier one[5] and this one which is newly printed (but typeset a while ago[6]) in your name. If this printing is still not fully corrected,[7] may your lordship excuse it, both on account of the brevity of time[8] and the ignorance of the foreign printers.[9] To your reverend lordship I humbly recommend myself, and I pray your lordship as much as I may that, by accepting happily the offered gift (such as it is), your lordship may also accept me among the number of his other servants and friends, for whose sake may God keep your lordship happy for a long time, and give your lordship the greatest good that your lordship desires.

From Florence, the eighth day of May of the year MDXXXII.

> Your most reverend lordship's,
> Ser Bernardo Giunta.

[3]Gaius Maecenas (d. 8 BCE) was the patron of the Roman poets Virgil, Horace, and Propertius.

[4]Giunta implies that for religious reasons *The Prince* was more difficult to publish than the *Discourses* and the *Florentine Histories.*

[5]Nifo's *On Skill in Ruling.*

[6]An attempt to claim priority, even though Blado's edition had appeared earlier.

[7]In fact Giunta corrected numerous errors in Blado's edition.

[8]This contradicts the assertion that the edition was "typeset a while ago."

[9]Some of the workers at Italian presses came from Germany.

8

AGOSTINO NIFO

FROM *On Skill in Ruling*

1523

Although Machiavelli's Prince *did not appear in print until 1532, five years after his death, Agostino Nifo published a rewriting of* The Prince *in Latin in 1523. Nifo was one of the most important Renaissance philosophers in the Aristotelian tradition. His treatise,* On Skill in Ruling, *was dedicated to Charles V, who in 1519 became Holy Roman Emperor. It was divided into five books, of which only the fifth was original; Nifo borrowed the first four books almost entirely from Machiavelli's* Prince. *The borrowings (or translations into Latin) were so extensive that scholars have frequently called Nifo's work a "plagiarism"—and certainly it would be considered such by modern standards. Close examination, however, has shown that although he fully plagiarized Machiavelli's distinctions and historical examples, Nifo effectively rewrote the work, plowing in much additional learning, and turning it into a treatise that was less critical of the church and that presented a traditional moral message.*

The circumstances that led to Nifo's adaptation of the still unpublished Prince *remain obscure. The volume contains no acknowledgment of Nifo's borrowing from Machiavelli, yet Nifo was closer to Machiavelli than one would know from reading* On Skill in Ruling. *Indeed the author of* The Prince *may well have been complicit in Nifo's adaptation of his work. By 1523, when Nifo's book was published, Machiavelli had returned to the good graces of the Medici family. At the behest of Cardinal Giulio de' Medici (later Pope Clement VII), Machiavelli received an appointment through the Florentine university in Pisa as official historiographer of Florence. Nifo was also a devoted follower of the Medici. In 1519, on Cardinal Giulio's request, Nifo had written a treatise,* On the Immortality of the Soul against Pomponazzi, *for which he was rewarded with a professorship at Pisa. Thus Nifo and Machiavelli were, in a way, university*

Agostino Nifo, *De regnandi peritia* (Naples, 1532), photographic reprint in Simone Pernet-Beau and Paul Larivaille, *Une réécriture du Prince du Machiavel: le "De regnandi peritia" de Agostino Nifo* (Nanterre: Université Paris X-Nanterre, 1987), 1, 5, 7–11, 117–21. Translated from the Latin by William J. Connell.

colleagues. It is also interesting that Machiavelli's extensive surviving correspondence never mentions Nifo's rewriting of The Prince, *even though Machiavelli was quite sensitive about receiving credit as an author. Thus it seems plausible that Machiavelli was in some way involved with Nifo's 1523 adaptation of* The Prince.[1]

Two epigrams by Girolamo Borgia, Nifo's dedicatory letter to Charles V, and two chapters of On Skill in Ruling *are translated below. The epigrams and dedication give a good feeling for the flowery classical rhetoric that was typical of Machiavelli's humanist contemporaries and quite different from Machiavelli's more direct, pungent style of writing. Book 1, chapter 1 of* On Skill in Ruling, *corresponding to chapter 1 of* The Prince, *presents a much expanded version of Machiavelli's opening distinction between republics and principalities. Book 4, chapter 11 of* On Skill in Ruling, *corresponding to chapter 18 of* The Prince, *transforms Machiavelli's famous discussion of the question of whether a prince should keep his word.*

Epigram by Girolamo Borgia

What makes peoples joyous and cities happy?
    What makes a king like a god on earth?
This is what Nifo teaches. You, Caesar,[2] perform this sacred task.
    You have a field in which you may be a god.

By the Same

How well Nifo shows the way to rule and the arts
    That make kingdoms last for a long time, and for what reason they
      fall.
And what makes a king, who manages public affairs, like a god,
    And at the same time makes kingdoms happy.
If kings follow well all of your precepts, Nifo,
    Plato will see the work that he wanted for so long.
O may either your mind belong to many kings,
    Or may fortune grant you a royal scepter!

---

[1]The case for Machiavelli's involvement is made by Sergio Bertelli, "Machiavelli riproposto in tutte le sue opere," *Archivio storico italiano,* 157 (1999): 789–800, esp. 792–93.
[2]The Holy Roman Emperor, Charles V.

Nifo's Dedicatory Letter to Charles V

Since previously, O most invincible Emperor Charles, I published under the name of your highness that small commentary that was titled *On the False Prediction of a Flood,* believing that I had made a thing more pleasant than useful, I have decided to dedicate this next one to you also, which is titled *On Skill in Ruling,* since indeed, on account of the many kingdoms you rule, I judge the work to be more necessary by far. Although skill in ruling is almost natural and inherent for you who come from a series of so many kings and emperors, nonetheless, so that I might give (as is said in the proverb) spurs to a running horse, I shall not hesitate to write for you all those things that we have taken that were known in ancient historical writings, and what we have found narrated by more recent historians, and what we have learned from the so many wars that were conducted for so many years in Italy. You will find briefly explained among these things deeds that are tyrannical and deeds that are kingly, just as in medical writings you find poisons and antidotes, the former so that you may avoid them, the latter so that you may follow after them. We have divided the whole of our material among five books. In the first book are narrated the ways by which private persons acquire kingdoms; in the second book, arms, soldiers and the ways in which kingdoms are defended against invasion by enemies; in the third book, the laws, the ruses, the deceits by which the same kingdoms are preserved against the attacks, defections and rebellions of subjects. In the fourth book certain things are narrated that are common to arms and to laws that are useful to both. In the fifth book, finally, there is shown the honest kind of ruling. I request no other prize for so many labors, o greatest Caesar, than that you diligently read these books. For I know that from that reading itself we, who are under your empire, will carry off a great profit. May Your Highness be well and rule happily for a long time.

Book I, Chapter 1: How many kinds of domination there are

The greatest philosophers, Plato and Aristotle, divided the domination by which man commands man into two kinds, of which one is called a "republic" and the other the "principality of one person." The Greeks call the republic a *politeia,* and they call the principality of one man a "monarchy." Where many people command, therefore, it is a republic; and where one man rules it is a monarchy. Now, where one man rules, either he procures the common good for himself and his subjects, which domination the Greeks called *basileia,* and our people a "kingdom"; or he procures his own good, which domination the Greeks said was a "tyranny" and the Romans a personal "domination," although "domination" later came to be used to refer to any kind of principality. But when more than one person rules, the domination is now subdivided among several forms. For aristocracy, which is said to be "the principality of the best men" is one form, and *demarchia,* in which the people command, is another. And if the latter defends its liberty with its own forces, and not with mercenary soldiers, it is called, as Polybius said, a "democracy." An oligarchy, in which the power belongs to a few men, is yet another form. But leaving aside the different forms of power in which more than one rules, we shall pursue the one that is called "monarchy," which is the principality of one person, for it is with this that we are chiefly concerned. The principality, therefore, is either ancient or new. If it is ancient, it is established by hereditary succession or it emerges from an election. A principality may be ancient that nevertheless is established by election, as are the principalities of the Roman pontiffs, and of the Emperors, and of the Egyptian kings who are called "Sultans." But a new principality is either completely new, as were those of Hiero of Syracuse and Francesco Sforza of Milan, which were thoroughly new; or it is new but not in all of its parts, since it comprises a new member annexed to a hereditary principality, just as the kingdom of Granada was connected to the kingdom of the Spain by your illustrious ancestor, Ferdinand the Catholic.

Book IV, Chapter 11: On giving one's word, and whether faith should be kept

Next, it may rightly be asked whether the faith given by princes should be kept, because, first of all, not a few kings, when they broke faith, achieved great things, like Philip, king of the Macedonians, who with dissimulations and lies accomplished great things. Hannibal, too, and Hamilcar, and almost all the other Africans never kept faith, although they accomplished great deeds. Ptolemy Ceraunus, although he accomplished a number of things worthy of note, rarely kept his sworn word. For this reason, not a few writers of histories affirm that there are two kinds of contest: one is waged by force and arms, the other is carried out with laws and reasonings. The contest that is waged by force and arms belongs to beasts; but the other contest that is waged by laws and reason belongs to men. They therefore assert, that if this second way proves sufficient, it should be kept to, and by no means should resort be had to the other way. But if it appears to be insufficient, they advise that it be abandoned, and not to persist in that which is founded on laws and reason. They say, indeed, that the prince is prudent who, in accordance with the logic of the times, knows how to use both the man and the beast. He uses the beast when he refuses laws, faith and sworn oaths and he resorts to arms and force. He uses the man, instead, when he observes all of the aforesaid. The writers who truly understood this matter wrote that Achilles and not a few other very ancient kings were raised by the centaur Chiron, since they wanted to signify—as I indeed interpret it—that depending on the times, places and persons, kings must make use of both natures: the human, when the king will have spoken true things, and will have kept faith and his sworn oath; the beastly, on the other hand, when a challenge to his rule compels him to violate his sworn oath. He is compelled, however, because not all those with whom he is in alliance are good and just. For if all men were good and just, only human nature would have to be used, but since many of those with whom one associates are wicked and faithless, the prince, too, is forced now and then to violate his sworn oath.

And therefore is it not worth wondering how a tyrant might observe the obligations of a king, which would be not to lie, to speak true things, not to violate sworn oaths, and not to break faith? For, as Apollonius says, to lie befits a slave rather than a free man. And among the Persians, too, as Herodotus has written, to lie was servile and not befitting kings. Furthermore, if the tyrant is caught violating his sworn oath, how will he be able to secure in faith the majority of the friends and confederates without whom he can hardly preserve his reign? The tyrant, therefore, as they say, may be seen to observe the obligations of kings. This may happen, in the first place, by dissimulation, for example, if he promises openly to all to observe true faith and religion, if he has punished those who have shown contempt for faith and sworn oaths, if, moreover, he shows himself zealous for the truth, a defender of the just, and a fierce enemy of injustices, then, even though he has dissimulated these things, the tyrant will be believed a truthful man by the people and a dissimulator by very few. For only the wise will understand that he dissimulates; all the rest will ignore it. I could add for you that certain kings and potentates in our memory and the memory of our fathers have been believed great and just by the people, while violating faith and law, but for honor's sake I shall omit them. For the people are moved more by their eyes than their mind, and more by their senses than by their intellect; yet dissimulation addresses the senses, while truth addresses the mind, which is why he will be judged truthful by the multitude and a dissimulator by very few.

The tyrant, therefore, should observe faith in all things, and violate his sworn oaths in a very few instances, namely in those in which his rule is at stake, which are certainly few. For this reason he will be believed truthful by most people.

Moreover, if the tyrant is caught violating his sworn oath, never will he lack an excuse for it, and witnesses in his support will be discovered, for, as Pliny says, no lie is so imprudent that a witness cannot be found to speak it. The Romans, therefore, ordered that in all cases sworn oaths and faith should be observed, for they asserted that a sworn oath was a religious affirmation, made as though God was witness. Hence Marcus Attilius Regulus, who, after being captured by the Carthaginians in the First Punic War, when he was ordered to come to Rome to the Senate, gave his word that, if captives were not given in exchange along the way, he himself would return to Carthage. This man came to Rome, and he did not approve that the captive Carthaginians should be given back. He preferred to return to be tortured and executed than to break the sworn oath and faith he had given the enemy. During the Second Punic War, one of the captives that Hannibal had sent to Rome in order to be exchanged went directly home. When it learned of this the Senate ordered that he should be arrested and likewise that he should be taken back to Hannibal—so much did the Romans hold faith and sworn oaths in consideration.

Moral philosophers concede that in just wars deceits may be used by princes so long as a sworn oath is not violated. Sertorius, however, in very difficult circumstances, dissimulated many things to his soldiers when dissimulation seemed to be useful. Caesar himself, as Cicero writes, used to say that if an oath is to be violated, it must be violated for the sake of ruling. And since those situations in which his rule is at stake are very rare, only in a few cases will the tyrant be judged a violator of sworn oaths, and these will be understood only by the wise, who are very few. Yet it is true that the saying of Caesar was tyrannical, while the deed of Marcus Attilius Regulus was religious and worthy of a king.

GIOVAN BATTISTA BUSINI

FROM *A Letter to Benedetto Varchi*

January 23, 1549

The Florentine Giovan Battista Busini (1501–d. after 1566) was in Florence at the time of Machiavelli's death. Years later, in the mid-sixteenth century, he shared a rich exchange of letters with a boyhood friend, Benedetto Varchi (d. 1565), who relied on him as an important source for his Florentine History. *In a letter to Varchi dated January 23, 1549, Busini responded to Varchi's questions concerning persons associated with the republican regime that was revived in Florence between 1527 and 1530. Among other matters, Busini described Machiavelli's last days and the reputation he had acquired as a result of* The Prince. *According to Busini, after the sack of Rome in 1527, when the Medici were again exiled from Florence, Machiavelli hoped to return to his old job as secretary to the Ten of Liberty and Peace in the Florentine chancery. This did not happen, and Machiavelli died soon after. Although Busini's letter emphasizes the popular feeling against* The Prince *in Florence in 1527, it is interesting to note that at that time* The Prince *had not yet been published. Busini's memory may have been affected by the book's later reputation; the letter was written more than twenty years after the fact, and Busini mistakes a few other details. More likely, however, The Prince really did acquire considerable notoriety before Machiavelli's death owing to the circulation of manuscript copies (see Documents 6 and 7). Thus the book's first publisher in Florence approached his work quite cautiously while preparing his edition in 1532 (Document 7).*

Magnificent and most honored Messer Benedetto.

Machiavelli fled Rome, and arrived here [in Florence] as [the city] was recovering its liberty. He tried with great insistence to enter into

---

Giovan Battista Busini, *Lettere di Giovambattista Busini a Benedetto Varchi sopra l'assedio di Firenze,* ed. Gaetano Milanesi (Florence: Le Monnier, 1860), 84–85. Translated from the Italian by William J. Connell.

his place with the Ten.[1] Zanobi [Buondelmonti] and Luigi [Alamanni] favored him very much, but Messer Baldassare [Carducci] and Niccolò di Braccio were against him. The populace hated him on account of *The Prince:* to the rich it appeared that his *Prince* was a document to teach the duke to take from them all of their property, to the poor it was to take all of their liberty. To the Savonarolans,[2] it seemed he was a heretic; the good thought he was dishonest; the wicked thought he was more wicked, or more effective, than they were; so that everyone hated him. But Zanobi and Luigi, as grateful men, remembered benefits they had received, and because of their own virtue they ignored his vices. For he lived most disgracefully in his old age, and other things aside, he had an uncontrollable appetite, on account of which he used certain pills, etc. . . . He fell ill, as it happens, partly from grief, partly in an ordinary way: the grief was from his ambition, since he saw his place taken by [Donato] Giannotti who was much inferior to him. . . . When he fell ill he began to take these pills, and to weaken, and to aggravate the sickness; whence he recounted that very celebrated dream[3] to Filippo [Strozzi], to Francesco del Nero, and to Jacopo Nardi and others, and in this way he died most unhappy, yet jesting. Messer Pietro Carnesecchi,[4] who came with him from Rome with a sister of his, said that after he heard that the city was free he heard him sigh many times. I believe that he regretted his ways, because in fact he loved liberty, and in a most extraordinary way, but he regretted that he had become involved with Pope Clement.

> Sent from Rome, the 23rd day of January, 1549.
> Yours,
> Il Busino.

---

[1]To be appointed Secretary to the Ten of Liberty and Peace, one of the positions he held from 1498 to 1512.

[2]Although Savonarola had been executed in 1498, there was a resurgence of Savonarolism in Florence in 1527.

[3]See Document 11.

[4]Pietro Carnesecchi (1508–1566) came from a prominent Florentine family and was favored in his ecclesiastical career by Pope Clement VII. He was executed as a Protestant heretic in Rome in 1566.

10

BENEDETTO VARCHI

FROM *Florentine History*

1565

Benedetto Varchi (1503–1565) was a prolific Florentine writer of the six-teenth century. He was originally a committed republican, and in 1529, under the last Florentine Republic, he enlisted in the militia. In 1537 he participated in an invasion of Florentine territory by republican exiles. But Duke Cosimo I de' Medici welcomed him back to Florence and in 1547 gave him the title of official historian, a position that had been vacant in Florence ever since Machiavelli had completed his Florentine Histories.

Varchi's own Florentine History, *which covered the years 1527–1538, was unpublished but nearly completed when the author died in 1565. Varchi drew on his own experiences, contemporary records, and discus-sions and correspondence with friends like Busini (Document 9), whose accounts he often checked and corrected. In the passage published here, Varchi describes Machiavelli's death in 1527, as well as the former secre-tary's unpopularity in Florence, which he ascribes to Machiavelli's authorship of* The Prince.

This election [of Donato Giannotti as secretary of the Ten of Liberty and Peace], which for many was unexpected, was (according to what is said and believed still today) a large reason that Niccolò Machiavelli, the writer of the *Florentine Histories,* died. For when he returned from serving the [papal] army with Messer Francesco Guicciardini, and when he had done everything possible in order to recover his former place as Secretary, and when he saw himself (although Luigi Alamanni and Zanobi Buondelmonti, very close friends of his, had greatly favored him) passed over for Giannotti, to whom he thought himself much supe-rior for an office of that kind (although one could hardly call Giannotti illiterate, but rather a man of letters), and when he realized how much the populace hated him, he became ill in such a way that after not much

---

Benedetto Varchi, *Storia fiorentina,* ed. Gaetano Milanesi, 3 vols. (Florence: Le Mon-nier, 1888), book 4, chapter 15, 1: 199–201. Translated from the Italian by William J. Connell.

time he weakened. And without wanting any other doctor or medicine, he took certain pills, for which Giovambatista Bracci, who enjoyed the same lifestyle and manners, had given him the recipe. And he recounted a made-up dream[1] of his to Filippo Strozzi and to Francesco del Nero and to Jacopo Nardi, who had come to visit him. As he had lived, making fun of himself and others and without any religion, so he died, without any religion whatsoever, ridiculing others and himself.

The reason for the hatred that was felt so greatly toward him, apart from his licentious tongue and his lifestyle, which was naughty and contrary to his rank, was the work that he composed and titled *The Prince,* which he addressed to Lorenzo di Piero di Lorenzo, so that Lorenzo could make himself the absolute lord of Florence. In that work (which is truly impious, and which ought not only to be blamed but eliminated, as he himself tried to do after the revolution of the state [in 1527], since it was not yet printed), it seemed to the rich that he taught how to take away their property, and to the poor it seemed that he taught how to take away their honor, and to both of them it seemed that he taught how to take away their liberty. For this reason there took place on his death what appears impossible to happen, namely that the good rejoiced in it just as the wicked. The good did this because they judged him wicked; and the wicked did it because they knew he was not just more wicked, but indeed more courageous than they. Machiavelli was nonetheless pleasant in conversation, obliging toward his friends, and the friend of virtuous men. In sum, he deserved that nature should have conceded him either less cleverness or a [morally] better mind.

And just as I have not wanted to omit what many affirm and what some wrote concerning the cause of the death of Niccolò, similarly I do not want to, nor should I, leave out that this was impossible, and, consequently, very false. For despite [what is said], Machiavelli, as a certain thing, died before . . . Giannotti was elected to the office of Secretary.

And if to anyone it should appear that I have digressed too diffusely or too particularly in writing about the manners of these two Secretaries [Machiavelli and Giannotti] of the Florentine Republic, let him know that in my judgment the former was, and the latter still is, among the rarest of men in the political affairs, not, I shall say, only of our city, but of our age. And just as for virtues one cannot give a more worthy reward than praise and honor, so for the vices there is no greater punishment than their blame and infamy, which remain after death.

[1] See Document 11.

11

ÉTIENNE BINET

FROM *On the Health of Origen*

1629

According to Busini (Document 9) and Varchi (Document 10), Machiavelli related a "dream" to some of his Florentine friends shortly before he died. Neither Busini nor Varchi recounts the details of the dream, but it must have circulated by word of mouth, for many later authors mention it, with the fullest account appearing in a book published by a French Jesuit, Étienne Binet, in 1629. Binet (1569–1639) was a prolific devotional writer and a good friend of St. Francis de Sales. His account of the dream appeared in a passage of a book titled On the Health of Origen, *published in Paris in 1629. Some have challenged the dream's authenticity, as well as many other details surrounding Machiavelli's death, yet the dream is so true to Machiavelli's character, and it corresponds so well with various passages in his writings, that most scholars accept it as genuine. The credibility of Binet's version is slightly enhanced by the fact that Binet spent thirteen years, from 1590 to 1603, in Italy, where he might well have heard the story.*

The dream describes alternative possibilities in the afterlife. The depiction of the souls in heaven is consistent with Machiavelli's frequent criticisms of the church. The noble ancients in hell are reminiscent of Machiavelli's description for Vettori of his evenings at Sant'Andrea (Document 3), and they certainly owe something to Dante's description, in Inferno *(canto IV), of the poet's visit with the noble ancients in the castle of Limbo. But at the back of Machiavelli's mind there was probably another, even more famous literary passage. In Plato's* Apology, *Socrates, like Machiavelli, gives alternatives for what happens after death, the second being the transportation of the soul to a place where it will be possible to converse with the dead. Machiavelli, like Socrates, was accused at various times of impiety and of corrupting the youth of his city. There is thus a good possibility that, in this deathbed dream, the founder of modern political science meant to liken himself to the founder of philosophy.*

Gennaro Sasso, *Machiavelli e gli antichi e altri saggi,* 4 vols. (Milan and Naples: Ricciardi, 1987–97), 3: 235. Translated from the French by William J. Connell.

Machiavelli . . . had the following vision shortly before yielding up his spirit. He saw a group of poor folk, like ruffians, who were in tatters, famished, wearing disguises, all out of order, and very few in number. It was said to him that these were the persons in Heaven of whom it is written, "Blessed are the poor, since theirs is the kingdom of Heaven."[1] When these had retired, there was made to appear an untold number of persons full of gravity and majesty. They appeared as though in a Senate, where one treats very serious affairs of state. He saw among them Plato, Seneca, Plutarch, Tacitus and others of this quality. He asked who these most venerable gentlemen were. It was said to him that these were the damned and that they were souls rejected by Heaven. "The wisdom of the world is enmity with God."[2] When this was done, he was asked to which of the groups he wished to belong. He replied that he would like much more to be in Hell with those great spirits, to discuss affairs of state with them, than to be with those verminous scoundrels he had been shown. And with that he died, and he went on to see how affairs of state are progressing in the next world.

[1]Luke 6:20, the first beatitude.

[2]M here adapts a biblical condemnation of prostitution ("the friendship of the world") that appears in James 4:4: "The friendship of the world is enmity with God." Condemnations of the "wise of the world" were common in Christian devotional literature. Thus M, in *Discourses*, 3.30, writes that Savonarola's sermons were "full of accusations against the wise of the world." Compare also John Bunyan's character, Mr. Worldly-Wiseman, in *The Pilgrim's Progress* (1678).

12

REGINALD POLE

FROM *Apology to Charles V*

1539

Reginald Pole, an Englishman who became a cardinal in 1536, was befriended by a number of Florentines who had known Machiavelli, including Francesco Guicciardini, Pietro Carnesecchi, and Niccolò Gaddi. Pole read The Prince *in the 1530s, and he claimed to despise it. His*

Reginald Pole, *Apologia Reginaldi Poli ad Carolum V. Caesarem super quatuor libris a se scriptis de unitate ecclesiae*, in Pole, *Epistolae*, ed. Angelo Maria Querini, 5 vols. (Brescia: Rizzardi, 1744–1757), 1: 151. Translated from the Latin by William J. Connell.

Apology to Charles V *(1539) includes a lengthy attack on* The Prince, *which he describes as "written by an enemy of the human race. . . . Even though the book presents itself in the pen and the name of a man, nevertheless, hardly had I begun to read, when I realized on the contrary that it was written with Satan's finger."* [1] *All the same, in the passage translated below, Pole included what his Florentine friends had told him was Machiavelli's own justification for writing* The Prince.

[B]ut as to what pertains to Machiavelli, if it is true what I heard last winter [2] when I was in Florence, when I made a detour there from my journey, concerning the occasion for [Machiavelli's] writing [*The Prince*] and his intention in writing it, then in some part he may be excused for its blindness and ignorance, just as his fellow citizens excused him when the subject of his book had been introduced and I had objected to his impious blindness. These Florentines replied with what they said Machiavelli himself had answered when they had previously confronted him: that indeed he had observed not only his own judgment in that book, but also that of the man for whom he was writing. And, since he knew him [Lorenzo] to be of a tyrannical nature, he inserted things that could not but most greatly please such a nature. Nevertheless, [Machiavelli] judged, as have all of the other writers who have written concerning how to make a man into a king or a prince, and as experience teaches, that if the prince did put these things into effect, his rule would be brief. This he greatly hoped for, since inwardly he burned with hatred toward that prince for whom he wrote. Nor did he expect from that book anything other than, by writing for the tyrant the things that please a tyrant, to give him, if he could, a ruinous downfall by his own action. So said these men to excuse the blindness of Machiavelli's mind. . . .

---

[1] Pole, *Apologia,* 1:136.
[2] Probably the winter of 1538–39.

INNOCENT GENTILLET

FROM *Discourses against Machiavelli*

1576

Innocent Gentillet (ca. 1532–1588), a French Protestant lawyer from Vienne, in southern France, who was living in exile in Geneva, wrote one of the most historically influential attacks on Machiavelli's writings. Gentillet had fled to Geneva after the St. Bartholomew's Day massacre of thousands of Protestants in France in 1572. He was one of a number of Huguenot writers who attempted to draw a connection between the persecutions that had caused them to flee and the doctrines of Machiavelli. The fact that the French regent, Catherine de' Medici, was from Florence, and that she was related to Lorenzo, the dedicatee of The Prince, *made the connection obvious in the minds of many. The prominent theologian Théodore Bèze reviewed a draft of Gentillet's* Discourses against Machiavelli *and the Genevan authorities approved it for publication on October 21, 1575. The first of many editions was published in 1576. Anti-Italian passages resulted in protests by Italians who were living in the reformed community of Geneva, and the author was physically assaulted twice by Italian Calvinists who objected to his characterizations of their people. The author was required to publish a clarification and apology, and removed most of the offending passages in later editions. Apart from these initial difficulties, however, Geneva's Calvinists showed a special interest in promoting the work, especially in a Latin translation that was widely distributed. In the past, scholars have exaggerated somewhat by disparaging Gentillet as the source of an unenlightened, moralistic anti-Machiavellism that shows little appreciation of Machiavelli's genuine insights. Gentillet's fiery rhetoric, full of insults, has not helped him in this regard, although this kind of passionate writing was typical of the period of the French religious wars. Gentillet was a learned man, and his lengthy work is both serious and sincere. When he denounces "these great cruelties that are committed against a large number of people," the St. Bartholomew's Day massacre is still fresh in his memory.*

Innocent Gentillet, *Discours contre Machiavel,* ed. Antonio D'Andrea and P. D. Stewart (Florence: Casalini, 1974), 10–11 (part 1, preface), 335, 337–38 (part 3, maxim 14). Translated from the French by William J. Connell.

It should not be imagined that all kinds of people are suited to manage the affairs of a public state, nor that everyone who jumps in to speak or write about them will know to say what is appropriate. One might, therefore, inquire whether I think so well of myself as to imagine that I could treat this material suitably. To this I reply, no, but also that this really is not the purpose I have in mind in the work I am undertaking. Rather, my goal is only to show that Niccolò Machiavelli, a former secretary of the Republic (now Duchy) of Florence, understood nothing, or little of the political science of which we speak, and that he chose maxims that were all wicked, and that he built on them not a political science, but a tyrannical science. This, then, is the purpose that I set for myself: to refute the doctrine of Machiavelli, but not thoroughly to treat political science, although I hope to make a few good points about it at certain places when the occasion presents itself. I hope, with God's help, to arrive at this goal with such good wind and with sails so full that all those who read my writings will form a good opinion of them, and they will understand that Machiavelli was completely ignorant in this science, and that the only purpose in his writings has been and is the creation of a true tyranny.

Furthermore, Machiavelli never had the necessary involvement to understand political science. For he can hardly have had experience in the management of public affairs, since he saw in his time only the quarrels of a few Italian potentates, and certain dealings and conspiracies of a few citizens of Florence. He also had little or no knowledge of history, as we shall show in greater detail in many passages of our *Discourses*. There we shall notice the grave errors and lapses he has committed in what little history he has wanted to treat sometimes in passing, and which he usually brings in inappropriately and often falsely.

Machiavelli possessed no fixed and solid natural judgment whatsoever, as is seen by the weak and inept explanations with which he usually supports the propositions and maxims he advances. Instead, he possessed only a certain subtlety, such as could give color to his wicked and damnable teachings. But when one examines his subtlety a little more closely, one discovers in truth that it is pure absurdity, albeit accompanied with stupidity and above all full of extreme wickedness.

I do not doubt that many persons at court, who manage affairs of state, and others of their kind, find it strange that I speak in this manner of their great "Doctor Machiavelli," whose books one could rightfully call "the Koran of courtiers," so much do they value it, since they follow and observe his teachings and maxims no less than the Turks follow and observe the Koran of their great prophet, Mohammed. But I beg them not to be angry if I speak in this way about a man who, as I shall reveal for everyone's eyes to see, was filled with all wickedness, impiety and ignorance, and to suspend their judgment as to whether I speak truthfully or not until they have read these *Discourses* of mine completely. For, when they have read them, I am certain that any man of sound judgment will say and judge that I speak only too modestly of the vices and the stupidity that are found in this Master Doctor. . . .

[Machiavelli writes,] "It is necessary for a prince to administer cruelty all at once, and to confer pleasure little by little."[1] . . . Continuing to give tyrannical precepts to the prince, Machiavelli teaches him by this maxim a very exquisite way to take possession of a people freshly brought into obedience and to enter into their good graces. He says that the newly arrived prince must, in one strike, make a great deluge of men, killing and murdering everyone who is suspect to him. As for the others who remain, he can gather them back afterward sweetly, reassuring them, and little by little doing them favors. But I beg you, is there a man in the world so brutish that he does not see the absurdity and wickedness of this doctrine? How would it be possible that a prince could make himself loved or obeyed in a newly conquered land by means of such barbarity, seeing as they are hardly able to achieve it who employ all possible sweetness? It is certain that there is no nation so effeminate and servile that it would not have itself cut to pieces sooner than submit to the yoke of whatever prince has seized dominion over it, if the prince made a beginning as cruel and bloody as Machiavelli advises. For even if some force compelled such a people to bear the yoke for a time, it would be impossible for the situation to last any longer than the force itself. The example he advances of Liverotto of Fermo shows this well, for he hardly lasted at all, no longer than Cesare Borgia who by similar means usurped rule in the Romagna, as was said elsewhere. Yet would one know how to imagine a deed more cruel and detestable than the one that Machiavelli relates concerning Liverotto of Fermo, who wickedly murdered his own relations and people who had given him every honor and all the hospitality that it was possible for them to give? And yet Machiavelli proposes this handsome example for the prince to imitate, just as he previously proposed the example of Cesare Borgia. And as for Agathocles, it is

---

[1]See *Prince,* chapter 8.

true . . . that he wrongfully seized the tyranny of Sicily by killing the principal men of Syracuse. But what became of him, too? He got what he deserved. For when he wanted to extend his rule to Italy he relied on conspirators there who did not keep their word. So that when his plans had failed, come to naught through the same means by which he had become great, by treason and perfidy, he died amidst disappointment and scorn. Is this not always the sentence of God, who ruins tyrants with the same methods by which he allowed them to advance? Nevertheless, even though Agathocles met an end that was as wicked as the life he led, Machiavelli dares to compare him with those who have been great and virtuous generals, and he proposes that the prince imitate him. The result is that one sees well how this wicked atheist has no other purpose in his books than to persuade the prince to become tyrannical and wicked by embracing all the vices and chasing away all virtue. . . .

Is it not an animal-like reasoning to say that cruelty should be administered all at once, so that it is not felt as frequently as when one administers it little by little over many occasions? How so? Will one feel the cruelty that is administered all at once only during the very hour in which it is being administered? On the contrary, one sees that these great cruelties that are committed against a large number of people so break the hearts and afflict the spirit of all the relations and friends of the murdered ones that they resent it all their lives, indeed the wound from such cruelties bleeds down to the third generation.

But the cruelties that are committed on many different occasions do not penetrate so deeply into the hearts of men, and they do not pierce them so sharply, although their continuation causes discontent to grow. Furthermore, one cannot deny that it is much more shocking and horrible to our senses to see a great butchery and a large number of persons murdered than to see only one or two of them. And it would be impossible that one could ever expect to be treated sweetly by a prince who had carried out a general execution such as Machiavelli recommends, regardless of any handsome display he may make of wishing to act humanely and with sweetness. For that first realization of his cruelty would be so strongly fixed and engraved in the minds of men that no demonstration of sweetness and humanity that followed could ever eradicate it.

14

CHRISTOPHER MARLOWE

FROM *The Jew of Malta*

ca. 1590

In sixteenth-century England, Machiavelli became a favorite villain of the playwrights who wrote for the Elizabethan stage. They portrayed Machiavelli as cynical, skillful in politics, and thoroughly wicked. One striking example of the Elizabethan interpretation of Machiavelli appears in Christopher Marlowe's play The Jew of Malta *(written in 1589 or 1590), which is introduced by a character named "Machiavel." In Protestant England some suggested that England's Catholic adversaries on the European continent were following the lessons of the Italian writer. This was also an argument in Gentillet's* Discourses against Machiavelli *(Document 13), which enjoyed a substantial readership in England. According to the speech of Marlowe's Machiavel, after Machiavelli's death, his soul went north of the Alps to France, where it possessed the duke of Guise, who was famous as one of those most responsible for the St. Bartholomew's Day massacre of French Protestants. The character declares that after the duke's assassination in 1588, Machiavelli left France, and he has now arrived in England.*

[Enter Machiavel].

Machiavel. Albeit the world think Machiavel is dead,
Yet was his soul but flown beyond the Alps,
And, now the Guise is dead, is come from France
To view this land and frolic with his friends.
To some perhaps my name is odious,
But such as love me guard me from their tongues,
And let them know that I am Machiavel,
And weigh not men, and therefore not men's words.
Admired I am of those that hate me most.
Though some speak openly against my books,

Christopher Marlowe, *The Complete Plays,* ed. Irving Ribner (New York: Odyssey Press, 1963), 178–79.

Yet will they read me and thereby attain
To Peter's chair;[1] and, when they cast me off,
Are poisoned by my climbing followers.
I count religion but a childish toy
And hold there is no sin but ignorance.
Birds of the air will tell of murders past;
I am ashamed to hear such fooleries.
Many will talk of title to a crown;
What right had Caesar to the empery?
Might first made kings, and laws were then most sure
When, like Draco's,[2] they were writ in blood.

[1]The papacy.

[2]Draco (seventh century BCE) was the first Athenian lawgiver and inspired the word "draconian." His laws were exceptionally severe, with death as the penalty for many crimes.

15

FREDERICK THE GREAT

FROM *The Refutation of Machiavelli's* Prince

1740

During the eighteenth century, Machiavelli's writings were among the most widely read and most influential texts of the Enlightenment, an intellectual movement that emphasized the superiority of reason and science over superstition and tradition. Frederick II, king of Prussia (r. 1740–1786), also known as Frederick the Great, exhibited an interest in the world of letters, and his treatise against Machiavelli's Prince, *which was published in 1740, just as he became king, achieved a wide distribution in Europe. Frederick's partner in this publication project was the great French writer, Voltaire (1694–1778). While crown prince of Prussia, Frederick had corresponded with Voltaire, who was in France. In 1738 Voltaire sent Frederick a draft of the introduction to his history,* The Age

Frederick the Great, King of Prussia, *La réfutation du "Prince" de Machiavel,* ed. Charles Fleischauer, in *Studies on Voltaire and the Eighteenth Century,* 5 (1958): 169–73, 271–76. Translated from the French by William J. Connell.

of Louis XIV. *In his reply to the draft, Frederick objected to Voltaire's calling Machiavelli a "great man," and he was pleased when Voltaire subsequently eliminated the Florentine from his text. The following year, Frederick revealed to Voltaire his plan to write a chapter-by-chapter refutation of* The Prince, *and with the French writer's encouragement, he began sending his chapters to Voltaire for editing. While Frederick was completing his treatise in 1739–40, Voltaire made arrangements for the work to be printed. He suggested the title* Anti-Machiavel; *he proposed printing Frederick's text in parallel columns with Machiavelli's text; and he found a printer in The Hague who agreed to take on the project. Yet Frederick, once he had finished writing, seems to have changed his mind. First he requested that Voltaire try to make the book less provocative, and, then, after the death of Frederick's father (May 31, 1740) and his own ascent to the throne, the new king asked Voltaire to buy up all copies of the book. The printer, however, went ahead. Voltaire then put out a second, revised edition, but Frederick complained that Voltaire had added too much, so that it was no longer his book. Fortunately, modern scholars have been able to reconstruct Frederick's original version, titled* The Refutation of Machiavelli's "Prince," *which does not include Voltaire's additions.*

Frederick states at the outset that Machiavelli has been to politics what the Dutch philosopher Benedict de Spinoza (1633–1677) has been to theology. Spinoza's writings had initiated a series of great controversies because they argued that God takes no willed part in nature and the world, and that human values derive not from God but from human experience. Like many men of the Enlightenment, Frederick has faith in the progress the human race has made through history. He writes, "in our day the fashion for sedition and revolution appears to be completely over." Probably he would have agreed that this progress shows both that there is a God who participates in the world's affairs, and that God encourages human reason to combat superstition and cruelty. Frederick is thus especially critical of the cruelty and duplicity Machiavelli praises in his work. It is paradoxical, then, that Frederick's work, in fact, did much to promote Machiavelli's fame in Europe. His publication of Machiavelli's work alongside his own, his stature as a renowned monarch who reigned for another forty-six years, and his endorsement of some of Machiavelli's views in his own text—Frederick, a Protestant, agreed, for example, with Machiavelli's criticism of the Roman church; and he admitted that unfortunate necessities may require that a prince break treaties—contributed to Machiavelli's celebrity in the world of letters. Frederick's preface and much of his chapter 17 are translated here.

Preface

The Prince of Machiavelli is to morality what the work of Spinoza is to matters of faith. Spinoza undermined the foundations of faith and aimed at nothing less than to overthrow the edifice of religion. Machiavelli corrupted politics and he undertook to destroy the precepts of sound morality. The errors of the one were only errors of speculation; those of the other regarded practice. It so happened that the theologians rang the warning bell and cried the alarm against Spinoza, his work was formally refuted, and divinity was established undeniably against the attacks of that impious man. Machiavelli, meanwhile, has only been harassed by a few moralists, and, in spite of them, and in spite of his pernicious morality, he remains in a seat of authority in politics down to our own day.

I dare to take up the defense of humanity against this monster who wishes to destroy it. I dare to oppose reason and justice to iniquity and crime. And I have put forth my reflections on Machiavelli's *Prince* at the end of each chapter, in order that the antidote may be found immediately next to the poison.

I have always seen *The Prince* of Machiavelli as one of the most dangerous works that have ever been foisted upon the world. It is in the nature of the book that it falls into the hands of princes and of those who have a taste for politics. Since it is very easy for a young and ambitious man, one whose heart and judgment are not formed sufficiently to distinguish securely the good from the bad, to be corrupted by maxims that flatter the impetuosity of his passions, any book that contributes to this should be regarded as absolutely pernicious and contrary to the good of mankind.

But if it is wicked to seduce the innocence of a single person who has only the slightest influence on the affairs of the world, it is so much more wicked to pervert the princes who are supposed to govern their peoples, administer justice and be an example of it for their subjects, who are supposed to be, in their goodness, their magnanimity, and their mercy, the living images of divinity, and who should be kings less by their greatness and strength than by their personal qualities and virtues.

The floods that ravage the countryside, the lightning that reduces towns to cinders, the deadly and contagious poison of the plague, are not so baneful for the world as are kings that have dangerous morals and unbridled passions. Heavenly scourges last only for a while, they only ravage some countrysides, and these losses, although painful, are repaired. But kings' crimes cause entire peoples to suffer, the state's misfortune worsens under their strong arm, and their oppressed peoples do not even have the feeble consolation of being able, without becoming criminals, to hope for an end to their miseries.

Just as kings have the power to do good when they are willing, similarly it is theirs to do evil when they have resolved upon it. How deplorable is the situation of the people when they have everything to fear from the abuse of the sovereign power, when their property is prey to the prince's avarice, their liberty to his caprices, their tranquility to his ambition, their security to his perfidy, their life to his cruelties! Such is the tragic picture of a state in which a monster, as Machiavelli would like to shape him, rules.

I have more to say. Even if Machiavelli's venom does not reach as far as the throne, even if it only spreads to the hearts of those ministers who are the means by which politics works, I affirm that a single disciple of Machiavelli and of Cesare Borgia in the world would be enough to cause the execrable principles of his frightening politics to be abhorred.

I should not conclude this preface without saying a word to those persons who believe that Machiavelli wrote what princes do, rather than what they ought to do. This thought has pleased many both because it is satirical and because it has some semblance of truth. People have been satisfied with a brilliant falsehood, and they have repeated it as soon as they have heard it uttered once. Let me take up the defense of princes against those who would slander them, and save from the most horrible accusation those whose sole purpose should be to labor for the happiness of mankind. The persons who pronounced this final judgment against princes no doubt were misled by the examples of certain wicked princes, contemporaries of Machiavelli, who are cited by the author, and by the lives of certain tyrants who earned the hatred of humanity, and perhaps by some somber, melancholy soul who likes only to criticize and takes pleasure in spreading slander. To these misanthropic critics I reply that in every country there are good and wicked people, that just as in all families there are persons who are handsome along with ones who are one-eyed, hunchbacks, blind, or crippled, so, among princes there have been and will always be some monsters who are not worthy of the sacred character with which they are vested. I beg these critics to consider that, since the seductive force of the throne is very powerful, it requires a more than common virtue to resist it, and that therefore it is not astonishing at all that within an order so numerous as the order of princes there are some who are wicked amid the good, and that even among those Roman emperors who included men like Nero, Caligula and Tiberius, the universe remembers with joy the names of Titus, Trajan and Antoninus, which have been consecrated by their virtues. Therefore it is a crying injustice to attribute to an entire body which is appropriate only to some of its limbs.

History should preserve only the names of the good princes, and allow forever to perish the names of the others, with their indolence, their injustice and their crimes. The history books would be much diminished with regard to the truth, but humanity would profit by it, and the honor of living on in history, of seeing one's name pass through future centuries on to eternity, would only be virtue's reward. Machiavelli's book would no longer infect the schools of politics, the pitiful self-contradictions in which he always finds himself would be despised, and the world would be persuaded that the true politics of kings, founded only on justice, prudence and goodness, is preferable in every way to the disconnected system, full of horrors and cruelty, that Machiavelli had the impudence to present to the public.

Chapter 17: On cruelty and compassion, and whether it is better to be loved than feared or the contrary

The most precious trust that is confided in the hands of princes is the life of their subjects. Their position gives them the power to condemn to death or to pardon the guilty; they are the supreme arbiters of justice. One word from their mouth causes the sinister ministers of death and destruction to march forth; one word from their mouth causes the agents of their favor to fly to the rescue, those ministers who announce good tidings. But a power so absolute requires circumspection, prudence and wisdom so as not to be abused! . . .

Good princes regard this unlimited power over the life of their subjects as the heaviest burden of their crown. They know that they themselves are men just like those they must judge. They know that wrongs, injustices and injuries can be repaired in the world, but that a hasty sentence of death is an irreparable evil. They only use severity in order to avoid a more troublesome hardship that they foresee if they act otherwise. They only make these sad decisions in cases that are desperate and equal to those in which a man, learning he has a gangrenous limb, despite the tenderness he feels toward himself, resolves to allow it to be cut off, to guarantee and at least to save the rest of his body by that painful operation. . . .

But Machiavelli is not yet finished. I follow him now to his most captious, most subtle and most dazzling argument. He says that a prince does better if he makes himself feared than if he makes himself loved, for the greater part of the world tends toward ingratitude, variability, dissimulation, cowardice and avarice. He says that love is a tie of obligation that the malice and the baseness of the human race have made very fragile, whereas the fear of punishment ensures in a much stronger way that people will do as they should. He says that men are masters of their good will, but not of their fear, so that the prudent prince will rather rely on fear than on other things.

I reply to all of this that I do not deny that there are ungrateful and dissimulating men in the world. I do not deny that fear, in certain moments, is very powerful. But I suggest that any king whose politics has making himself feared as its only end will rule over slaves. He will not be able to expect great deeds from his subjects, because everything done out of fear and timidity has always shown its character. A prince who has the gift of making himself loved will rule over men's hearts, since his subjects find it advantageous to have him for a master. There are a great number of examples in history of great and beautiful actions that have been done out of love and fidelity. I say further that in our day the fashion for sedition and revolution appears to be completely over. One sees no kingdom, save England, where the king has the least reason to suspect his people, and even in England the king has nothing to fear unless he himself a raises a storm.

I conclude, therefore, that a cruel prince exposes himself to being betrayed more than a good-natured one, since cruelty is intolerable. People are quickly weary of cruelty; goodness is always lovable, and no one grows weary of loving it. It might be wished, for the happiness of the world, that the princes would be good without being too indulgent, so that goodness would always be a virtue in them and not a weakness.

16

JEAN-JACQUES ROUSSEAU

FROM *On the Social Contract*

After 1762

Enlightenment thinkers were especially impressed by Machiavelli's analysis of Roman history in the Discourses, *and they agreed with most of his criticisms of the Roman church. The political doctrine of* The Prince *remained troubling, however, because Machiavelli's treatise appeared to openly endorse tyranny. In defense of Machiavelli, many Enlightenment writers accepted and developed the idea that he wrote* The Prince *with the secret intention of undermining princely rule, and that it was not really the manual for princes it purported to be.*

The suggestion that Machiavelli had a hidden, antimonarchical motive for writing The Prince *was first recorded by Reginald Pole on the evidence of his 1534 discussion with friends of Machiavelli's in Florence (Document 12); and Riccardo Riccardi attributed a similar view to Machiavelli (Document 5). On the basis of these reports, it seems quite possible that Machiavelli encouraged this interpretation later in life, although, as his letter to Vettori (Document 3) makes clear, it was almost certainly not the reason he originally wrote* The Prince *in 1513–14.*

Later in the sixteenth century, the Oxford jurist and law professor Alberico Gentili (1552–1608) endorsed the idea that The Prince *contains a secret, antityrannical message and the early Dutch Enlightenment philosopher Benedict de Spinoza seconded this view. When Pierre Bayle (1647–1706) wrote the entry "Machiavelli" in his* Historical and Critical Dictionary *(first published in 1697), he quoted Gentili's interpretation approvingly, and he attacked many of Machiavelli's critics.[1] Denis Didérot (1713–1784), in an article, "Machiavellism," published in the* Encyclopédie *in 1765, explained, "When Machiavelli wrote his treatise on the prince, it was as if he had said to his fellow citizens, 'Read this work well.*

---

[1]Pierre Bayle, *Political Writings,* ed. Sally L. Jenkinson (Cambridge: Cambridge University Press, 2000), 162–71, gives an excerpt.

Jean-Jacques Rousseau, *Du contrat social,* ed. Robert Derathé, in Rousseau, *Oeuvres complètes,* 3 (Paris: Pléïade, 1964), 409, 1480–81 (book 3, chapter 6). Translated from the French by William J. Connell.

If you ever accept a master, he will be such as I paint him for you. See here the ferocious beast to which you will abandon yourselves.'"[2]

The foregoing writers were well known to Jean-Jacques Rousseau (1712–1778), the philosopher from Geneva, who was also a close reader of Machiavelli's Prince *and* Discourses. *In a famous brief passage that appeared in Rousseau's book* On the Social Contract, *he restated the thesis of a hidden purpose in* The Prince *while also giving it meaning for the princes and people of his own day.*

While pretending to give lessons to kings, he gave some great ones to the people. *The Prince* of Machiavelli is the book of republicans.[3] Machiavelli was an honest man and a good citizen; but because he was attached to the Medici house, he was forced, during his fatherland's oppression, to disguise his love of liberty. The choice of his execrable hero [Cesare Borgia] alone sufficiently shows his secret intention; and the comparison of the maxims of his book on *The Prince* with those in his *Discourses* on Titus Livy and his history of Florence demonstrates that this profound political thinker has had until now only readers who were superficial or corrupt. The court of Rome has severely prohibited his book, and I believe this is well done, since that is the court that he paints the most clearly.

---

[2]Denis Didérot, "Machiavellisme," *Encyclopédie,* 9 (Neufchastel, 1765), 793.
[3]The remainder of the passage appears in a footnote, inserted at this point by Rousseau himself, as a clarification to the text that was published in the first edition.

17

BENITO MUSSOLINI

A Prelude to Machiavelli

1924

In 1924 the University of Bologna offered Benito Mussolini (1883–
1945), the founder of Italian Fascism, an honorary doctorate in juris-
prudence. Italy's leader, known as Il Duce, had only recently come to
power, after his followers had marched on Rome in 1922. Prior to seizing
power, Mussolini had had a prominent career as a journalist and political activist. Although he had read widely on philosophical and cultural
topics and was a prolific writer, he had never earned a university degree,
which remained something of a sore point with him. Therefore, Mussolini informed the university that he did not wish to earn an honorary
degree, but a true one, and to do this he proposed to write a thesis on
Machiavelli. In the negotiations that ensued, it became clear that taking
Mussolini away from the business of governing to write a doctoral thesis
would be inappropriate, and, to its credit, the university insisted on up-
holding its standards. To show how serious he was, Mussolini actually
wrote an introduction to the thesis, and promised to complete the thesis
after he retired from political life. In the end, however, the university
never conferred the degree. In the meantime, Mussolini's introduction,
titled, "A Prelude to Machiavelli," took on a life of its own. The essay was
published in the Fascist magazine Gerarchia, which Mussolini directed,
and later it was published as the foreword in Fascist editions of Machiavelli's Prince.

Mussolini wrote and published his essay on Machiavelli shortly before
consolidating his dictatorship with the kidnapping and brutal murder of
the leader of the parliamentary opposition, the Socialist Giacomo Matteotti (1885–1924). Mussolini's essay openly endorses The Prince as a
guide to the exercise of power, so it is quite possible, as some have suggested, that Mussolini thought he was following Machiavelli's advice

Benito Mussolini, *Opera omnia,* 44 vols., ed. Edoardo and Duilio Susmel (Florence: La
Fenice, 1956–80), 20: 251–54. Translated from the Italian by William J. Connell.

when he arranged the killing of his opponent, Matteotti. Mussolini, the "new prince," would thus have been taking Cesare Borgia or Liverotto of Fermo as his model.

"A Prelude to Machiavelli" reminds us of some of the grim messages about power in The Prince. *It is also revealing about the twentieth-century political movement known as Fascism. Fascists like Mussolini were opposed to the democratic ideals that had originated with Enlightenment authors like Rousseau (Document 16) and that spread throughout Europe and the Americas in the nineteenth and early twentieth centuries. Mussolini's essay shows how Fascists believed that the ideal of popular sovereignty, on which democratic theory is based, is just a myth used to manipulate the masses. In the end, Mussolini writes, it is always leaders, not the people, who make important political decisions.*

Mussolini's essay begins in the form of a composition to be submitted for grading by a panel of university professors.

It so happened that one day there was announced to me from Imola, from the Black Legions [Fascists] of Imola, the gift of a sword inscribed with Machiavelli's maxim, "States are not preserved with words." This cut short my procrastination and determined absolutely the choice of the composition that today I submit to you for grading. I could have called it, "A Comment of the Year 1924 on *The Prince* of Machiavelli" — part of a book I would like to call *A Companion Guide for the Statesman.* I am obliged, moreover, out of intellectual honesty, to add that this work of mine has a scanty bibliography, as will be seen in what follows. I have reread *The Prince* carefully, and the rest of the works of the great Secretary, but I did not have the time and will to read all that has been written in Italy and in the world about Machiavelli. I wanted to put between Machiavelli and myself as few intermediaries as possible, whether old or new, Italian or foreign, so as not to spoil my making direct contact between his doctrine and my life as it has been lived, between his observations of men and of things and mine, between his experiences in government and mine. What I am honored to read to you, therefore, is not a cold scholarly dissertation, bristling with the citations of others. It is instead a drama—if it may be considered, in a certain way, dramatic (as I believe it may) to attempt to throw a bridge, built out of spirit, over the abyss of generations and events.

I shall say nothing that is new.

The question is posed: At a distance of four centuries, what is there that is still alive in *The Prince*? Could the counsels of Machiavelli have some kind of usefulness for rulers even of modern states? Is the value of the political system of *The Prince* restricted to the epoch in which the book was written, and therefore necessarily limited and in part decayed? Or is it not instead universal and valuable now? Is it especially valuable now? My thesis replies to these questions. I argue that the doctrine of Machiavelli is more alive today than four centuries ago. For if the external aspects of our life have changed greatly, profound changes have not been evidenced in the spirit of individuals and of peoples.

If politics is the art of governing men, that is, of guiding, using and educating their passions, their selfishness, their interests with a view to goals of a general nature, goals that almost always transcend the life of the individual because they are projected into the future, if this is politics, there is no doubt that the fundamental element in this art is man. From here it is necessary to begin. What are men in the political system of Machiavelli? What does Machiavelli think of men? Is he an optimist or a pessimist? And when we say "men," must we interpret the word in a restricted sense, as referring to the Italians that Machiavelli knew and pondered because they were his contemporaries? Or does it refer to men without regard for time and space, "under the species of eternity," to put it in learned parlance? I think that before proceeding to a more analytical examination of the system of Machiavellian politics as it appears condensed for us in *The Prince,* it is necessary to establish exactly what concept Machiavelli had of men in general, and perhaps, of Italians in particular. Now, of course, what comes out clearly, even from a superficial reading of *The Prince,* is the acute pessimism of Machiavelli concerning human nature. Like all those who have had the opportunity for continuous and vast commerce with men like themselves, Machiavelli is scornful of men, and he loves to present them to us, as I shall document shortly, in their most negative and embarrassing guises.

Men, according to Machiavelli, are wicked. They are more affectionate toward things than toward their own relatives. They are ready to trade away sentiments and passions. In chapter 17 of *The Prince,* Machiavelli expresses himself thus:

> For the following may be said generally about men: that they are ungrateful, changeable, pretenders and dissemblers, avoiders of

dangers, and desirous of gain, and while you do them good they are wholly yours, offering you their blood, their property, their life, and their children, as I said above, when the need is far off, but when it comes close to you they revolt. And that prince who has founded himself wholly on their words, because he finds himself naked of other preparations, is ruined. . . . Men have less fear of offending one who makes himself loved than one who makes himself feared, since love is held in place by a bond of obligation that, because men are wicked, is broken at every opportunity for utility to oneself, but fear is held in place by a fear of punishment that never abandons you.

Regarding human selfishness, I find among his *Various Papers* the following:

Men complain more about a farm that is taken from them than about a brother or father who is killed, because death is forgotten sometimes, but property never. The reason is easy, since anyone knows that with the revolution of a state your brother cannot be resuscitated, but you can certainly get his farm back.

And in [book 1,] chapter 3 of the *Discourses*:

It is demonstrated by all those who reason about the civil life, and every history is pregnant with examples of it, that it is necessary for whoever lays out a Republic and ordains laws for it to presuppose that all men are evil, and that they will always reveal the malignity of their spirit whenever they have free opportunity. . . . Men never achieve anything that is good without necessity, but where liberty abounds, if license is permitted, suddenly everything becomes full of confusion and disorder.

The citations could continue, but it is not necessary. The passages quoted are sufficient to demonstrate that a negative judgment on men is not accidental but fundamental in the spirit of Machiavelli, and in all of his writings. It stands as a deserved and discouraging conviction. This initial and essential point has to be kept in mind in order to follow all of the subsequent developments in the thought of Machiavelli. It is also evident that Machiavelli, when he was passing judgment on men in this way, was not referring only to the men of his time, to the Florentines, Tuscans and Italians who lived on the cusp of the fifteenth and sixteenth centuries, but to men without any boundaries of space and time.

Time has passed, but, if it were permitted for me to pass judgment on men who are like myself and are my contemporaries, I could not in any way soften the judgment of Machiavelli. I ought, perhaps, to make it harsher. Machiavelli does not delude himself, and he does not delude the prince. The opposition between prince and people, between state and individual, is, in the conception of Machiavelli, inevitable. What has been called utilitarianism, pragmatism, Machiavellian cynicism, springs logically from this initial position. The word "prince" should be understood as "state." In the conception of Machiavelli, the prince is the state. Although individuals, motivated by their selfishness, try to be socially tone-deaf, the state stands as an organizing and a restraining force. The individual tries continually to avoid. He tries to disobey the laws, to not pay taxes, to not go to war. Few are they, heroes or saints, who sacrifice their own selves on the altar of the state. The revolutions of the seventeenth and eighteenth centuries attempted to resolve the fissure that exists in the foundation of every state's social organization, by making power surge upward, as though it were emanating from the free will of the people. And there is yet one more fiction, one more illusion. From the beginning "the people" were never defined. As a political entity, it is an entity that is entirely abstract. One doesn't know exactly where it begins, or where it ends. The adjective "sovereign," when applied to the people, is a tragic joke. The people, at very most, delegate, but they certainly cannot exercise any sovereignty whatsoever. Representative systems have more to do with mechanics than with morals. Even in the countries where these mechanisms have been in full use for centuries and centuries, there come solemn hours when nothing more is requested of the people because it is felt that their reply would be fatal. Their paper crowns of sovereignty—good in normal times—are ripped away, and it is ordered unhesitatingly that they should accept a revolution or a peace, or that they should march off into the uncertainty of war. All that remains for the people is the single syllable by which they agree and obey. You see that the sovereignty that was graciously extended to the people is taken away from them in the moments in which they might feel its need. It is permitted for them only when it is harmless or is so reputed, that is, in periods of ordinary administration. Can you imagine a war declared by referendum? A referendum is great when it is a question of selecting the most suitable place for locating the village fountain. But when the supreme interests of a people are at stake, even the governments that are ultrademocratic defend themselves against submission to the judgment of the real people. There is, therefore, an inherent dissidence, even in the regimes that were dished up for us in the *Encyclopédie* (which erred, thanks to Rousseau, in its immeasurable excess of optimism) between the organized force of the state and the fragmentary tendency of individuals and of groups. Regimes that are exclusively consensual have never existed, do not exist, and probably will never exist. Long before the publication of my by-now famous article, "Force and Consent" [published in March 1923], Machiavelli wrote in *The Prince* [chapter 6]:

> From this it arose that all the armed prophets were victorious and the unarmed ones were ruined. For ... the nature of peoples is changeable, it is easy to persuade them of one thing, but it is difficult to keep them in that persuasion. For this reason it is suitable for them to be ordered in such a way that, when they no longer believe, one can make them believe by force. Moses, Cyrus, Theseus and Romulus would not have been able to make their peoples observe their constitutions for long if they had been unarmed.

18

ANTONIO GRAMSCI

FROM *Prison Notebooks*

1932–1934

While in prison in the early 1930s, Antonio Gramsci (1891–1937), a leader and theorist of the Italian Communist Party, developed one of the more influential twentieth-century readings of Machiavelli. Gramsci was elected party secretary and also a deputy in Parliament in 1924, just as the Fascist Party strengthened its hold over the Italian government. Gramsci called for a general strike against the Fascists, and he became a vocal leader of the parliamentary opposition. In 1926, Mussolini's government outlawed all opposition parties and arrested Gramsci. Two years later the government tried him in Rome on a charge of subversion, and sentenced him to twenty years in prison. While in prison, Gramsci

Antonio Gramsci, *Quaderni del carcere*, ed. Valentino Gerratana, 4 vols. (Turin: Einaudi, 1975), 3: 1555, 1556, 1558, 1598–1601, 1690–91. Translated from the Italian by William J. Connell.

maintained a lengthy and important correspondence with his Russian sister-in-law, Tatiana Schucht (1880–1943), who followed his case, visited him, and, after his death, preserved the Prison Notebooks *that Gramsci had been permitted to write while incarcerated. Much of the time he was in prison, Gramsci, who suffered from poor health, lived in lamentable conditions. Meanwhile, outside, he fell under the suspicion of Stalinist Communist Party officials, who thought he harbored Trotskyite sympathies. In 1933 he appears to have learned that even his wife Julia, who lived in Moscow with their two children, had denounced him to party officials in Russia. Gramsci continued to receive a certain level of support from Communist friends, however; due to their efforts, the government eventually granted him a conditional release from prison in 1934. His health remained precarious, and he died in 1937. Tatiana deposited Gramsci's papers with the Soviet embassy in Rome; from there they were sent to Moscow; and after the war they were returned to Italy, where for decades the Communist Party carefully managed their publication, eliminating traces of the tensions that had existed between Gramsci and the party in the 1930s.*

In several famous passages on Machiavelli in the Prison Notebooks, *Gramsci sets forth a very positive interpretation of Machiavelli's* Prince, *which, like Mussolini (Document 17), he reads as offering a model for political action. But whereas Mussolini thought the book offered valuable instruction for a single ruler, Gramsci argues that it was intended for an entire revolutionary social class, and that its aim was to instruct this class in the need to coalesce around a leader or "prince" capable of acting boldly and not in accordance with the received morality of the time. In Machiavelli's day, the desired prince was a "captain," a military leader; instead, the "modern prince," as Gramsci calls him, will not be a single man, but rather a political party expressing the interests of the revolutionary class. Gramsci thus uses Machiavelli's* Prince *to provide both a model and intellectual justification for the bold and seemingly immoral actions he believes it will be necessary for the Communist Party to take.*

The fundamental character of *The Prince* is that it is not a systematic treatment, but a living book, in which political ideology and political science are fused in the dramatic form of a myth. Out of the utopia and the scholastic treatise, the two genres in which political science expressed itself before Machiavelli, this writer gave his concept a form both imaginative and artistic, in which the doctrinal and rational element is realized in a captain, who represents in a plastic and anthropomorphic way the symbol of the "collective will." The process of forming a specific collective will, directed toward a specific political end, is represented not through disquisitions and pedantic classifications of the principles and criteria for a plan of action, but as the qualities, characteristic traits, duties and necessities of a concrete person. This is something that sets in motion the artistic fantasy of whoever wants to convince himself and it gives a more concrete form to the political passions. Even the conclusion of *The Prince* is tied to this mythic character of the book. After having represented the ideal captain, Machiavelli, in a passage of great artistic efficacy, invokes the real captain who should embody historically the ideal one. This passionate invocation is reflected in the whole book, conferring on it its dramatic character. . . .

Throughout his small book Machiavelli discusses what the prince should be in order to lead a people to the foundation of the new state, and the discussion is conducted with logical rigor, with scientific detachment. In the conclusion, Machiavelli himself becomes the people, mixes himself with the people, but not with a people understood generically, but with the people Machiavelli has convinced in his previous discussion, of whom he becomes and feels himself to be the consciousness and the expression. . . .

The modern prince, the mythic prince cannot be a real person, a concrete individual. It can only be an organism, a complex element of society, in which there has already begun to take place the concretization of a collective will that has been seen and partially confirmed through action. Historical evolution has already created this organism. It is the political party, the first cell in which the seeds of the collective will are gathered, seeds that aim to become universal and total. . . .

The fundamental innovation brought by the philosophy of praxis [Marxism] to political science and history is the proof that there exists no abstract "human nature," fixed and immutable (a concept that surely derives from religious thought and from [the idea of] transcendence), but that human nature is the sum of social relations as they are historically determined, that it is a historical fact that is measurable, within certain limits, through the methods of philology and criticism. For this reason political science ought to be understood, with regard to its concrete subject matter (and also its logical formulations), to be like a growing organism. All the same, it needs to be noted that the interpretation given by Machiavelli to the question of politics—that is, the affirmation, implicit in his writings, that politics is an autonomous activity, which has its own principles and laws different from those of morality and religion, a proposition that has great philosophical consequences, because implicitly it revolutionizes the concept of morality and religion, that is, it revolutionizes the whole concept of the world—is still today debated and contradicted. It has not succeeded in becoming "common knowledge." What does this mean? Does it mean only that the intellectual and moral revolution whose elements are contained in seed-form in the thought of Machiavelli has not yet been realized? Or does it instead have a simple political meaning for the present, indicating the existing gulf between rulers and ruled, indicating that there exist two cultures, one of the ruling and one of the ruled, and that the controlling class, just like the Church, has a policy of its own for the simple folk, dictated by the necessity, on the one hand, of not separating itself from them, and, on the other, of keeping them convinced that Machiavelli is nothing more than a diabolical apparition?

In this way the problem is posed concerning the significance that Machiavelli had in his own time and the ends he set for himself when writing his books, especially *The Prince*. Machiavelli's teaching was not, in its own day, a purely scholarly thing, the monopoly of a few isolated thinkers, a secret book that circulated among the initiated. Machiavelli's style is not that of a systematic treatise typical of the Middle Ages and of Humanism. It is completely different. It is the style of a man of action, of someone who wants to incite to action, it is the style of a party "manifesto." The "moralistic" interpretation offered by Foscolo is certainly mistaken; all the same, it is true that Machiavelli has *revealed* something, and not just theorized about reality.[1] But what was the purpose of this revealing? Did it have a moralistic or a political end? It is customarily said that Machiavelli's rules for political behavior "are observed but not discussed." The great statesmen, it is said, begin by cursing Machiavelli, by declaring themselves anti-Machiavellian, precisely so that they can observe his rules in a "saintly" way. Would not Machiavelli, in this case, have been a poor Machiavellian, one of those who "know the game" and stupidly let others in on it, whereas Machiavellianism, as it is commonly understood, teaches how to do the contrary? Croce's assertion[2] that, since Machiavellianism is a science, it is useful for both reactionary and democratic politicians,

---

[1]The poet Ugo Foscolo (1778–1827), in his poem, "On Tombs," described Machiavelli as "that great man who, even as he strengthens the rulers' scepter, plucks away the laurel and reveals to their peoples the tears and blood that trickle down it."

[2]The philosopher Benedetto Croce (1866–1952) famously argued that Machiavelli discovered "the autonomy of politics," that politics operates by its own rules, independent of religion and morality.

just as the art of fencing is useful for noblemen and for brigands, for defense and for assassination, and that Foscolo's judgment should be understood in this sense, is, in an abstract way, true. Machiavelli himself notes that the things he writes are practiced and have always been practiced by the greatest men in history. It does not appear, for this reason, that he wants to suggest them to those who already know these things, since his is not the style of a disinterested scientific work, . . . [A]nd one cannot imagine that he arrived at his theses concerning political science by means of philosophical speculation. . . . One may therefore suppose that Machiavelli has in mind "those who do not know," and that he intends to give a political education to "those who do not know": a political education that is not negative, for becoming the haters of tyrants, as Foscolo seems to understand it, but positive, for whoever needs to realize necessary, specific means, even the means of tyrants, if he wants to achieve specific ends.

A person who is born into the traditions of men in government, because of the totality of the education that he absorbs from his family environment, in which dynastic and patrimonial interests are predominant, acquires almost automatically the characteristics of a political realist. Who, therefore, "does not know"? The revolutionary class of the time, the "people," and the Italian "nation," the urban democratic movement that gives from its breast Savonarolas and Pier Soderinis, and not Castruccios and Valentinos. One can imagine that Machiavelli wanted to persuade these forces of the necessity of having a "leader" who knows what is needed and how to obtain what is needed, and to accept him with enthusiasm, even if his actions might be or appear to be contrary to the general ideology of the time, namely religion. . . .

It seems that Machiavelli's intentions in writing *The Prince* were more complicated and even more democratic than the "democratic" interpretation[3] would have them be. Machiavelli, that is, believes that the need for a unified national state is so great that everyone will accept that to achieve this highest end the only means that are capable of achieving it should be used. It may be said, therefore, that Machiavelli proposes "to educate the people," but not in the meaning that is usually attributed to this expression, or at least that certain democratic circles have attributed to it. "To educate the people," for Machiavelli, can have meant only making them more convinced and conscious that there may exist only one policy, the one that is realistic,

---

[3]Of Rousseau (Document 16), for instance, and Foscolo.

for achieving the desired end, and that therefore it is necessary to adhere to and to obey expressly the prince who employs such methods for achieving this end. For only someone who desires the end will desire the means that are capable of achieving it. Machiavelli's position, according to such a reading, should be likened to those of the Marxist theoreticians and politicians who have also tried to create and to sow a "realism" that is popular and for the masses....The "democracy" of Machiavelli is of a kind adapted to his own times. It consists in the active consent of the popular masses for the absolute monarchy, insofar as the monarchy limits and destroys feudal and lordly anarchy and priestly power, and insofar as it establishes large, territorial, national states, a function that absolute monarchy could not perform without the support of the bourgeoisie, and of a standing army that is national, centralized, etc.

A Niccolò Machiavelli Chronology
(1469–1527)

1469   *May 3:* Niccolò Machiavelli is born in Florence.

1478   *April 26:* The Pazzi conspiracy erupts against the Medici in Florence. Lorenzo de' Medici, known as "Lorenzo the Magnificent," escapes, but his brother Giuliano is killed.

1492   *April 8:* Lorenzo de' Medici dies. His son, Piero, assumes the role of unofficial leader of Florence.

August 11: Alexander VI (Rodrigo Borgia) is elected pope.

1494   Charles VIII of France invades Italy. Piero de' Medici surrenders Pisa, Livorno, and a number of fortresses to the French without consulting the Florentines, and he is chased out of Florence. With encouragement from Girolamo Savonarola, a popular constitution is enacted.

1498   *May 23:* Girolamo Savonarola is executed.

June 15: Machiavelli is elected secretary and second chancellor of the Florentine Republic.

1500   *July:* Machiavelli leaves on a diplomatic mission to France.

1501   *April:* Cesare Borgia is made duke of the Romagna. He invades Florentine territory but leaves soon afterward.

August: Machiavelli marries Marietta di Luigi Corsini.

1502   *June 4:* Borgia's captains encourage the rebellion of Arezzo and the Valdichiana from Florentine rule. The revolt is put down after several months.

June 24: Machiavelli's first diplomatic mission to Cesare Borgia, as assistant to Cardinal Francesco Soderini.

September 22: Piero Soderini is elected as standard bearer for life of the Florentine Republic.

October 5: Machiavelli's second diplomatic mission to Cesare Borgia.

December 26: In Cesena, Machiavelli sees the exposed body of Remirro de Orco, executed by command of Cesare Borgia.

December 31: Machiavelli is with Borgia at Senigallia when he orders the arrest of his captains, Vitellozzo Vitelli, Liverotto of Fermo, and two of the Orsini. The first two are strangled that night. The Orsini are executed later.

1503 *August 18:* Pope Alexander VI dies.

September 22: The College of Cardinals elects Pope Pius III, who dies unexpectedly on October 18. Machiavelli is sent to Rome to report on the conclave.

November 1: The College of Cardinals elects Pope Julius II.

1504 *January:* Machiavelli's second mission to France.

1506 *August:* Machiavelli's mission to Julius II in Rome. He follows Julius' army to Perugia, Cesena, Forlì, and Imola, returning to Florence in October.

1507 *January 12:* Machiavelli is appointed chancellor of the Nine of the Militia.

December: Machiavelli's mission to Maximilian I in the Tyrol.

1509 *June 8:* Pisa surrenders to Florence. Machiavelli participates in the negotiations.

November: Mission to Maximilian I in Mantua.

1511 *September:* Mission to the French court.

1512 *August 29:* Papal army sacks Prato, a subject town of Florence.

August 31: Piero Soderini is forced to leave office as Florence's standard bearer for life. The Medici return to Florence.

November 10: The new Medicean government of Florence fires Machiavelli from his position as secretary and second chancellor and requires that he remain in Florentine territory for one year.

1513 *February:* A conspiracy to overthrow the Medici is uncovered. Machiavelli is arrested as a possible accomplice, tortured (although he denies knowledge of the plot), and imprisoned.

February 20: Pope Julius II dies.

March 11: The College of Cardinals elects Pope Leo X (Giovanni de' Medici). Machiavelli is freed from prison in a general amnesty declared in Florence to celebrate the election.

December 10: Machiavelli states in a letter to Francesco Vettori that he is writing a treatise *On Principalities.*

1515 Machiavelli begins to frequent the Rucellai Gardens, where he reads to his friends from his *Discourses on the First Ten Books of Titus Livy,* mostly composed in the period 1515–17.

1516   *June:* Lorenzo de' Medici the Younger is made duke of Urbino by his uncle, Pope Leo X.

1519   *May 4:* Lorenzo de' Medici the Younger, duke of Urbino, dies.

1520   *November 8:* Machiavelli is commissioned to write a history of Florence.

December: Machiavelli writes his *Discourse on Florentine Affairs after the Death of Lorenzo de' Medici the Younger.*

1521   *August:* Machiavelli's *Art of War* is published in Florence by the Giunta press.

December 1: Pope Leo X dies.

1522   *January 9:* The College of Cardinals elects Pope Adrian VI.

May–June: A Florentine conspiracy against Cardinal Giulio de' Medici is exposed. The plot involves Zanobi Buondelmonti, to whom Machiavelli dedicated his *Discourses,* and several other friends of Machiavelli's.

1523   *March:* Agostino Nifo publishes *On Skill in Ruling* in Latin under his own name, although much of the book consists of borrowings from Machiavelli's *Prince.*

September 14: Pope Adrian VI dies.

November 19: The College of Cardinals elects Pope Clement VII (Giulio de' Medici).

1525   *May:* Machiavelli presents his *Florentine Histories* to Pope Clement VII.

1527   *May 6:* Rome is sacked by the troops of Emperor Charles V.

May 17: Florence chases out the Medici, beginning a final period of republican rule that lasts until 1530.

June 21: Machiavelli dies in Florence.

Questions for Consideration

1. The title *The Prince* was chosen by the work's first publisher, after Machiavelli's death. During his lifetime Machiavelli used the title *On Principalities.* Which title do you think is more appropriate?

2. In the dedicatory letter to Lorenzo de' Medici the Younger, what does Machiavelli say his book offers a prince? Does he expect a reward?

3. In chapter 1, Machiavelli writes that all states are either republics or principalities. This use of the word *state*—representing an abstract, generic form of government—is very much like our modern usage. Does Machiavelli always use the word *state* in this way?

4. Machiavelli states at the beginning of chapter 2 that he treats republics elsewhere, referring to his *Discourses on Titus Livy.* Yet republics are discussed in a number of passages of *The Prince* (chapters 5 and 9, for example). Why are they included?

5. Why does Machiavelli include Moses in his list of ancient founders of states (chapter 6)? Does Machiavelli believe that Moses received instructions from God?

6. What qualities does Machiavelli find admirable in Cesare Borgia?

7. In his discussion of Agathocles of Syracuse (chapter 8), Machiavelli uses the word *virtue* (*virtù*) several times. Does he consider Agathocles virtuous? Why?

8. In chapter 11 Machiavelli writes that because ecclesiastical principalities "are exalted and maintained by God, it would be the office of a presumptuous and rash man to discuss them." Nevertheless, he discusses them here, and he appears to discuss the church further in chapter 19, when he likens the papacy to the sultanate in Mameluke Egypt. What strengths did Machiavelli find in the Christian church?

9. A reading of the chapter titles suggests that there are three general subjects in the main text of *The Prince:* the various kinds of principalities (chapters 1–9 and 11); military matters (10, 12–14, 20, and 24); and the prince's conduct (chapters 15–19 and 21–23). There appear to be two concluding chapters (25–26). Do you think *The Prince* is organized in a coherent and effective way?

10. How does Machiavelli's advice concerning the prince's conduct in chapters 15–19 conflict with the advice previous writers would have given?

11. What does Machiavelli mean by "the effectual truth of the thing"? (See chapter 15.)

12. What does Machiavelli think of human nature? (See chapter 17.)

13. Machiavelli describes "virtue" and "fortune" as opposing forces. What does he mean by these terms? How much control do humans have over fortune? (See chapter 25.)

14. In Italian, *fortuna* is a feminine noun, and "fortune" was always depicted as a woman. Is there still something shocking about the closing passage of chapter 25?

15. How do Moses, Cesare Borgia, "virtue," and "fortune" reappear in chapter 26, the "Exhortation to seize Italy and to set her free from the barbarians"? Does Machiavelli believe that religion has a role to play in the liberation of Italy?

Selected Bibliography

MACHIAVELLI'S OTHER WRITINGS

Art of War. Translated by Christopher Lynch. Chicago: University of Chicago Press, 2003.

The Discourses on Livy. Translated under the title *The Sweetness of Power* by James B. Atkinson and David Sices. DeKalb, Ill.: Northern Illinois University Press, 2002.

Florentine Histories. Translated by Laura F. Banfield and Harvey C. Mansfield Jr. Princeton: Princeton University Press, 1988.

Lust and Liberty: The Poems of Niccolò Machiavelli. Translated by Joseph Tusiani. New York: Ivan Obolensky, Inc., 1963.

Machiavelli: The Chief Works and Others. 3 vols. Translated by Allan Gilbert. Durham, N.C.: Duke University Press, 1965. Especially good for Machiavelli's diplomatic missions and his minor political treatises.

Machiavelli and His Friends: Their Personal Correspondence. Translated and edited by James B. Atkinson and David Sices. DeKalb, Ill.: Northern Illinois University Press, 1996. Machiavelli's private correspondence.

Mandragola. Translated by Mera J. Flaumenhaft. Prospect Heights, Ill.: Waveland Press, 1996.

BIOGRAPHIES OF MACHIAVELLI

Ridolfi, Roberto. *The Life of Niccolò Machiavelli.* Translated by Cecil Grayson. London: Routledge and Kegan Paul, 1963. Still the best biography.

Villari, Pasquale. *The Life and Times of Niccolò Machiavelli.* 2 vols. Translated by Linda Villari. 1892. Reprint, New York: Greenwood Press, 1968.

Viroli, Maurizio. *Niccolò's Smile.* Translated by Antony Shugaar. New York: Farrar, Straus & Giroux, 2000.

ON *THE PRINCE*

Baron, Hans. "Machiavelli the Republican Citizen and Author of *The Prince.*" 1961. Reprinted in Baron, *In Search of Florentine Civic Humanism: Essays on the Transition from Medieval to Modern Thought.* 2 vols.

Princeton: Princeton University Press, 1988. A classic essay distinguishing phases in Machiavelli's thought.

Clough, Cecil H. *Machiavelli Researches*. Naples: Istituto Universitario Orientale, 1967. A valuable treatment of Machiavelli's intentions and the textual tradition.

Coyle, Martin, ed. *Niccolò Machiavelli's Prince: New Interdisciplinary Essays*. Manchester: Manchester University Press, 1995. A good collection.

de Alvarez, Leo Paul. *The Machiavellian Enterprise: A Commentary on The Prince*. DeKalb, Ill.: Northern Illinois University Press, 1999. A chapter-by-chapter commentary.

Gilbert, Allan H. *Machiavelli's Prince and Its Forerunners: The Prince as a Typical Book de Regimine Principum*. Durham, N.C.: Duke University Press, 1938. Shows how *The Prince* resembles similar manuals for princes.

Gilbert, Felix. "The Humanist Concept of the Prince and *The Prince* of Machiavelli." 1939. Reprinted in Gilbert, *History: Choice and Commitment*. Cambridge, Mass.: Harvard University Press, 1979. Shows how *The Prince* differs from its forerunners.

Mattingly, Garrett. "Machiavelli's *Prince:* Political Science or Political Satire?" *The American Scholar,* 27 (1958): 482–91. Argues that *The Prince* was a satire.

INTERPRETATIONS OF MACHIAVELLI

Ascoli, Albert Russell, and Victoria Kahn, eds. *Machiavelli and the Discourse of Literature*. Ithaca, N.Y.: Cornell University Press, 1993. Excellent collection of literary essays.

Bock, Gisela, Quentin Skinner, and Maurizio Viroli, eds. *Machiavelli and Republicanism*. Cambridge: Cambridge University Press, 1990. Good treatments of the historical and intellectual background.

Connell, William J. "Machiavelli on Growth as an End." In Anthony Grafton and J. H. M. Salmon, eds., *Historians and Ideologues: Essays in Honor of Donald R. Kelley*. Rochester, N.Y.: University of Rochester Press, 2001, 259–77. Machiavelli on empire.

de Grazia, Sebastian. *Machiavelli in Hell*. Princeton: Princeton University Press, 1989. Explores the role of religion (and many other things) in Machiavelli's writings.

Hulliung, Mark. *Citizen Machiavelli*. Princeton: Princeton University Press, 1983. Shows similarities between *The Prince* and *Discourses*.

Kahn, Victoria. *Machiavellian Rhetoric: From the Counter-Reformation to Milton*. Princeton: Princeton University Press, 1994. Machiavelli's later influence.

Mansfield, Harvey C. *Machiavelli's Virtue*. Chicago: University of Chicago Press, 1996. A strong collection of essays.

Masters, Roger D. *Fortune Is a River: Leonardo da Vinci and Niccolò Machiavelli's Magnificent Dream to Change the Course of Florentine History.* New York: Free Press, 1998. Argues for Leonardo's influence on Machiavelli.

Najemy, John M. *Between Friends: Discourses of Power and Desire in the Machiavelli–Vettori Letters of 1513–1515.* Princeton: Princeton University Press, 1993. Brilliant study of Machiavelli's correspondence with Vettori.

Parel, Anthony J. *The Machiavellian Cosmos.* New Haven: Yale University Press, 1992. Astrology, magic, medicine: Machiavelli as a man of the Renaissance.

Pitkin, Hanna Fenichel. *Fortune Is a Woman: Gender and Politics in the Thought of Niccolò Machiavelli.* 2nd ed. Chicago: University of Chicago Press, 1999. Gendered dimensions of Machiavellian politics.

Pocock, J. G. A. *The Machiavellian Moment: Florentine Political Thought and the Atlantic Republican Tradition.* Princeton: Princeton University Press, 1975. The history of an important strand of republican thought.

Skinner, Quentin. *Machiavelli: A Very Short Introduction.* 1981. Reprint, Oxford: Oxford University Press, 2000. A brief overview, focusing on the essentials.

Strauss, Leo. *Thoughts on Machiavelli.* 1958. Reprint, Chicago: University of Chicago Press, 1995. An elegant interpretation.

Viroli, Maurizio. *Machiavelli.* Oxford: Oxford University Press, 1998. Survey of Machiavelli's ideas.

HISTORICAL CONTEXT

Becker, Marvin B. *Florentine Essays.* Edited by James Banker and Carol Lansing. Ann Arbor: University of Michigan Press, 2002.

Brucker, Gene. *Renaissance Florence.* 2nd ed. Berkeley and Los Angeles: University of California Press, 1983. Florentine society during the Renaissance.

Burckhardt, Jacob. *The Civilization of the Renaissance in Italy.* Translated by S. G. C. Middlemore. Notes by Peter Murray. Introduction by Peter Burke. New York: Penguin, 1990. Still the standard introduction.

Butters, Humfrey C. *Governors and Government in Early Sixteenth-Century Florence, 1502–1519.* Oxford: Oxford University Press, 1985. Political developments in Florence.

Chabod, Federico. *Machiavelli and the Renaissance.* Translated by David Moore. Introduction by A. P. D'Entrèves. 1958. Reprint, New York: Harper & Row, 1965.

Connell, William J. "The Republican Idea." In James Hankins, ed., *Renaissance Civic Humanism: Reappraisals and Reflections.* Cambridge: Cambridge University Press, 2000. Machiavelli's pivotal role in the history of republicanism.

Connell, William J., ed. *Society and Individual in Renaissance Florence.* Berkeley and Los Angeles: University of California Press, 2002. Essays on Florentine society and culture.

Connell, William J., and Andrea Zorzi, eds. *Florentine Tuscany: Structures and Practices of Power.* Cambridge: Cambridge University Press, 2000. Essays on the Florentine state.

Gilbert, Felix. *Machiavelli and Guicciardini: Politics and History in Sixteenth-Century Florence.* 1965. Reprint, New York: Norton, 1994. On the role of historical writing.

Godman, Peter. *From Poliziano to Machiavelli: Florentine Humanism in the High Renaissance.* Princeton: Princeton University Press, 1998. Humanism between politics and high culture.

Grendler, Paul F., ed. *Encyclopedia of the Renaissance.* 6 vols. New York: Scribners, 1999. A basic reference work.

Hale, J. R. *Florence and the Medici.* London: Thames & Hudson, 1977. An excellent narrative.

Kirshner, Julius, ed. *The Origins of the State in Italy, 1300–1600.* Chicago: University of Chicago Press, 1996.

Kristeller, Paul O. *Renaissance Thought and the Arts.* Princeton: Princeton University Press, 1990.

Landucci, Luca. *A Florentine Diary from 1450 to 1516.* Translated by Alice de Rosen Jervis. London: Dent, 1927. Daily life in Renaissance Florence as recorded by a shopkeeper.

Martines, Lauro. *Lawyers and Statecraft in Renaissance Florence.* Princeton: Princeton University Press, 1968.

Polizzotto, Lorenzo. *The Elect Nation: The Savonarolan Movement in Florence, 1494–1545.* Oxford: Clarendon Press, 1994. Religion and politics in Machiavelli's Florence.

von Ranke, Leopold. *History of the Latin and Teutonic Nations (1494 to 1514).* Translated by G. R. Dennis. London, 1909. An older but still splendid political narrative.

Index

Machiavelli's vocabulary is a source of continuing interest. To allow readers to trace Machiavelli's use of "fortune," "liberty," "state," and "virtue," the page numbers after these words are printed in **boldface** when the pages indicated refer to the text of *The Prince* (as opposed to supplemental matter). When the word appears more than once on a page, the number of occurrences is indicated in parentheses.

Achaean League, 46, 86, 110
Achilleid (Statius), 94*n*
Achilles, 86, 94, 157
Adages (Erasmus), 11, 146*n*
Adda River, 49*n*
Adrian VI, pope, 192
Adriani, Marcello Virgilio, 32, 110*n*
Aeneid (Virgil), 91*n*
Aesop's Fables, 94*n*, 130*n*
Aetolian League, 46, 110
Africa, 6, 65, 103, 108, 157
Agathocles, tyrant of Syracuse, 65–68, 168–69, 193
Agnadello, battle of, 49*n*. *See also* Vailate
Agricola, Rudolph, 10
Alamanni, Luigi, 160–61
Alba Longa, 56
Albergaccio, 135
Alberico da Barbiano, count of Cunio, 80
Alberti, Leon Battista, 112*n*
Albinus, Decimus Clodius, 101
Alessandria, 121
Alexander, Roman emperor. *See* Severus, Alexander
Alexander the Great, 51–53, 77*n*, 84, 86, 90, 116
Alexander VI (Rodrigo Borgia), pope, 4, 8, 13, 15, 48–50, 57*n*, 59, 61*n*, 62–63, 66–67, 74–75, 77*n*, 94, 190–91
Alexandria, 102, 132
Alighieri, Dante. *See* Dante
allegory, 94*n*
allies (*amici*), 87*n*
Alviano, Bartolomeo, 79
Amboise, Georges d', cardinal of Rouen, 50, 64
Americas, 6. *See also* New World
Ammianus Marcellinus, 84*n*, 132
Amphitryon, 137
Annals (Tacitus), 84*n*

Anne of Brittany, queen of France, 50*n*
Antiochus III, ruler of Asia Minor, 46–47,110
Antoninus Pius, Roman emperor, 175
Apollonius of Tyana, 156
Apology (Plato), 163
Apology to Charles V (Pole), 24, 164–65
Appian of Alexandria, 132
Appiano, Jacopo IV, lord of Piombino, 48*n*
Aquileia, 103
Aragon, 64, 78
archery, 55, 80
Ardinghelli, Pietro, 18, 132, 139
Aristotle, 11, 25, 92*n*, 112*n*, 156
Arezzo, 105*n*, 143–45, 190
Art of Love (Ovid), 119*n*
"art of memory," 83*n*
Asia, 51, 53, 101
Asola, 150
Athens, 54, 56, 120, 171*n*
Austrians, 79*n*
auxiliary arms, 81–84
Avignon papacy, 7

Baglioni, Giampaolo, 60*n*
Baglioni, lords of Perugia, 63
balance of power, 7–8, 74, 106*n*
barbarians (*barbari*), 119, 122
Bargello, Palace of. *See* Florence
barons, 51–52, 74–75, 109
basileia, 156
Bayle, Pierre, 26, 177
Bellacci, Pandolfo, 145–46, 150
Bene, Tommaso del, 137, 138*n*
Bentivoglio, Annibale I, 97
Bentivoglio, Annibale II, 97
Bentivoglio, Ermes, 60*n*
Bentivoglio, Giovanni II, 60*n*, 98, 118, 127
Bentivoglio, lords of Bologna, 48, 97–98, 108, 118

Bergamo, 79
Bertini, Paolo, 139
Bèze, Théodore, 166
bible
  Exodus, 56*n*, 121*n*
  James, epistle, 164*n*
  Luke, gospel, 164*n*
  New Testament, 12
  Old Testament, 83
  Pentateuch, 13
  Romans, epistle, 148*n*
  Samuel, 83*n*
Binet, Étienne, 163
  On the Health of Origen, 163–164
Biondo, Flavio, 10
Birria, 137*n*
Black Death, 7
Black Legions, 180
Blado, Antonio, 33, 147–50, 152*n*
  Dedicatory Letter to Filippo Strozzi, 147–50
Bohemia, 12
Bologna, 48*n*, 60, 75, 97–98, 108, 118, 121, 127
  University of, 26, 179
Bonaparte, Napoleon, 26
bonfire of vanities, 14
Borgia, Cesare (Valentino), duke of
  Valentinois, 4–5, 15–16, 18, 21, 29,
  50, 58–64, 67, 75, 82, 84*n*, 90, 107–8,
  120*n*, 168, 174, 178–79, 188, 190–91,
  193–94
Borgia, Girolamo, 154
Boscoli, Andrea, painter, 3
Bracceschi, 78
Bracci, Giovambatista, 162
Braccio da Montone (Andrea Fortebracci),
  78, 80
Bracciolini, Poggio, 10–11
Brancacci, Giuliano, 131–32
Brescia, 79*n*
Brittany, 44
Bruni, Leonardo, 10
Bunyan, John, 164*n*
Buonaccorsi, Biagio, 20, 126*n*, 145–46, 150
  Prefatory Letter to Pandolfo Bellaci, 145–46
Buondelmonti, Zanobi, 160–61, 192
Burgundy, 44
business, modern, 4, 9
Busini, Giovan Battista, 159–61, 163
  A Letter to Benedetto Varchi, 159–60
Bussone, Francesco (Il Carmagnola), 79
Butler, Samuel, 31*n*

Caesar, Julius, Roman emperor, 86, 89–90,
  158–59, 171
Calabria, 93*n*
Caligula, Gaius, Roman emperor, 175
Calliano, battle of, 79*n*
Calvinism, 24–25, 166
Cambrai, League of, 49*n*
Camerino, 48
Canetoli family of Bologna, 98*n*
Canneschi, 98

Caos (Fantaguzzi), 62*n*
Capua, 54, 121
Caracalla, Antoninus, Roman emperor, 99,
  101–2, 104
Caravaggio, battle of, 78
Carducci, Baldassare, 160
Carnesecchi, Pietro, 25, 160, 164
Carthage, 54, 57*n*, 65, 77, 91*n*, 158
Casavecchia, Filippo, 126–27, 136, 139
Cascina, battle of, 78*n*
Castile, 109
Castruccio Castracane, tyrant of Lucca, 188
Catholic Church. *See* church
cavalry, 103, 122
centaur, 94
Cesena, 62, 190–91
Chaeronea, battle of, 77*n*
chancery. *See* Florence
Charles V, Holy Roman emperor, 8, 151*n*,
  153–55, 192
Charles VII, king of France, 83, 84*n*
Charles VIII, king of France, 8, 47–48, 50*n*,
  54*n*, 74, 76, 80, 190
Chiron, 94, 157
Christianity, 3, 13, 20, 26, 73–74, 103*n*, 108,
  109*n*, 193–94
church, the, 3, 13, 48–50, 59, 62, 73–75, 78,
  80, 108, 120, 187, 193
  reform, 8, 11–13
Cicero, Marcus Tullius, 12, 14, 94*n*, 119*n*, 158
Città di Castello, 60*n*, 107
civil principality, 68–71
civil society, 30–31
Clement VII (Giulio de' Medici), pope, 18, 21–
  23, 33, 132–33, 148, 153–54, 160, 192
Coligny, Admiral Gaspard de, 24
collective will, 186
collectivities, 30, 100, 111, 119
College of Cardinals, 62, 64, 75, 104, 191
Colleoni, Bartolomeo, of Bergamo, 79
Colloquies (Erasmus), 12
colonies, 45–46, 49
Colonna, Giovanni, cardinal, 64
Colonna family and faction, 59–60, 64, 74–75
Colonnesi, 59
Commodus, Roman emperor, 99–102, 104
Communist Party, 29, 184–85
Commynes, Philippe de, 77*n*
Company of Piety, 32
compare, 130
confraternity, 13, 32
conspiracy, 17, 20, 97–98, 130, 136*n*, 142, 191
Constantinople, 81
contado, 14
Corno, Donato del, 133
Corsini, Marietta di Luigi, 15, 33, 190
Cortona, 105*n*
Counter-Reformation, 24
Croce, Benedetto, 28–29, 187–88
Cynoscephalae, battle of, 46
Cyrus, king of Persia 13, 55–57, 84*n*, 86, 90,
  120, 184

Dante, 94*n*, 136*n*, 138–39, 163
Darius I, king of Persia, 58
Darius III, king of Persia, 51–52
David, king of the Hebrews, 83, 84*n*
da Vinci, Leonardo, 1
de Cordoba, Gonzalvo, 126
Dedicatory Letter to Filippo Strozzi (Blado),
    147–50
Dedicatory Letter to Giovanni Gaddi
    (Giunta), 150–52
de Lorqua, Ramiro (Remirro de Orco), 5,
    61–62, 190
democracy, 26–27, 31, 156, 187–88
De officiis (Cicero), 94*n*
Devil, 3–4, 24
    as "Old Nick", 3–4, 31*n*
    Satan, 24, 165
Didérot, Denis, 26, 177–78
Dido, queen of Carthage, 91
Dioscorides, Pedanius, 11
diplomacy, 7–8, 15–16, 74*n*
Discourses against Machiavelli (Gentillet),
    25, 166–69
Dovizi, Bernardo, of Bibbiena, cardinal, 133
Draco, 171
Draft of a Letter to Giovan Battista Soderini
    (Machiavelli), 125–29
drawing, art of, 40

Education of Cyrus (Xenophon), 86*n*, 87*n*, 94*n*
Egypt, 13, 56, 103–4, 120
Elizabeth I, queen of England, 26
empire, 41*n*, 63*n*, 66*n*, 74*n*. *See also* Holy
    Roman Empire; Roman Empire
Encyclopédie, 177, 184
ends and means, 95, 127
England, 3, 25–26, 83, 170, 176
Enlightenment, 171–72, 177, 180
Epaminondas, 77
Epicureanism, 10–11
Erasmus, Desiderius, 10–13, 146*n*
Este, Alfonso I, duke of Ferrara, 42
Este, Ercole I, duke of Ferrara, 42, 48*n*
Euffreducci, Oliverotto (Liverotto of
    Fermo), 4, 25, 29, 60*n*, 61*n*, 66–67,
    143–44, 168, 179, 191

Fabius Maximus Cunctator, 92–93
factions, 7, 59–63, 104–6
Faenza, 48, 60
Fantaguzzi, Giuliano, 62
fascism, 29, 179–80
Fates, 128–29, 133. *See also* fortune
Ferdinand II of Aragon (Ferdinand the
    Catholic), king of Spain, 6, 8, 13, 18,
    41, 49*n*, 80, 81, 96*n*, 108, 126, 156
Fermo, 4, 66–67, 143–44
    Liverotto of. *See* Euffreducci, Oliverotto
Ferrara, 14, 18, 42, 48, 57*n*, 74, 79*n*, 81
few, the, 53–54, 95, 96, 98. *See also* great, the;
    oligarchy
Ficino, Marsilio, 12

Fifth Lateran Council, 12
figura, 83*n*
First Punic War, 77*n*, 158
Flamininus, Titus Quinctius, Roman general,
    46*n*, 110*n*, 116
Florence, 6–7, 10, 14–19, 21–22, 30, 48, 54,
    63, 71, 74, 81, 87*n*, 90, 98, 127, 129,
    150, 152, 159–62, 165, 166, 167
    Bargello, Palace of, 83*n*, 139
    chancery of, v, 14, 20, 31*n*, 33, 83*n*, 159
    Ciompi regime, 71*n*
    duchy of, 167
    Nine of the Militia, 15–16, 127*n*, 191
    Palace of the Signoria, 83*n*, 135
    people of, 71, 81*n*, 90, 127, 160–61
    republic of, 7, 14–17, 21–22, 48, 54, 63, 71,
        74, 78, 81, 90, 111, 159–62, 167, 190,
        192
    Signoria, 14, 71*n*
    Ten of Liberty and Peace, 15, 132, 159–61
    territorial state of, 7, 14–17, 105*n*
    university of, in Pisa. *See* Pisa
Florentine History (Varchi), 159, 161–62
Florus, Lucius, 132
Fogliani, Giovanni, of Fermo, 66–67
Foix, Gaston de, 44*n*
"Force and Consent"(Mussolini), 184
Forli, 48, 82, 108, 191
Fornovo, battle of, 121*n*
fortresses and fortifications, 72, 104, 105,
    107–8, 128, 190
fortune (*fortuna*), ix, **40(2), 41, 44,
    55(4), 57(2), 58(6), 59(3),
    60(1), 63(2), 64(1), 65(2),
    66(1), 68, 70, 73, 74, 78, 81,
    83, 84(2), 86, 92, 95, 106, 110,
    111, 116(3), 117(4), 118,
    119(2),** 119*n*, **120(2), 121,** 126,
    128–29, 136, 138, 154, 194
fortunate (*fortunata*), **68**
    See also Fates
Foscari, Marco, 105*n*
Foscolo, Ugo, 188–89
foxes, 94, 101–2, 130
France, 8, 24–26, 41*n*, 43–44, 47–53, 60, 62,
    64, 74–75, 82–83, 89, 101, 109, 111,
    117–18, 119*n*, 122, 166, 170–71,
    190–91
    institutions of, 44, 52, 83, 89, 98–99
    Parlement, 98–99
    provinces, 44
Francis I, king of France, 8
Francis de Sales, saint, 163
Frederick I of Aragon, king of Naples, 49*n*
Frederick II (Frederick the Great), king of
    Prussia, 171–76
    The Refutation of Machiavelli's Prince,
        171–76
Frederick III, Holy Roman emperor, 114*n*
freedom. *See* liberty
free will, 113*n*, 117, 121
French Revolution, 26

Gabburra, butcher, 137
Gaddi, Giovanni, monsignor, 150–51
Gaddi, Niccolò, 164
Gascony, 44
Gaul, 53n
Geneva, 25, 166, 178
Genoa, 7, 48, 121
Gentili, Alberico, 25, 33, 177
Gentillet, Innocent, 25, 166–70
    Discourses against Machiavelli, 25, 166–69
Geradadda, battle of, 49n. *See also* Vailate
Gerarchia, 179
Germany, 8, 72, 117, 119n, 122, 152n
Geta, 136
Ghibellines, 7, 10, 106
Giannotti, Donato, 160–62
Ginori, Filippo, 137
Giordani, Antonio, of Venafro, 60n, 112
Giovanna II, queen of Naples, 78
Girolami, Giovanni, 132
Giunta, Bernardo, 21, 150–52
    Dedicatory Letter to Giovanni Gaddi,
      150–52
Giunta press, 192
God, 55, 68, 74, 76, 116, 120–21, 164, 169,
      172, 193
Goliath, 83
Gonzaga, Francesco, marchese, 48n
Goths, 84
Gracchus, Gaius Sempronius, 71
Gracchus, Tiberius Sempronius, 71
Gramsci, Antonio, 29, 184–89
    Prison Notebooks, 184–89
Granada, 109, 156
    treaty of, 41n, 49n
great, the, 69–70, 98–99, 115. *See also* few,
      the; oligarchy
Great Schism, 7
Greece, 9, 10, 44, 45n, 46, 53–54, 58, 70, 82,
      93n, 110, 116, 156
Guelfs, 7, 106
Guicciardini, Antonio, 137
Guicciardini, Battista, 137–38, 144
Guicciardini, Francesco, 47n, 112n, 138n,
      143, 144n, 161, 164
Guicciardini, Jacopo, 144
Guicciardini, Luigi, 143–45
Guicciardini, Niccolò, 20, 143–45
    A Letter to Luigi Guicciardini, 143–45
Guicciardini family of Florence, 20, 143–45
Guise, Henri, duke of, 170
gunpowder weapons, 6, 16, 31n

Habsburg, house of, 114n
Hamilcar, 65, 157
Hannibal, 92, 93n, 127, 157–58
Hawkwood, John, 78
Hebrews, 120, 121n. *See also* Israel; Jews
Heliogabalus, Roman emperor, 99, 103
Hellespont, 58
Henry VII of Luxembourg, Holy Roman
      emperor, 7

heresy, 10, 12–13, 25
Herodian, 99n, 132
Herodotus, 56n, 157
Hesiod, 112
Hiero II of Syracuse, 57, 82–83, 84n, 149n,
      156
Historical and Critical Dictionary (Bayle),
      177
history, 9–11, 40, 86, 105, 132, 146, 155, 157,
      175, 186
History of Italy (Guicciardini), 143
Holy League, 44n
Holy Roman Empire, 7, 70, 72, 80, 114, 115
Huguenots, 3, 24, 166, 170
humanism, 9–12, 14, 154, 187
hunting, 19, 85, 137, 142
Hus, Jan, 12

Iago, 25
Imola, 48n, 82, 180, 191
imperio, 41n
Index of Forbidden Books, 22, 24
India, 6
indulgences, 75n
infantry, 6, 8, 16, 83–84, 103, 122
Inferno (Dante), 94n, 163
Innocent VIII, pope, 75n
Inquisition, 12, 24
Ionia, 58
Islam, 103
Isocrates, 39
Israel, 56, 120. *See also* Hebrews; Jews
Italy, 7–8, 16, 18, 25, 27–29, 44, 47–50, 59,
      74–75, 76–82, 109, 115–17, 119–23,
      127, 129, 155, 167, 188, 194

Janiculum hill, 131
janissaries, 103n
Jerome of Prague, 12
Jesuit order, 25, 163
Jew of Malta, The (Marlowe), 25, 170–71
Jews, 109n. *See also* Hebrews; Israel
Joan of Arc, 83n
John VI Cantacuzene, Byzantine emperor,
      81–82
Julianus (Didius Julianus), Roman emperor,
      99, 101
Julius II (Giuliano della Rovere), pope, 8,
      12–13, 42, 63–64, 74n, 75, 81, 89, 111,
      114n, 118–19, 125, 128, 191
Justin, 57

Kamenev, Lev, 31n
Koran, 167–68

Ladislaus, king of Naples, 78n
Lampridius, Aelius, 132
language, 10, 22, 44, 87, 149, 152
Leonardo da Vinci, 1
Leo X (Giovanni de' Medici), pope, 12,
      17–18, 42n, 75, 120n, 129, 133n,
      191–92

Letter to Benedetto Varchi, A (Busini), 159–60
Letter to Francesco Vettori (Machiavelli), 134–40
Letter to Luigi Guicciardini, A (Guicciardini, N.), 143–45
Letter to Niccolò Machiavelli (Vettori), 129–33
liberality, 88–90
liberty (*libertà*), ix, **53, 54(2), 66, 69, 77, 98**, 160, 162, 178
 free, in freedom (*libero*), **41, 44, 53, 54(3),77, 117**
 freedom (*libertas*), **119**
 to free (*liberare*), **65**
 very free (*liberissimi*), **72, 77**
lions, 94, 101–2, 130
Liverotto of Fermo. See Euffreducci, Oliverotto
Livy, Titus, 14, 19, 41*n*, 45*n*, 86*n*, 87*n*, 92*n*, 93*n*, 120*n*, 178
Locris, 93
Lodi, Peace of, 7–8, 74*n*, 79*n*
Lombardy, 48–49, 78, 111, 120
Louis IX, king of France, 98*n*
Louis XI, king of France, 83
Louis XII, king of France, 8, 15, 19, 33, 41*n*, 43–44, 47–50, 62–63, 64, 74, 80, 89
Lucca, 21, 48, 63, 78*n*
Lucretius, 11, 32
Luther, Martin, 11

Macbeth (Shakespeare), 25
Macedonia, 46, 116
Machiavelli, Bernardo, 14, 32, 135
Machiavelli, Giovanni, 133
Machiavelli, Margherita, 14
Machiavelli, Niccolò
 Art of War, 31*n*, 78*n*, 83*n*, 192
 Capitolo on Fortune, 119*n*, 126
 Clizia, 119*n*
 composition of *The Prince*, 17–19
 death, 21–22, 159–64, 192
 deathbed confession, 13, 32
 "A Description of the Method Used by Duke Valentino in Killing Vitellozzo Vitelli, Liverotto of Fermo and Others," 61*n*
 Discourse on Florentine Affairs after the Death of Lorenzo de' Medici the Younger, 192
 Discourses on the First Ten Books of Titus Livy, 5–6, 10, 13, 19–20, 25, 27, 29, 31*n*, 33, 41*n*, 45*n*, 57*n*, 65*n*, 72*n*, 86*n*, 90*n*, 92*n*, 93*n*, 97*n*, 107*n*, 108*n*, 120*n*, 128*n*, 149*n*, 151, 164*n*, 178, 182, 191, 192
 Draft of a Letter to Giovan Battista Soderini, 125–29
 "dream" of, 160, 162–64
 early career, 14–17, 190–91
 Florentine Histories, 6, 10, 21, 71*n*, 78*n*, 80*n*, 98*n*, 111*n*, 120*n*, 151, 161, 178, 192
 later career, 19–22, 192
 Letter to Francesco Vettori, 134–40
 marriage, 15, 33, 190
 Mandrogola, 94*n*
 On Pistoiese Affairs, 90*n*
 posthumous reputation, 1–6, 22–29, 140–89
 Prince, The
  chapter numbers, 41*n*
  chapter titles, 41*n*
  composition of, 17–19
  Machiavelli's embarrassment with, 20–21
  prefaces of, 145–52
  publication of, 20–22, 147–54, 162
  as satire, 5
  title of, 39*n*, 139,193
  translation of, ix–xi
 Report on Things in Germany, 72*n*, 114*n*
 "Thrushes, The," 17–18, 140–41
Machiavelli, Primavera, 14
Machiavelli, Totto, 14
Machiavelli family of Florence, 14, 135, 190
Machiavelli's Presentation of The Prince *to Lorenzo de' Medici* (Riccardi), 142
Macrinus, Roman emperor, 99, 103
Maecenas, Gaius, 152
Maffei, Raffaello, 11
Magione, 60
"magnificent" (honorific), 39*n*
Malatesta, Pandolfo, lord of Rimini, 48*n*
Mamelukes, 103–4, 193
Manfredi, Astorre, lord of Faenza, 48*n*
Mantinea, battle of, 77
Mantua, 48, 150*n*, 191
Marcus Aurelius, Roman emperor, 99–100, 102, 104
Marlowe, Christopher, 25, 170–71
 The Jew of Malta, 25, 170–71
Marranos, 109
Marxism, 186, 189
masses, the, 95, 189. *See also* people, the; plebs
Matteotti, Giacomo, 34, 179
Maximilian I Habsburg, emperor-elect of the Holy Roman Empire, 8, 15, 106*n*, 114, 191
Maximinus, Roman emperor, 99, 101–4
Medes, 56, 120
Medici, Catherine de', queen and regent of France, 24, 166
Medici, Cosimo I de', duke of Tuscany, 161
Medici, Giovanni de', cardinal. *See* Leo X
Medici, Giuliano de', 17–21, 139–41
Medici, Giulio de', cardinal. *See* Clement VII
Medici, Lorenzo de' (the Magnificent or the Elder), 1, 30, 105*n*, 111*n*, 127, 190
Medici, Lorenzo de' (the Younger), 17, 19, 24, 39–40, 142, 148–50, 162, 165, 192–93

Medici family of Florence, 14, 16–17, 20–22, 129, 140, 145, 154, 159, 191–92
Mehmet II (Mehmet the Conqueror), sultan of the Ottoman Turks, 44
mercenary troops, 7, 16, 76–84, 105
Mercenary War, 77n
Messer, 61n
Mestre, battle of, 121
Michelangelo, 1
Middle Ages, 7, 106n, 187
Milan, duchy and city, 7, 41, 43, 48, 58–59, 74, 78–79, 85, 108, 111, 115, 156
　Ambrosian Republic of, 78n
　Castello Sforzesco, 108
　militia of citizens, 7, 15–16, 77, 79–80, 83, 127n
"mirrors of princes," 5
Mochi, Teofilo, 147
　Preface to a Manuscript of The Prince, 147
Modena, 18, 42n, 143
Mohammed, 168
Molinella, battle of, 79n
Molise, 112n
Montaigne, Michel de, 32
Montefeltro, Guidubaldo da, duke of Urbino, 60n, 107, 127–28
Montevarchi, 14
morality, 1, 10–11, 26, 28–29
More, Thomas, 87n
Moses, 13, 55–57, 74n, 84n, 184, 193, 194
Muslims, 109n
Mussolini, Benito, 29, 34, 179–84
　A Prelude to Machiavelli, 179–84

Nabis, 70, 97
Nantes, 50
Naples, kingdom and city, 7–8, 12, 18, 21, 41, 49, 50, 62, 78, 79n, 109, 115, 120
Napoleonic wars, 26
Nardi, Jacopo, 160, 162
Nasi, Giovambatista, 132
Nelli, Bartolomea, 14
Nero, Francesco del, 160, 162
Nero, Roman emperor, 131, 175
New World, 28
Nifo, Agostino, 21, 151, 153–59, 192
　On Skill in Ruling, 21, 51, 153–159, 192
Nine of the Militia. See Florence
Ninety-Five Theses (Luther), 11
nobles, 14, 60, 62, 79, 80. See also barons
Normandy, 44
Numantia, 54

"Old Nick." See Devil
oligarchy, 53n, 156. See also few, the; great, the
On Skill in Ruling (Nifo), 21, 151, 153–59, 192
On the Discoverers of Things (Vergil), 11
On the Health of Origen (Binet), 163–64
On the Immortality of the Soul Against Pomponazzi (Nifo), 153

On the Social Contract (Rousseau), 26, 177–78
Oran, 109n
orders (ordini), 54n, 59n, 84n
Orsini, Francesco, duke of Gravina, 60n, 61n
Orsini, Giambattista, cardinal, 60n
Orsini, Niccolò, count of Pitigliano, 79
Orsini, Paolo, lord of Mentana, 60, 61n
Orsini family and faction, 59–61, 67, 74–75, 191
Othello (Shakespeare), 25
Ottoman Empire, 44, 51–52, 82, 103, 167
Ovid, 95n, 119n, 138
Oxford, University of, 25, 177

Palmieri, Matteo, 112n
Panzano, Fruosino da, 130, 137
papacy, 7–8, 12–13, 15, 48, 59–64, 73–75, 80, 104, 171–72, 178
Paradiso (Dante), 139n
Parlement. See France
parricide, 67
Peloponnesian War, 54n
Pentateuch. See bible
people, the, 26, 52, 57, 58, 61, 62, 69–71, 73, 97–104, 108, 111, 115, 122, 127, 173, 183, 188. See also masses, the; plebs
Persia, 56, 120, 157
Pertinax, Roman emperor, 99–100, 104
Perugia, 60, 62, 125, 127n, 128n, 191
Pesaro, 48
Pescennius Niger, Gaius, 101
Petrarch (Francesco Petrarca), 10, 123, 136n, 138
Petrucci, Pandolfo, 60n, 107, 112
Philip II, king of Macedon, 77, 84, 116, 156
Philip V, king of Macedon, 45n, 46–47, 116
Philistines, 83
Philopoemen, 86
Pico della Mirandola, Giovanni, 12
Piombino, 48, 62, 126
Pisa, 16, 48, 54, 62, 63, 66n, 78–79, 81, 105, 190, 191
　Florentine university in, 11, 21, 153
Pistoia, 90, 104
Pius III, pope, 191
Plato, 12, 34, 87n, 154–56, 163–64
plebs, 30, 72, 79. See also people, the
Pleminius, Quintus, 93n
Pliny the Elder, 158
Plutarch, 132, 164
Pole, Reginald, cardinal, 24, 164–65, 177
　Apology to Charles V, 164–65
politeia, 156
Politics (Aristotle), 25, 92n
Poliziano, Angelo, 10, 99n
Polybius, 57n, 77n, 156
Pomponazzi, Pietro, 153
pope. See papacy
Possevino, Antonio, 25
Praetorian Guard, 101n

Praise of Folly (Erasmus), 12
Prato, 16, 138, 191
Preface to a Manuscript of The Prince
(Mochi), 147
Prefatory Letter to Pandolfo Bellacci
(Buonaccorsi), 145–46
Prelude to Machiavelli, A (Mussolini),
179–84
Priest Luca. *See* Rinaldi, Luca
Princeton University, 25
principalities
civil, 68–71
ecclesiastical, 73–75, 193
hereditary, 41–42
mixed, 43–54
new, 54–71
printing press, 6, 148, 152
Prison Notebooks (Gramsci), 184–89
Procopius, 132
Prussia, 171
Ptolemy Ceraunus, 157
Ptolemy of Alexandria, 129n
Punic War, First, 77n, 158
Punic War, Second, 46n, 65n, 158
Purgatorio (Dante), 136n
Pyrrhus, king of Epirus, 53

Ravenna, battle of, 44, 81, 122
Reformation, Protestant, 3, 11–12, 24–25,
160, 166
Refutation of Machiavelli's Prince, The
(Frederick the Great), 171–76
Reggio, 42n, 143
Regulus, Marcus Attilius, 158–59
Remirro de Orco. *See* de Lorqua, Ramiro
Republic (Plato), 34, 87n
republics, 2, 5, 19–22, 27, 29–30, 65, 77, 80,
87, 156, 193
Riario, Girolamo, count of Imola and Forlì,
108
Riario, Raffaello, cardinal, 64n, 95n
Riccardi, Riccardo, 142, 177
Machiavelli's Presentation of The Prince *to*
Lorenzo de' Medici, 142
Ricordi (Guicciardini), 47, 112
Ridolfi, Angelo, 26
Rimini, 59
Rinaldi, Luca (Priest Luca), 114
Romagna, 5, 15, 48–49, 59–62, 75, 80, 82, 90,
168, 190
Roman Empire, 53, 58, 84, 99–104
ruin of, 84
Rome
ancient, 9–10, 20, 29, 46–47, 53–54, 56,
57n, 70–71, 77, 84, 89, 93, 99–104,
110, 116, 127, 156, 158, 175, 177,
178–79, 184–85
modern, 179
Renaissance, 18, 22, 24, 59n, 60, 62–63,
74–75, 118, 130–36, 147–48, 150,
159–60, 177–78, 191–92
Romulus, 13, 54, 56–57, 84n, 184

Rosso Fiorentino, painter, 3
Rousseau, Jean-Jacques, 26, 177–78, 180,
184, 188
On the Social Contract, 26, 177–78
Royal Roman Road, 135
Rucellai, Giovanni, 132
Rucellai Gardens, 191
Russia, 3, 185

Sacchetti, Franco, 109n
Sallust, 132
Salutati, Coluccio, 10
San Casciano, 138
sanjaks, 51
Sanseverino, Roberto da, count of Caiazzo,
79
Sant'Andrea in Percussina, 17, 134–35, 163
Satan. *See* Devil
Saul, king of the Hebrews, 83
Savonarola, Girolamo, 12–14, 57, 77n, 160,
164n, 188, 190
Scali, Giorgio, 70n, 71
Schucht, Julia, 185
Schucht, Tatiana, 185
Scipio Africanus, 65n, 86, 92–93, 127, 129
Second Punic War, 46n, 65n, 158
Segni, Bernardo, 25
Selim I, sultan of the Ottoman Turks, 103n
Senate, 92–93, 101, 103, 158, 164
Seneca, 133n, 164
Senigallia, 61, 67, 191
Sernigi, Cristofano, 130
Sertorius, Quintus, 158
Severus, Alexander, Roman emperor,
99–100, 103–4
Severus, Septimius, Roman emperor, 99,
101–2, 104
Sforza (Muzio Attendolo), 78, 80
Sforza, Ascanio, cardinal, 64, 85n
Sforza, Francesco, 41, 58, 78, 85, 108, 128,
156
Sforza, Galeazzo Maria, 85n
Sforza, Gian Galeazzo, 85n
Sforza, Giovanni, lord of Pesaro, 48n
Sforza, lords of Milan, 85, 108
Sforza, Ludovico Maria (Il Moro), 43, 59, 85n
Sforza Riario, Caterina, countess of Forlì, 48,
108
Shakespeare, William, 25
Shakur, Tupac, 3
Sicily, 65, 169
Siena, 48, 60n, 63, 107, 147
Signoria. *See* Florence
Sisyphus, 140n
Sixtus IV (Francesco della Rovere),
pope, 74
Slavonia, 101
Socrates, 163
Soderini, Francesco, cardinal, 139n, 190
Soderini, Giovan Battista, 125–29
Soderini, Pier, 125, 139, 188, 190–91
Soderini family of Florence, 139

Spain, 6, 18, 53, 62–64, 81, 108–9, 111, 117–18, 119n, 122, 127, 129, 143, 156
Sparta, 52, 70, 77
Spartianus, Aelius, 132
Spinoza, Benedict de, 26, 172–73, 177
St. Bartholomew's Day Massacre, 3, 24–25, 166, 170
Stalin, Joseph, 3, 31n
state (*stato*), ix–xi, 7, **40**, 40n, **41(2), 42, 44(4), 45(5), 46(2), 47(3), 48, 49, 50, 51(7), 52(4), 53(5), 54, 55(2), 56, 58(3), 59(4), 63, 67, 68(2), 70, 71(5), 73(3), 74, 76(3), 79, 80(2), 84, 88(2), 95(3), 96, 97, 98(2), 100, 101(2), 104(5), 105(6), 106(2), 107(7), 108(2), 109, 111(2), 112, 113, 114, 115(3),** 115n, **116,** 181–83, 188–89, 193
Statius, 94n
Strozzi, Filippo, 147–49, 162
Suetonius, 132
Sultan. *See* Egypt
Switzerland, 8, 77, 80–81, 83, 122, 144
Syracuse, 57, 64, 82, 169

Tacitus, Cornelius, 84n, 132, 164
Taro River, 121
Ten of Liberty and Peace. *See* Florence
territorial states, 7, 32, 79, 189
Thebes, 54, 77
Theseus, 13, 55–57, 84n, 120, 184
Thirty Tyrants, 54
Thrace, 103
Tiberius, Roman emperor, 175
Tibullus, 119n, 138
Titus, Roman emperor, 128, 175
To Nicocles (Isocrates), 41n
Trajan, Roman emperor, 175
Trecentonovelle (Sacchetti), 109n
Trent, 132
Trieste, 114n
Tripoli, 109n
Trojans, 91n
tu, xi, 39n
Tuscany, xii, 14–15, 60, 62, 85, 87, 120, 147, 149
tyranny, 25–27, 54n, 57n, 65n, 70n, 156–59, 165, 169, 174, 188
Tyrol, 114n, 191

universals, 117n, 128
Urbane Commentaries (Maffei), 11
Urbino, 39n, 60–61, 107, 128, 192
utopias, 87, 185

Vaglienti, Piero, 70n
Vailate, battle of, 49n, 79, 106, 121
Valentino. *See* Borgia, Cesare
Valentinois, duchy of, 50n
Valla, Lorenzo, 10, 12
Varano, Giulio Cesare, lord of Camerino, 48n
Varchi, Benedetto, 21, 159–61, 163
  Florentine History, 159, 161–62
Venafro, Antonio of. *See* Giordani, Antonio
Venice, 7, 22, 41, 47–49, 50, 59, 78, 106, 111, 118
Vergil, Polydore, 11
Verrocchio, Andrea del, sculptor, 83n
Vespucci, Amerigo, 31n
Vettori, Francesco vi, 17, 20, 26, 89n, 110n, 130, 141, 163, 177, 191
  Letter to Niccolò Machiavelli, 129–33
Vettori, Paolo, 136
Vienne (France), 166
Virgil, 91
virtue (*virtù*), ix–x, **41, 41n, 47, 53, 54, 55(7), 56(2), 57(2), 58(4), 59, 63(2), 64, 65, 66(2), 67, 68, 73, 75, 79, 80, 82, 83, 84(3), 88(2), 92(3), 99, 100, 101(2), 104, 111, 116, 117(2), 120(3), 121(3), 122, 123,** 160, 162, 174–76, 193, 194
  most virtuously (*virtuosissamente*), **79**
  very virtuous (*virtuosissimo*), **79**
  virtuous (*virtuoso*), **55, 56, 59, 77, 78, 111, 115, 119**
  virtuously (*virtuosamente*), **88**
Visconti, Bernabò, lord of Milan, 109
Visconti, Filippo Maria, 78–79
Visconti, Galeazzo II, 109n
Visconti, Giangaleazzo, 109n
Visconti, lords of Milan, 109
Visconti, Matteo II, 109n
Vitelli, lords of Città di Castello, 60n, 61n, 67, 127
Vitelli, Niccolò, 107
Vitelli, Paolo, 66, 78, 107n
Vitelli, Vitellozzo, 61, 63, 66–67, 107n, 191
voi, xiii, 39n
volgare, 22
Voltaire, 171–72
Volterra, 105n

Waterloo, battle of, 26
Wittenberg, 11
wolves, 94
women, 92, 96, 119

Xenophon, 86, 87n, 94n